WITHDRAWN
UTSA LIBRARIES

Eros and Psyche

Strindberg and Munch in the 1890s

Studies in the Fine Arts
The Avant-Garde, No. 27

Stephen C. Foster, Series Editor

Associate Professor of Art History
University of Iowa

Other Titles in This Series

No. 20	*The Société Anonyme's Brooklyn Exhibition: Katherine Dreier and Modernism in America*	Ruth L. Bohan
No. 21	*Robert Delaunay: The Early Years*	Sherry A. Buckberrough
No. 22	*The Theatrical Designs of George Grosz*	Andrew DeShong
No. 23	*Endless Innovations: Frederick Kiesler's Theory and Scenic Design*	R. L. Held
No. 28	*The Symbolist Art of Fernand Khnopff*	Jeffery W. Howe
No. 29	*Eugène Carrière—His Work and His Influence*	Robert James Bantens
No. 30	*Aristide Maillol in the 1890s*	Wendy Slatkin
No. 33	*The Art of Gustave Moreau: Theory, Style, and Content*	Julius Kaplan
No. 35	*The Art of Mikhail Vrubel (1856-1910)*	Aline Isdebsky-Pritchard

Eros and Psyche

Strindberg and Munch in the 1890s

by
Reidar Dittmann

LIBRARY
The University of Texas
At San Antonio

Copyright © 1982, 1976
Reidar Dittmann
All rights reserved

Produced and distributed by
UMI Research Press
an imprint of
University Microfilms International
Ann Arbor, Michigan 48106

Library of Congress Cataloging in Publication Data

Dittmann, Reidar.
Eros and Psyche: Strindberg and Munch in the 1890s.

(Studies in fine arts. The Avant-garde ; no. 27)
"A revision of the author's thesis, University of Washington, 1976"–Verso of t.p.
Bibliography: p.
Includes index.
1. Strindberg, August, 1849-1912–Friends and associates. 2. Strindberg, August, 1849-1912–Influence–Munch. 3. Munch, Edvard, 1863-1944–Influence. 4. Authors, Swedish–19th century–Biography. 5. Artists–Norway–Biography. I. Title. II. Series.

PT9815.D5 1982 839.7'26 [B] 82-4923
ISBN 0-8357-1319-9 AACR2

1. Edvard Munch: *Portrait of Strindberg.* 1896.

2. Edvard Munch: *Self-Portrait with Skeletal Arm.* 1895.

Contents

List of Plates

Preface

In my childhood, spending summers in Åsgårdstrand, the Oslofjord village so prominently featured in Munch's paintings throughout his creative life, I had occasion to see the artist and somehow sense his greatness. This no doubt was in part because I was vaguely aware of his fame, but more so, I am sure, because there was something decidedly impressive—and odd—in his very appearance as he moved, lost in thought, along the cobblestoned streets. From this early and direct exposure to the person came a gradually evolving interest in his art, maturing with the years and growing in depth and familiarity, particularly with its nearly unlimited accessibility through the 1963 opening of the Munch Museum in Oslo.

More recent is my interest in Strindberg's works, beginning with my first structured studies in the Scandinavian drama in the 1950s with such eminent scholars as Dr. Sverre Arestad and Dr. Walter Johnson, both now professors emeriti of the University of Washington. It was Dr. Johnson who encouraged me to pursue the Strindberg-Munch topic in detail, and without his interest and confidence it is doubtful the project would have been undertaken in this manner.

During my recent year of study at the University of Washington I was deeply inspired by Dr. Martha Kingsbury's lectures and seminar on nineteenth- and twentieth-century art, and by Dr. Raymond Jarvi, whose Strindberg seminars were among the highlights of a very fruitful year. Dr. Jarvi's special interest in Strindberg and music paralleled my own relative to the visual arts, and it was therefore natural that he should become my dissertation advisor. As such he offered many valuable suggestions regarding research approach and style of writing. Moreover, during my brief stay in Stockholm he generously gave of his time; through his special insight and contacts he made my visits to the Strindberg archives of the Royal Library, the Strindberg Museum, and the Thiel Collection particularly meaningful.

In the Munch Museum I received courteous assistance from the librarian, Frida Tank, and other members of the staff; in the company of its former director, Johan Langaard, I had the unique opportunity of visiting private collections which otherwise would have been inaccessible. The one person in Norway who contributed most substantially to my research, however, was Ingrid Langaard, not only through her singularly impressive monograph on Edvard Munch but also in personal correspondence and conversation.

Throughout the writing and the rewriting of the volume I received continuous support from my wife, a librarian, whose insight into bibliographical matters was an invaluable asset in my research.

Northfield, Minnesota
(March 15, 1982)

Reidar Dittmann

Introduction

Much has been written about the lives and works of August Strindberg and Edvard Munch, and it is not uncommon that the consideration of one prompts a reference to the other. When the principal subject of investigation is Strindberg, the Munch reference—unless the visual arts are in the spotlight, as in *Strindberg och bildkonsten* by Göran Söderström, or *Strindbergs måleri* edited by Torsten Måtte Schmidt—more often than not is of very limited scope, amounting to a mere sentence, or at the very most a single paragraph of rather noncommittal consequence. Many Strindberg biographers—scholars as thorough as Martin Lamm or loquacious as V.J. McGill—find it possible to discuss his activities in Berlin and Paris without once referring to Munch; others tend to include him only in the roster of the numerous walk-on players who at one time or another appeared on stage in the turbulent drama that was Strindberg's life. Even Gunnar Brandell, whose volume *Strindberg in Inferno,* is concerned with a period in that life when the subject's relationship to Munch might appear essential in the probing of his psyche, makes only the most casual reference to the moody artist Strindberg had come to consider a key conspirator in a complex plot against his life—the person to whom he once wrote: "The last time I saw you you looked like a murderer or at least a murderer's handyman."

Munch's biographers have been more generous in their allotment of space to Strindberg, although it is only recently that such generosity has resulted in a more meaningful assessment of the relationship between the two. Traditionally, it has been treated in terms of anecdotes and with scant relevance to each artist's creative development. Cases in point are certain chapters in two volumes published separately on the occasion of Munch's seventieth birthday, Pola Gauguin's *Edvard Munch* and Jens Thiis's *Edvard Munch og hans samtid.* Gauguin, placing little more importance on Munch's exposure to the Scandinavian artist community in Berlin than referring by name to its principal members, suggests that Strindberg's presence made a particularly trying period in Munch's life even more difficult. Jens Thiis, discussing the same crucial period, during which he himself happened to be in Berlin, garrulously carries on about his private encounters with Strindberg to the extent that he barely finds time and space for the issue at hand.

In 1960, however, a new and far more meaningful monograph on Norway's one claim to fame in the world of the visual arts appeared: Ingrid Langaard's pioneering *Edvard Munch: Modningsår.* Among the many outstanding features of this volume is its presentation of the relationship between Munch and Strindberg. Though only part of a much greater totality, it is viewed in the broad perspective of the times and the creative forces, individual and sociocultural, that determined the direction of the development of each artist, and the extent to which they may have been able to influence each other.

A major work, Ragna Stang's *Edvard Munch, the Man and His Art,* appeared in Norway in 1977. Although greater in scope than Ingrid Langaard's volume, the more recent book does not add anything new to our knowledge of the period presently considered. However, as director of Oslo Municipal Collections from 1969 to 1976, Stang had unlimited access to the Munch Museum archive. Therefore, her use of documents and citations add a new and valuable resource to Munch material in print.

The purpose of the present study, finished in 1976 and revised in 1982, is to trace the development of Munch and Strindberg in chronological order, and in relationship to concurrent and shifting cultural trends. In chapters devoted alternately to each artist it will be shown how, separately but simultaneously, they were drawn in the same creative direction and, motivated by instincts and external circumstances strikingly similar, came to reject the *status quo,* moving from the prevailing emphasis on social realism into an artistic probing of the human psyche as revealed to them in an agonizing but uncompromising unveiling of their inner selves. Few other artists have possessed the courage or the compulsive desire so to bare their souls in their creative works. A meaningful tracing of their artistic development is therefore to a great extent dependent upon a proper interpretation of their persistent personal trials and tribulations: Strindberg's total failure to bring his own "pre-Inferno" house in order, Munch's never-ending struggle against family sickness and death and an unceasingly hostile public. It is shown how these experiences, so negative on the personal level, when pitted against each artist's boundless creative energy and imagination were transformed into dynamic sources of inspiration leading to some of the most significant single contributions to the literary and visual arts of the 1880s and 1890s.

On the Strindberg side of the ledger attention is focused on his early interest in the visual arts as shown in his critical writings, his direct relationship with artists, and his predilection for painting, initially as a pastime but later as a more determined effort in creative expression.

His more intimate personal relationships are discussed, that with his first wife, Siri von Essen, and in greater detail that with Frida Uhl, his second wife, whom he met and courted in Berlin simultaneously with the cultivation of his friendship with Edvard Munch, through whom he met the intriguing Dagny Juell.

It is shown how in his early Berlin period he abandoned his writing career in favor of scientific studies interspersed with painting and freewheeling revelry in the circle of friends gathering at *Zum schwarzen Ferkel,* and how his relationship with Frida initially made him turn over a new leaf and give up the *Ferkel* and its frivolities. Not long thereafter, however, weary of domesticity, he was to turn his back on his young wife and their newly born child to rejoin his friends, first in Berlin, then in Paris. There, after a futile attempt at reconciliation, the marriage would come to an end. Indeed virtually all of his various friendships were to terminate through his isolated preoccupation with pseudoscientific research and religious broodings, topics beyond the scope of the present investigation.

On the Munch side it is shown how his early contact with the Norwegian Bohème group led by Hans Jaeger and Christian Krohg helped free him from his inherited inhibitions, while Paris and his artistic encounters there freed his painterly approach. Through his contact with Strindberg he would radically alter his view on the relationship between man and woman, and it will be pointed out how decisively this change affected his creative activities for a brief period of time.

Dagny Juell's ambivalent role in the lives of Munch, Strindberg, and others within the *Ferkel* circle, in particular Stanislaw Przybyszewski, is presented in the perspective of the emerging independent woman Munch considered her to be rather than the scheming *femme fatale* portrayed by Strindberg in his letters and writings. By the same token, Stanislaw Przybyszewski, whose wife she would become shortly after her initial relationship with Strindberg, is viewed in a light quite different from that focused upon him by Strindberg in *Inferno,* where he takes on the character of a reckless criminal and an avenging demon.

During their brief period of friendship, Strindberg and Munch must have felt comfortable in each other's company and in that of their greater circle of friends with whom they formed an avant-garde group closely resembling those they had each associated with in their early creative years. Yet their principal meeting ground was still the interest they shared in each other's chief activity. Strindberg's close affinity with painters dated from the earliest days of his career, as did Munch's with writers. However, while Munch's fascination with literature is reflected far better in his pictures than in the few pieces of writing he left behind, Strindberg made serious attempts at expressing himself in painting. It was during his period of friendship with Munch that he reached his greatest accomplishments in that field. Considerable attention is therefore devoted to Strindberg as a painter and to his and Munch's technical and emotional approaches to the visual arts, as shown in retrospective works completed both before and during their days of association. It will then become apparent, perhaps surprisingly, that in terms of technique and painterly preferences they were actually so far apart that their obvious emotional affinities were quite inadequate to compensate for such differences. This may in part account for Strindberg's final and devastating judgment of Munch's artistic efforts: "... masterpieces in the grotesque, which I abhor."

Those of Strindberg's literary works which fall within the time span of this study are discussed in some detail. It so happens, however, that during much of that period his literary activities remained at a virtual standstill. Even so, his other pursuits, his thoughts, and his shifting points of view are clearly documented in his incredibly prolific correspondence. His letters, now in print through the year 1904, are generously quoted. These quotes, as well as all others not originally in the English language, have been translated throughout the text.

Munch's letters, the few presently in print and those available in the archives of the Munch Museum, shed little light on his actual thoughts and activities. Mostly writing either to his aunt or his sister, both genteel members of the decaying upper middle class, he must deliberately have toned down the extent of his personal problems and involvements which, judging from the character of his paintings, must have been both numerous and complex. More convincing and revealing than these sparse letters are his scattered notes, for the most part undated epigrammatic observations on his own paintings and the emotional experiences behind them. Now accessible in the archive of the Munch Museum, these documents have been scrutinized carefully and are liberally quoted. In the final analysis, however, neither Munch's letters nor such sporadic literary efforts are as sweepingly illuminating as are his visual records; for with his senses continually keyed to the potential visualizing of all their stimuli, he found little satisfaction in verbal expression. Therefore, whatever another person might have committed to a diary or a letter—thoughts, visions, experiences—Munch recorded in his sketchbook, and from his sketchbook came his paintings, from the paintings his graphics. Consequently, his enormous creative output—more than 2,000 paintings and some 700 separate graphic works—came to represent a uniquely complete documentation of everything that occupied his mind, hence the considerable space devoted in the present context to illustrative plates and detailed analyses of the most significant of these works of art.

Implicit in the chronologically oriented pursuit of the activities of Strindberg and Munch, which forms the backbone of this analysis, is the assumption that the major artistic achievements of each are directly rooted in their personal experiences. Yet once molded by each artist's profound perception and committed to his special medium of expression, these physical and emotional realities attain a significance extending far beyond the immediate artistic renditions they happened to inspire. Raised to the level of universally valid creative metaphors, they become verbal or visual manifestations of some of the most intimate and crucial aspects of the human condition.

Art is a fragment of nature seen through a temperament, Zola is quoted to have said. It is two such temperaments, and their separate yet often common views and interpetations of human experiences, that should emerge from these pages and shed some light not only on the aims, activities, and destinies of those directly involved, but on the creative atmosphere of a significant cultural era in which Strindberg and Munch were among the most dominant figures on the Scandinavian scene.

1

A Year of Exile and Entry

Two separate and entirely unrelated events occurred in close chronological sequence in the capitals of the twin kingdoms Sweden and Norway in the autumn of 1883. They may, in retrospect, be viewed as the first in a series of episodes that over the next several years would be paving the way for a direct and personal contact between the key figures in early Scandinavian expressionism.

In Stockholm, the event concerned August Strindberg, then thirty-four years old and a writer of considerable notoriety. At that time, abruptly it may have seemed, he decided to pull up stakes and abandon his homeland in favor of a career abroad, thereby hoping to find a more appreciative response to his creative efforts. His deliberately private departure went largely unnoticed. Not so with the Kristiania[1] event, the Second Annual Autumn Exhibit of Arts. It was very much a public affair, of particular significance in the present context because it marked the first formal showing of a work by Edvard Munch, then not quite twenty years old and virtually unknown except within a circle of enthusiastic friends.

Strindberg's decision to leave Sweden was in reality not all that sudden. A craving to try his luck abroad has been prodding him for quite some time, the intensity varying with his rapidly shifting moods and circumstances. But late that summer, once more facing the dreaded seasonal abandoning of his beloved vacation place in the Stockholm archipelago to return to the stuffy capital, he must have felt incapable of repressing the urge to try something new and better. His letters, up to that time containing occasional hints that he might go abroad, now clearly reveal that he is quietly making the necessary preparations. Quietly, indeed, for it is amply documented that this was a matter not intended to become public knowledge. "I'll be rushing through Stockholm like a wind to vanish without a trace," he buoyantly declares in one letter, while another, addressed to his brother and containing information on his immediate destination—Grez near Namours in the Fontainebleau region of France—closes on a cautioning note: "Do not hand out this address needlessly."[2] But no sooner is he settled in his new and inspiring surroundings, secure and happy among friends and admirers—"I believe all parties will gain from my exile, even my enemies"[3]—than he throws all caution to the wind and eagerly proclaims his whereabouts to his many correspondents. Among them was the editor of Kristiania's ultraliberal daily, *Verdens Gang,* Ola Thommessen, who had written to report on the tumultuous reception members of the Norwegian Student Society had given his own reading of a Strindberg poem from 1876 entitled *Landsflykt* [Exile]. Small wonder these radicals and intellectuals had roared their approval. In a section featuring Kristiania, Strindberg had taken his own countrymen to task bemoaning the intrusion of the Swedish element into the daily life of the Norwegian capital, while at the same time decrying the local conservatism that had made leading Norwegians—he must have thought in particular of Ibsen—prefer to reside abroad:

> Norwegian people,
> I see law breakers and lackeys
> Crowd your sidewalks,
> While you, the masters,
> Wearily tramp
>   the cobblestoned streets.
> But nowhere do I see
>   your great men,
> Forced into exile,
>   Men great enough to be sufficient
> Even for us immense Swedes . . .[4]

Thommessen, having chosen the poem not only to call attention to Strindberg's own recent exile but to cite this rare Swedish contribution to Norway's quest for independence, requested and received permission to print it in *Verdens Gang* alongside a projected article on Strindberg and his works.[5]

In October—November 1883 while this exchange of letters took place, the art community in Kristiania, spurred by Frits Thaulow and Christian Krohg, leading exponents of the realist movement in Norwegian painting, was assembling the most comprehensive show of contemporary art in Norway's history. Included were recent works by such aging romantics as Adolph Tidemand and Hans Gude; the latest efforts of the realists, among them the two in charge as well as Erik Werenskjold, Harriet Backer, Gerhard Munthe, and others; and those of a great many newcomers.[6]

Edvard Munch's debut work (Plate 7)—a working girl sleepily making up the morning fire in the stove—generated some interest. A few critics, finding the subject acceptably representative of current trends, nodded their approval, while others observed that it lacked detail and finesse. As for Munch himself, he was encouraged by the reaction of his fellow artists. "They all liked it exceptionally well," he proudly reports in a letter. "Krohg found it 'superb.'"[7]

So impressed was Erik Werenskjold that he decided to call special attention to Munch in an article published in *Dagbladet* a month later.

Favorable press reaction to his work would be a rare experience for Munch in his early career. Already at next year's Autumn Exhibit he incurred the wrath of the critics with the painting *Morning* (Plate 10). In subject matter differing little from that of the preceding year, it once more shows a working girl, now seated on the edge of her bed, the bright sun, diffused by the white lace curtains of the window, pouring in over her. This time, however, the realistic rendition of the model is of secondary importance; instead the artist focuses attention on light and color, organizing these elements into a shimmering pattern of clearly defined spaces of contrasting keys.

Yet those viewing the painting thought it messy, tasteless, technically inept, and replete with inexcusable errors. Even the subject was no longer acceptable: "A simple seamstress no educated person would want on his wall."[8]

For more than ten years—in fact, until safely reassured by favorable reviews from abroad—the conservative press would persist in treating Munch's efforts with similar disdain, thereby arousing in him a steadily mounting bitterness that would ultimately alienate him from his hometown establishment and make him join ranks with "the great men forced into exile." This would lead to his face-to-face meeting with Strindberg and other members of a northern avant-garde of which these two would become the nucleus.

2

Strindberg's Decision

The Stockholm from which Strindberg had chosen to absent himself had, with the exception of a brief period when he was a student in Uppsala, been his permanent place of residence since his birth in 1849. At that time numbering around 100,000 inhabitants, it was on the threshold of such rapid development that in three decades its population would more than double. To the casual visitor this ceaseless state of expansion and change may have been much less in evidence than the city's ceremonial splendor and serenely beautiful setting, as described in a popular guidebook of the day:

> Crisscrossed by clear waterways which in undulant motion seek their way toward the great deeps, surrounded by wooded hills and green meadows, it presents a prospect which must make a splendid impression on the visitor.[1]

Strindberg, too, had an eye for the obvious attractions of his hometown—more so when he was away during his student days in Uppsala. Having abandoned his studies, however, and returned to Stockholm with no special academic accomplishments to his name, he found its splendor and setting to be poor compensations for its stale bourgeois climate and lack of viable opportunities for a livelihood. He tried his hand at teaching, acting, journalism, and of course freelance writing; then in 1874 he received an appointment to the staff of the Royal Library, where he would remain employed for the next eight years. While several works date from the 1870s, among them his first important play, *Master Olof,* and his harshly realistic stories from Uppsala, *Från Fjårdingen och Svartbäcken,* he gained little recognition until he chose to give vent to his cumulative frustrations with Stockholm and his own lot in the novel marking his artistic breakthrough, *The Red Room,* published in 1879.

Though presuming to take place in the 1860s *The Red Room* provides in reality a faithful commentary on the author's own experiences as an active member of the Stockholm avant-garde in the mid-1870s. By that time a new and aggressive spirit had been injected into Scandinavian intellectual and artistic life through the crucial lectures on *Main Currents in Nineteenth Century European Literature* delivered at Copenhagen University in the fall of

1871 by Georg Brandes, and by the dramas of Norway's Henrik Ibsen who, though soon to become the target of Strindberg's greatest scorn, was then one of his much admired exiles "great enough to be sufficient even for us immense Swedes."

The scathing artist who had flayed his people with that phrase in the poem of 1876 is hard at work in *The Red Room,* now laying bare the widespread hypocrisy he considered to be characteristic of Stockholm's bourgeois society with its pompous patriotic clamor, its shallow acceptance of orthodox religious views, its deplorable addiction to political expediency and fiscal corruption, and, first and last, its rigid resistance to new ideas. The main character is Arvid Falk, a government worker and soon-to-be-published poet. He supplied a journalist with some sensational data concerning waste and inefficiency in his particular government agency; when this material is made public and the disclosure is led back to Falk, he is promptly dismissed from the civil service.

Now better able to concentrate on his creative work, he does so within a circle of freewheeling Bohèmes gathering regularly in the restaurant providing the novel with its title. Yet Falk, whose youthful idealism had first been shaken and eroded by the bourgeois society he had rejected, soon discovers that not even those in his own inner circle remain immune to the social pressure. In the face of potential success or failure they yield one by one, either to resignation—"Lundell . . . since having finished his altar painting . . . has become a fat Epicurean"[2]—or to despair, as in the case of Olle Montanus, Falk's closest friend, sculptor, and dedicated proletarian, who commits suicide. But when the protagonist himself is on the verge of seeking the same way out he is allowed instead to find solace in a love relationship, calmly balanced yet far from traditional, for in their forthcoming marriage the partners are to be free and equal.

The Red Room, a milestone in Swedish literature, clearly points the way to a new era in prose writing. Influenced by Charles Dickens, Gustave Flaubert, and Brandes, Strindberg presents first and foremost an artistic account of his own experiences and does so by providing fascinating insight into the creative atmosphere in which he was working at that particular time in his career. "So obviously similar are Falk's and Strindberg's experiences," says a Swedish scholar, "that no reader can help being struck by it."[3] Even Falk's final destiny, that of occupying a schoolmaster's position while on the side dabbling in numismatics, has its parallel in Strindberg's acceptance of a position in the Royal Library, where he had the opportunity to pursue some rather esoteric hobbies. That this relatively happy ending reflects a temporary state of affairs, for the protagonist as well as for Strindberg, is suggested on the final page in a letter from one character to another:

> Falk is a political fanatic, who knows he would be consumed if he fanned his flame, and therefore he keeps it under control with rigid, dry studies. But I don't think he will succeed, because no matter how he confines himself he is, I'm afraid, headed for an explosion.[4]

The improvements in Strindberg's life had begun with his appointment to the Royal Library staff in 1874. They continued during his often turbulent but ultimately successful courtship of Siri von Essen, an aspiring actress of Finnish birth, initially the wife of Baron Carl Gustaf von Wrangel but in 1877 Strindberg's bride. Two years thereafter, with the publication of *The Red Room,* their fortune appeared to have been made, for despite mixed critical reaction, the novel "fared well with the public, stabilized Strindberg's economy, and made him a well-known writer almost overnight."[5] However, these were rewards earned in a decade of uphill struggle, his first serious literary effort having been made in 1869, and *Master Olof,* one of his finest achievements, still gathering dust in his desk drawer. So his bitterness was deep and abiding. All the same, as he entered the 1880s his situation was clearly a good deal better than it had ever been; his marital happiness, culminating with the birth of a healthy child,[6] added to his other fortunes. Responding to these favors of destiny with an incredible surge of creative energy, he produced within the next three years a body of work in prose, poetry, and the drama which in quantity might have sufficed a lesser spirit for a lifetime.

It is rather strange that so little of this output seems to reflect his new and favorable state of affairs. Even his domestic bliss, so pronounced in much of his correspondence, is discernible only in the play *Sir Bengt's Wife,* written exclusively as a vehicle for his own wife. There the serenity is broken already in the second act, when on the morning following the wedding night Sir Bengt, calling his bride's attention to the way she has strewn her clothes about, glumly observes, "I've been raised in a home where order was the first and last rule." More broadly indicative of Strindberg's attitude at that particular time is the play's closing statement: "Let us teach our children that heaven is up there, but down here is the earth."[7] It was surely in that spirit he resumed the battle he had begun in *The Red Room,* when in a highly controversial work, *Det nya riket* [The New Kingdom], he launched his most massive broadside against Swedish society and its members, aiming his guns at the living and even the dead. On one extreme his target was his soon-to-be publisher, Albert Bonnier, on the other the revered eighteenth-century poet and balladier, Carl Michael Bellman.[8]

Though his creative energy seemed to prevail his marital happiness and economic stability were far more fragile phenomena, and at the height of this productive period his letters begin to reflect a gradual change in mood and a groping for something new and better. In the spring of 1882, writing to his brother Oskar, he bemoans his own health, saying his brain is so badly shaken he doesn't dare show himself in public. "Between us, I have felt such symptoms," he secretively adds "—purely physical, mind you—that I'm seriously frightened."[9] Initially, only his brothers are allowed to share in such apprehensions. To Siri, then visiting her family in Finland, he writes cheerful, loving letters, and those to friends and associates are still warm and often buoyantly jovial. To Carl Larsson, a key member of the younger generation of Swedish painters and at that time in the process of illustrating Strindberg's *Svenska folket* [The Swedish People], he composes some rather bawdy notes inspired by a delicate matter on which Larsson had sought his advice.[10] But in much of his correspondence there is an undercurrent of restlessness sufficiently persistent to suggest a disenchantment with the *status quo*. In fact, as early as June of 1881 he had told Edvard Brandes, younger brother of the critic and himself a principal figure in Danish progressive circles, of his intention to go abroad, although a full year would pass until the subject was broached again:

> In the fall I will definitely be leaving Sweden, for I can no longer endure being so alone. You people in Denmark have your party, while I stand here utterly abandoned, having one pack of dogs after the other sicked on me.

Then, responding to Brandes' subsequent inquiry, he explains that it is not the fear of critics that is behind his dissatisfaction and projected departure but an intense desire to get away from "friends" and make it possible for wife and children to escape the "rude persecution" to which they seem to be subjected.[11]

That the hostility toward Strindberg so rampant in certain circles may also have been reflected in a negative attitude toward Siri is of course entirely possible. However, the "rude persecution" was no doubt felt much more keenly by him than by members of his family and may have been a veiled reference to a group of professional history scholars who had expressed their resentment at his invasion into their domain with his two-volume *Kulturhistoriska studier* [Studies in Cultural History] in 1881. It is likely that the irately anti-intellectual tone so pronounced in *Det nya riket* was the result of this group's negative reaction to certain aspects of his scholarship, although a contributory factor may well have been the attitude of members of his own coterie, the "friends" he refers to in his Brandes letter. These artists and intellectuals had greeted *The Red Room* with unqualified enthusiasm only to become disillusioned with his subsequent efforts, in particular *Sir Bengt's Wife* and the fairytale play, *Lucky-Per's Journey,* none of which appeared radical enough to justify their hope of a position of political leadership on the part of the young author.

Yet despite his apparent determination to leave, 1882 and most of 1883 passed with no dramatic changes taking place. And as long as he remained at his summer haven at Kymmendö the creative avalanche roared on with undiminished force. Cooped up in his apartment in the dreary Stockholm fall and winter, however, he felt his spirits sadly deflated. "I haven't been able to write anything for two weeks!" he laments to a friend. To his publisher he paints a series of grim pictures of his existence—concluding one letter with a pronouncement that must have taken the recipient by surprise:

> Could you rescue me today with some money? My entire life is nothing but a delayed hanging. But on the first of April the great reformation begins, and this fall I intend to become a farmer.[12]

The reformation must have implied his moving to the archipelago, a passionately desired annual change, that year actually delayed by several weeks. As to his becoming a farmer, it was a suggestion not quite as outrageous as it might appear, for the preceding season at Kymmendö he had been in frequent consultation with his nephew, the agronomist Olle Strindberg, on a variety of matters concerning seeding and planting. When he arrived back at Kymmendö early in the summer he did in fact dig about in the dirt, but the nearest he would come to anything agricultural that fall would be through an appreciative observation of the pastoral activities unfolding in the fields and meadows between the shore of the Loing river and the edge of the Fontainebleau Forest in France.

His mounting interest in having his works translated into French may be viewed as an indication of a desire to pave the way for his own appearance in the French-speaking parts of Europe, or at least a plan for the building up of a reserve fund in the form of royalties to finance a possible stay in such countries. Discussing with his publisher the translation of *Sir Bengt's Wife* he stressed that by the time the French manuscript would be finished he would himself be working in France. He is badly in need of a change, he maintains:

> My head seems to be seriously affected, and that tends to work in all directions. It will lead to hell sooner or later. Nothing seems to help. I till the soil until, stooped over, I have to struggle toward a fence to be able to haul myself up. I sleep and eat, but I don't drink. Yet nothing seems to help.[13]

This was written in May of 1883. Then in July, following some apparently successful negotiations with his new publisher, Albert Bonnier, through which his financial prospects loomed both brighter and more predictable, he told his brother, Axel, that he would be taking his family abroad "this September. Irrevocably."[14]

Time was certainly ripe for such a move, and there can be little doubt that he would have left Sweden no matter where he would have been headed. His decision to go to France, however, was the direct result of his correspondence with Carl Larsson, now the proud recipient of a gold medal at the Paris *Salon.* This artist's glowing reports of life in Paris and among Scandinavians in a village where they tended to congregate had so intensified Strindberg's desire to become part of it all that he could no longer contain himself. Therefore, throughout the month of August, while finishing the manuscript for *Dikter på vers och prosa* [Poems in Verse and Prose], which soon was delivered to Bonnier to become the first work issued by his new publisher, he was also in the process of taking care of business matters so that he might leave Sweden with things in reasonable order. Next, he sent wife and children ahead to Stockholm, following them by mid-September, but only to collect his family and, as he had already vowed, "rush through . . . to vanish without a trace."

A tedious and tiring journey brought them to Paris, and after a few days there they continued to Grez on the Loing, where their arrival, though eagerly anticipated by Carl Larsson and others, momentarily caught all by surprise:

> I got a letter from Strindberg dated the day before, stating that he and wife Siri would be arriving the next day. Great excitement. All I could do was to set out for the station in the nearby village without delay. But only halfway there I saw them coming, the two promenading so prudently arm in arm along the monotonous French highway.[15]

Grez is not far from the much more famous Fontainebleau village, Barbizon, where Corot, Millet, Rousseau, Daubigny, and a great many other Frenchmen had taken up residence in the 1830s and '40s to escape the rapid urbanization of Paris and devote themselves to open-air painting. While declining in importance as the century passed its midpoint, Barbizon continued to attract artists until the end of the 1870s, then more often painters from other parts of Europe. Among them were three distinguished Swedes who in those surroundings produced some of their most memorable canvases: Carl Skånberg's shimmering *Interior from the Fontainebleau Forest,* Alfred Wahlberg's *Romantic Late-Summer Landscape,* and Carl Fredrik Hill's many scenes from Montigny, Isle-Adam, and Champagne.

Subsequently other villages in the region, such as Moret and Grez, both on the shore of the Loing, began to draw painters from abroad, and it was then that Grez became popular with the Scandinavians—initially for no other reason, it seems, than that there was a local innkeeper willing to offer accommodations on credit. At the time of Strindberg's arrival an entire colony was enjoying that hospitality. In addition to Carl Larsson, there were his fellow Swedes, Karl Nordström and Bruno Liljefors, the Dane, Peter Krøyer—better remembered for his sunbaked canvases from Jutland's Skagen peninsula than any French landscapes—two Norwegians, Christian Krohg and Christian Skredsvig, and Krohg's moody German friend, Max Klinger, whose emotion-charged paintings and graphics seem totally incompatible with the rustic poetry of the Fontainebleau landscape. But among all these painters in a social and creative setting totally devoted to the visual arts, Strindberg not only held his own but immediately became the focus of attention.

Not that he was unprepared for that select company. In the 1870s he had been painting quite regularly, mostly marine landscapes inspired by his stay in the Stockholm archipelago and executed with a skill far beyond that of the able amateur. In his journalist days he had written reviews and essays on art, gradually gaining insight and authority. Moreover, he was intimately familiar with the artist milieu, as clearly demonstrated in his portrayal of it in *The Red Room.* Also, he was not without knowledge of contemporary French trends, for on his first visit to Paris—a three-weeks stay in 1876 ostensibly on behalf of the Royal Library—he had occasion to see works both by members of the Barbizon group and the impressionists. Of the former he wrote an unequivocally enthusiastic appraisal, while his assessment of the latter was more ambivalent. Calling their efforts anemic, colorless, nonsensical, he suggested that Manet might have been suffering from an eye disease,[16] and yet a detailed analysis of a Sisley canvas seems exceptionally perceptive. On the whole, however, his art opinions were decidedly more orthodox than those of his companions who, with the exception of Klinger, were all influenced by the impressionists, and one may easily imagine how animated the discussions over the punch bowls must have been during those first weeks of Strindberg's stay in Grez.

3

Edvard Munch's Childhood and Youth

The Norwegians, throughout the nineteenth century deprived of true political freedom, had sought to manifest their spirit of independence through an active engagement in cultural pursuits. Consciously and subconsciously, this served to compensate for the depressing reality that the partriotically conceived and enthusiastically endorsed constitution of May 17, 1814, providing for the dissolving of a less than happy four-hundred-year union with Denmark, failed to provide freedom and instead led to a new and equally undesirable union with Sweden, which was to last for ninety-two years. During that period of time, however, the nation fostered several generations of creative personalities whose composite contribution served to make the nineteenth century a golden age of Norwegian culture.

Beginning in the first half of the century with the poets and popular leaders Henrik Wergeland and Johan Sebastian Welhaven, the painter Johan Christian Dahl, the violinist Ole Bull, and the historian Peter Andreas Munch, this mobilization of *åndskrefter* [powers of the spirit] reached its zenith in the later decades with such imposing figures as Henrik Ibsen, Bjørnstjerne Bjørnson, Edvard Grieg, and Edvard Munch.

Some of these found it necessary to spend major portions of their lives abroad where conditions on the whole were more favorable, but this did not prevent them from exerting their influence on developments at home, nor did the geographic distance separating them from Norway terminate their own dependence on their native environment. This was most pronounced, perhaps, in the case of Johan Christian Dahl. Following a frugal childhood and youth in Norway he soared into fame after periods of study in Denmark and Germany and an extensive stay in Italy, becoming a distinguished professor of landscape art at the prestigious Dresden Academy, where he served as teacher and guiding spirit of nearly every member of the next art generation in Norway. As for himself, he returned home at frequent intervals to scoop up inspiration, producing out in the open the rapid charcoal sketches and limpid watercolors from which he composed his vast shimmering studio paintings unveiling for his continental viewers the awesome scenic grandeur of his homeland. (Plate 3).

And there is Ibsen, in twenty-seven years of exile never ceasing to write about his own people. His plays are populated with men and women, some trying to cope with life in small coastal cities with views of wintry fjords and islands, others shivering in frigid country estates on the edge of somber evergreen forests, or withering away in the murky gloom of narrow valleys while yearning for the liberating vastness of the mountian plateaus. Although Ibsen's influence on literary developments in Norway was to be profound it asserted itself more slowly than did that of Bjørnson who, though frequently visiting Germany, Austria, and France, never really settled abroad. Instead, he established court at Aulestad, a rustic manor house in Gausdal, where visitors, foreign and domestic, were received in grand style.

As with Bjørnson, the great majority of Norwegian artists and intellectuals maintained their residence at home, not necessarily as a matter of choice but because they found it difficult to finance extended stays abroad. This situation then favored Kristiania which, in a union of separate but supposedly equal kingdoms, in reality was the capital of a strictly secondary realm and as such was slow in developing much beyond the state of a provincial center. Most of the features that made Stockholm a decidedly royal residential city were lacking or existed only in the most eclectic and diminutive forms: architectural monumentality and refinement, social ceremony and sophistication, an atmosphere of political intrigue and importance. Even so, life in the Norwegian capital was not entirely without its exciting aspects, and as the nineteenth century moved into its final quarter and the nation's avant-garde began to make itself felt, the city may in some ways have been offering more directly challenging opportunities than its grander sister capital to the east. With a population of only 100,000, no nobility, a minimal military presence, and a government bureaucracy of rather manageable proportions it featured on the whole much less clearly delineated social strata, therefore allowing a far more rapid penetration of ideas and events to all levels of the population.

There was really only one street of more than the most utilitarian importance, Karl Johan's Gate, incongruously named for the French founder of the Swedish Bernadotte dynasty, whose bronze likeness in an equestrian pose pranced at the north end of the street on a promontory in front of the rarely occupied Royal Palace. Closer to the people was the University—actually the Royal Frederik University, a reminder of the Danish period. Opposite and southward all the way to the neo-Renaissance Parliament Building stretched the green lawns of the Student Park, promenade ground of the citizenry, and facing the expanse was the new Grand Hotel, the street-level café of which served the local avant-garde as its headquarters

Edvard Munch, destined to make this urban setting known far beyond the borders of Norway, was born in rural Løyten but was only an infant when the family moved to the city and was therefore as much a product of the Norwegian capital as was Strindberg of the Swedish. There were other interesting similarities between the two. In his autobiographical novel, *The Son of A Servant,* Strindberg calls attention to the polar opposites in his parental background, describing his father, a less than successful businessman, as "an aristocrat to the core," while his mother was nothing better than "a poor tailor's daughter sent into domestic service by her stepfather."[1]

Munch, on his paternal side, had impeccable aristocratic credentials. Born into one of the most distinguished families of his nation he counted among early ancestors great landowners, high-ranking military officers, parish ministers of legendary standing, bishops, and in more recent times Norway's first important portrait painter, Jacob Munch, the nation's foremost historian, Peter Andreas Munch, and Andreas, a poet and dramatist whose works had inspired Ibsen. On his mother's side, however, he was of plainer stock, farmers and seamen. So in the make-up of their ancestral charts Strindberg and Munch had something in common, but in attitudes toward their ancestry they differed radically, Strindberg saying, "The boy has seen the splendor of the upper class from a distance. He longs for it as if it were his native home."[2] Munch, on the other hand, decried his aristocratic background, blaming it for his physical weakness and emotional instability. "From father's side of the family we inherited poor nerves," he said. "Grandfather became mad, you know."[3]

In the premature loss of a mother the two also shared destiny. The young August, having vied for her love throughout his early childhood—"my mother never loved me, she had other favorites"—felt his entire world collapsing when that goal became irrevocably unattainable:

> When at last there was stillness in the room, and his father had said, "Mother is dead," he was not to be comforted. He shrieked like a drowning man.[4]

Munch, who rarely attempted to express his emotions in words, did so in his paintings, revealing in his early works a nearly pathological preoccupation with death. Some recalled the vividly remembered struggle of his sister, Sophie, who died at the age of fifteen—when he was fourteen—others, such as the ghastly canvas *The Odor of Death,* derived from the memory of a more remote event, his mother's death when he was five. In *The Son of A Servant* Strindberg recalls an experience from *his* bleak childhood which could well have been a description of a Munch painting:

> When Johan had grown older and his mother was dead, it seemed he could not think of her without seeing first her and then a geranium, or else both together. She was pale. Her face was like the transparent white leaves of the geranium with its crimson veins, which grew darker toward the pistil where they seemed to form an almost black pupil, black as his mother's.[5]

For to Munch, too, flowers would evoke bitter memories. To him, as later to Strindberg, it was the hyacinth that brought the odor of death, and one evening, finding a bouquet of them in his living room, "he flared up angrily and stalked into the kitchen to berate his housekeeper: 'Haven't I told you I want no hyacinths in the house?' "[6]

Sickness, death, poverty, and extreme religious piety were as much part of the Munch household as they had been of the Strindberg family. Christian Munch, a physician practicing in the slums of Kristiania and emotionally incapable of charging for his services, sought comfort for his own frustrations and household shortages through a devout reading of scripture. Edvard, his oldest son, who would later react against his pietist upbringing by remaining aloof to religious issues, was no rebel at home and dutifully participated in daily reading and prayer. Also, when Dr. Munch considered the engineering profession the most suitable for his son, Edvard made no objection. It was only his frequent and prolonged illnesses, which affected his school records, that rescued him from that fate. Illnesses and his beloved aunt, for it was she, charged with the household duties after her sister's death, who discovered the boy's talent and was instrumental in having him enroll in the Municipal School of Art. As he approached twenty he was given free instruction by Christian Krohg. At that time he was sharing with other young artists a studio near Karl Johan's Gate, a setting that to him became what Montmartre had been to some of the impressionists. At one point in his career he used the street and its surroundings in the same deliberate manner, painting the same scenes at various seasons and times of day, in sunshine and rain, now meticulously dotted, now boldly streaked, and sometimes in carefully juxtaposed surfaces of radiantly pure, clearly delineated colors. Featured in these paintings are the people of Kristiania, hurrying to and from work, promenading along the Student Park or gaily following the military band on its Sunday parade. Most attractively depicted are the women, coyly peering up from under their wide-brimmed straw hats, swinging their brightly colored parasols or, caught in a sudden downpour, prudently lifting their skirts as they daintily skip across suddenly formed puddles (Plate 26).

So much a part of him did this setting become during his experiments with impressionism that he demonstratively returned to it in his deliberate repudiation of that approach—and of his townspeople, for that matter—in his stunningly different, ominously eerie, *Evening at Karl Johan's Gate* (Plate 27) from 1892, where the pallid faces and vacuous stares of the passers-by, the glaring color intensity of the sky as heightened in the windows of the Parliament Building and reiterated in agitated splashes in hat bands and eye sockets, and the piercing perspective of the disappearing street, need only be further synthesized and stylized to suggest his expressionist masterpiece of a year later, *The Shriek*.

4

Trial, Triumph, and Grez

Strindberg's first stay in Grez was of short duration, and despite his obvious pleasure at the company, his decision to remain abroad for an indefinite period seemed quickly shaken. In fact, less than a week after his arrival he writes back to Stockholm suggesting that from such distance it was already possible for him to view Swedish matters more calmly and with less bitterness, and that Sweden in comparison with the overrated countries abroad came through as an easy winner. "When it turns cold here we'll be going to Paris," he continues, "to some peaceful spot in Passy or Neuilly, and then most likely back to Sweden in the spring."[1] Of these tentative plans only the first was carried out. Early in October the Strindbergs were in Paris, remaining there for three months, the time divided equally between Passy and Neuilly. Then in January, 1884, they proceeded to Switzerland to settle in Ouchy near Lausanne. A return to Sweden that spring was financially out of the question, but late in the fall Strindberg did indeed return, alone and under the most bizarre circumstances.

Most of the works completed in these productive years were essays and other less formal observations on a variety of topics. In 1884, however, he wrote a collection of short stories intended to depict the reality of womanhood and the marital state, one of the stories taking its title from and intended as a satire on Ibsen's *A Doll's House,* a play Strindberg considered blatantly feminist. That his stories, published in September under the title *Giftas I* [Married I] and in tenor so contrary to the prevailing quest for women's equality, would be controversial Strindberg had fully anticipated, but the actual course of events still came as a shock to him. In a note dated Geneva, October, 1884, he records:

> Received this morning a telegram from Albert Bonnier stating that *Married* had been confiscated, for which reason he urges me to return home. Home? How strange the word sounds! Where is my home? Here in the hotel where through the wall I can hear my wife chatting with my children. Home? Since a year ago I have had no home. I have used other people's furniture, slept in other people's bedding, eaten at strange tables. I will not go home! What effect this will have on my existence I do not know, but I feel the ground rocking under me.[2]

Bonnier had good reason to ask for Strindberg's return, for he had himself been served with a summons to appear in court on a charge of "blasphemy against God's word or sacrament." In his autobiography, *The Son of A Servant,* Strindberg expresses his astonishment at such interpretation: "Religion? That he could not comprehend. It was Woman he had written about."[3] It was the first story in the collection, *The Reward of Virtue,* interpreted by conservative politicians and religious pietists as a brutal attack on the holy communion, that was at the root of the indictment.

Despite both gentle persuasion and more intense pressure exerted upon him by friends at home and abroad Strindberg was determined not to yield:

> A shower of telegrams! The dominent issue seems to be this: you will be considered a coward! Cowardly or brave, what does it matter? The confiscation, an act of violence by the upper class, makes Sweden twice as foreign to me.[4]

While he had visions of imprisonment and martyrdom few of his friends believed he would be convicted. Therefore they viewed his potential return as a unique opportunity to show the establishment the extent of his support among the rank and file, while they expected the trial to turn into a self-defeating mockery of an archaic bureaucracy. Among those most eager to see this process run its course was Carl Larsson, at that time a fiery political radical who with Ernst Josephson, most gifted of all the painters of the younger generation, was then organizing a massive opposition to the traditional art society. When Strindberg finally decided to take up the challenge it was to Carl Larsson he first disclosed his intention: "Now I'm going home! But how I shall rile them! A speech at the station . . . and a gala spectacle at *Nya Teatern.*"[5] During his long and solitary journey northward, however, such buoyancy was quickly deflated:

> In Hamburg where the travelers rested a while after a trying overnight train trip he burst into tears. But when he was about to board the steamer in Kiel and discovered it was named *August Victoria* . . . he took that as a good omen . . .
>
> In Copenhagen he received a telegram from his wife stating that she had received warnings of his arrest the moment he stepped on Swedish soil.[6]

Yet he knew there was no turning back. Once in Stockholm, met by vast cheering crowds, he must have felt that in some ways these were his finest hours. Next day, however, relating it all in a letter to Carl Larsson, he views the proceedings in a rather sober mood:

> My table is full of petitions, proclamations, poems . . . flowers and a laurel wreath. . . . If I were an idealist I'd have been duped by now, but I've never felt less ambitious—or smaller than I do now.[7]

The laurel wreath was the remaining evidence of the public's enthusiasm at his return, reaching a soaring climax at the conclusion of his first day in Stockholm in a well-timed "gala spectacle" at his own request: *Nya Teatern's* performance of *Lucky-Per's Journey,* during which the accolades had risen to a level of mass adulation. Years would pass until his fellow citizens would again so unequivocally acclaim his contribution to modern Swedish life.

All the same, neither such overt demonstrations of support nor his ultimate acquittal of all charges could induce him to remain in Sweden a minute longer than was absolutely necessary. The entire process, having left him weary, drained, had served only to reconfirm his totally negative opinion of Swedish officialdom. He was soon on his way to rejoin his family in Switzerland.

For the remainder of 1884 and into the spring of 1885, while in Ouchy, Strindberg continued his effort at having certain works translated into French and at the same time tried to improve his own fluency in the language. His only diversion was a hurriedly arranged trip to Italy with his new friend, Verner von Heidenstam, then an artist vacillating between painting and poetry. In Rome they met with Julius Kronberg, friend and painter whose famous *Hunter's Nymph* Strindberg had reviewed very favorably back in 1876, and Alfred Nyström, a sculptor from that circle of friends in the 1870s who had provided character inspirations for *The Red Room.* Otherwise Strindberg reaped little benefit from the venture. "Went to Venice and Rome," he notes in a letter. "Expected little, found less. Returned home sick in body and soul."[8]

And so it continued. His stay in Ouchy was plagued by sickness, not only his own but that of family members, and by severe financial distress accompanied by deteriorating marital relations. In early April, reluctant to leave the Alpine climate behind but urgently in need of a more active creative atmosphere, he once more brought his family to Paris, having then gained enough confidence in his language ability to be working on a sequence to *Married I* in French. Not that he intended to become a Frenchman, he reassured Carl Larsson in a letter. Claiming to be much too old to be transplanted he gave as the reason for his efforts in French a desire to be able to address, for once, a public sufficiently sophisticated to appreciate his works. An ominously morbid note brings the letter to a close:

> My strength has gone and my will to live as well. I have seen through all the sham and wish only to go to rest... When a man has been the object of contempt for so long he begins to look at himself as a contemptible creature, and then life is miserable.[9]

Those spring months in Paris with few friends within reach, continued illness, and ever worsening financial straits compelling him to send humiliatingly pleading letters to potential Swedish benefactors did nothing to alleviate his bleak mood, nor did the snail's pace at which his work proceeded. His attempt to write in French tended to complicate rather than facilitate matters, for although he was doing this to open up direct access to the French public the procedure resulted in the most cumbersome and continually fruitless negotiations with publishers both at home and abroad.

Then in June, while aching for the rocky skerries of his beloved Kymmendö, he had to accept as an uninspiring substitute a summer holiday on the sandy shore at Normandy, at Luc-sur-Mer which a decade earlier had been favored by his countryman, Carl Fredrik Hill, but which to Strindberg turned out to be "the most stupid of all places I have seen."[10] His spirits dropped to a new low. In this state, no matter what the source of his immediate or cumulative misery, he could direct his blame at one target only: "How I hate Sweden and despise its miserable population!... Exile is a terrible form of punishment. And yet! Yet I'm about to make this exile—permanent."[11]

Toward the end of July, his patience with the Atlantic seaside totally exhausted—his funds, too—he abandoned the beaches and retreated to a more familiar haven, Grez, where his prospects of friendly relations and generous credit seemed a good deal brighter. He had no sooner set foot in the village than he sent off a letter to Carl Larsson—then in Stockholm assisting in preparing the first exhibit of the so-called "opponents"—reflecting the total reversion of his mood: "Here I feel resurrected. Everything is beautiful—nature, dwellings, people, the food. It's a blessed place. Why I don't know."[12]

5

New Tendencies in Munch's Paintings

Strindberg's persistent disenchantment with Stockholm society, the public uproar at the *Married* trial, and in a broader context Ernst Josephson's and Carl Larsson's activities on behalf of the "opponents," all had their exact parallels in the life of the secondary capital of the realm, where reactionary politics, the church and other bureaucratic agencies, and the entire question of public versus private morality were hauled into the spotlight by a group of radicals calling themselves the Bohèmes. Among them was no mature literary genius who might have produced a Norwegian counterpart to *The Red Room,* but the group's composite activities had an effect on Kristiania activities far more profound than that of any Strindberg work, or even his trial, on Stockholm society.

Inspired by the same progressive trends from abroad that had influenced Strindberg, and also—as Ola Thommessen's reading of *Landsflykt* had demonstrated—by Strindberg himself, the loosely composed group numbered at one time or another most of the progressives congregating in Kristiania in the 1880s. Passionately devoted to all aspects of freedom, they might have preferred anarchy to any existing system of public order. Most gifted among the writers in the group were Arne Garborg, Gunnar Heiberg, and Sigbjørn Obstfelder, among the painters Krohg and Munch. Of all these only Krohg was along from the outset, and he was decidedly overshadowed by the movement's most articulate spokesman in public debate and polemics, Hans Jaeger (Plate 17), minor government functionary and a writer of modest talent. His rambling novel, *Fra Kristianiabohèmen* [From the Kristiania Bohème], was the decade's most sensational, though by no means most creative product. Published in 1885, a year after Strindberg's *Giftas I,* it was as expeditiously confiscated and placed in evidence in a trial strikingly similiar to that of Strindberg, with Jaeger indicted for "blasphemy and violation of modesty and morality." The Norwegian judiciary, perhaps less sophisticated and certainly less lenient than the Swedish, found the accused guilty and sentenced him to a prison term.

In the prolonged debate that ensued, Krohg, as active in journalism as in painting, was particularly outspoken in his condemnation of the authorities, and in what appeared to be a bold challenge he published his own Bohème novel, *Albertine,* in 1886, describing a young woman's path from poverty to prostitution. To no one's great surprise this too was confiscated and Krohg sentenced to pay a fine. Appeals to the Supreme Court on behalf of both authors were of no avail. The verdicts were upheld.

Before the end of the decade Krohg would present visual interpretations of sections of his novel in a series of paintings. Central among these is the monumental *In the Waiting Room of the Police Physician* (Plate 5), picturing a selection of the city's prostitutes lined up for their monthly checkup. This remarkable social and artistic document, in its days a sensation and a scandal, is now a treasured possession of the Norwegian National Gallery, where, perhaps deliberately, it has been placed on the wall facing the archway leading into the principal Munch Room.

Jens Thiis, one of Munch's early biographers, makes the astonishing claim that the Bohème group contributed little to Munch's development. "The movement was social and literary," he reasons, "and in these areas Munch was an outsider." How a scholar that well informed could brand Munch an outsider in literature is rather difficult to understand. Not only was Munch an avid reader of traditional and contemporary writings, as his large and well-worn book collection bears out, but in the period of his life when he maintained social contacts he invariably chose these from among writers. Thiis himself must have had second thoughts about the matter, for a few paragraphs further on he contradicts his previous claim, now saying that Munch as a close friend of the principal figure in the movement, Hans Jaeger, hardly could have remained unaffected.[1]

In his assessment of Munch's relationship with the Bohèmes, Thiis, apparently for reasons of propriety, is very anxious to separate their day-to-day mode of life, their overtly radical behavior, from their attitude toward the creative process. It seems well documented that Munch, although very much at ease in the company of individual members, was a more passive participant in the group's social rebellion. His paintings from the mid-1880s, however—most demonstratively his uncompromising portrayal of sexuality in *Puberty* and *The Day Thereafter*[2]—are simply unthinkable without direct reference to his exposure to the uninhibited social and creative attitude of the Bohèmes. That *The Day Thereafter* is a visual manifestation of human compassion and has no reference to social issues, as Thiis points out, is no doubt quite correct. That in no way alters the fact that Edvard Munch, shy, inhibited, even prudish, derived his courage to bare his human compassion in that radical manner from the influence exerted upon him by the very core concern of members of the Bohème group, sexual honesty.

Munch was always reluctant to reveal how or from whom he had acquired his technical approach to painting, but despite his own denial of any influence from Christian Krohg the effect of that student-teacher relationship is clearly evident in his early works, first of all his 1883 debut canvas, but also *Morning* and several other works from that period. Krohg, only five years Munch's senior, was already a widely recognized artist when he offered free instruction to Norwegian painters in the early 1880s. Educated in Berlin under the renowned realist, Carl Gussow, and in the daily company of Max Klinger—whose preoccupation with the morbid he did not share—he painted with a strong social consciousness but always in bright shimmering colors, acquired in part at the Skagen peninsula of Denmark where he worked with Anna and Michael Ancher and Peter Krøyer in the late 1870s. It was Krøyer who had brought Krohg and Klinger to Grez when Strindberg happened to be there. Later, Krohg had continued to Paris where his palette was further brightened by his exposure to the impressionists.

Returning to Norway at regular intervals he soon became one of Munch's principal mentors. So did Frits Thaulow, a frequent and successful contributor to the Paris *Salon* and Norway's only painter of international recognition. It was he who had offered Munch a personal grant for a visit to Paris in the spring of 1885.

In May of that year, while Strindberg was still in Paris struggling for his existence, Munch arrived in the French capital. Their paths could have crossed, for they both sought company in Scandinavian circles. On May 19, Strindberg, writing to Jonas Lie, says, "For fourteen consecutive evenings I went to the brasserie but did not see you."[3] Had Munch been there he would no doubt have recognized Strindberg from the photo in *Verdens Gang* the year before but would have been too shy to introduce himself to the now famous writer. Besides, he had only three weeks at his disposal and must have spent most of his time in the galleries. His letters provide no clues as to what he may have seen of art, except that he visited the Louvre where he was awed by the works of Delacroix, and the annual *Salon* that had opened shortly before his arrival. The press agreed that there was little to excite anyone in the *Salon* that year, although Munch may well have paused at *The Martyrdom of St. Denis* by the widely acclaimed academician, Leon Bonnat. When Munch returned to Paris to study in earnest some years later it was to Bonnat he went for instruction. The works of another artist may have impressed him—as it did Strindberg who, in an occasional piece of writing produced years later,[4] reveals that he, too, had visited the 1885 *Salon* and been particularly moved by the paintings of Puvis de Chavannes. It seems only logical that Munch, also, must have been intrigued by these crisply composed yet mysteriously moody works of which some of his own would soon evoke a faint echo.

The impressionists were not represented in the *Salon,* nor did they mount their own exhibit that year. In fact, by then the various members of the group had gone their separate ways, and while another impressionist show would open a year later these artists could no longer represent a unified front. More than ten years had passed since Pissarro, Monet, Renoir, Sisley, Degas, Cézanne, Morisot, and Guillaumin had formed the core of a larger group exhibit in which these eight had been singled out for special venom by the critics. One of the more stridently satirical of these arbiters of public taste, Louis Leroy, taking his cue from Monet's *Impression—Surprise,* had dubbed the group the impressionists, a designation intended to be derisive and initially not appreciated by any of its members.

That public and critics found it difficult to reconcile their established tastes with the novel efforts of these young painters becomes somewhat more understandable with the recollection that even Manet, pioneer in the deliberate usage of "the bright tones and luminous brilliance, which were adopted by the impressionists,"[5] refused to exhibit with them that first time because he found their works sloppy. Even so, in retrospect the merciless critical assaults on these deeply sincere artists seems downright cruel. Of Monet it was said that he had declared war on beauty, while Degas, having left himself wide open with one of his subject choices, was ridiculed in a pun: "How badly laundered his laundresses are!" As for Berthe Morisot, she was taken most severely to task by one of her former lady teachers who "told on her" in a letter to the young painter's aristocratic mother: "When I saw your daughter's paintings in such pernicious surroundings my heart failed me." But the most brutal criticism was reserved for Cézanne who, accused of being an incorrigible drunkard, was described as "a madman painting in the midst of delirium tremens."[6]

While most of these artists had gained some ground between those turbulent days and Munch's first Paris visit they were still so much the outsiders in proper French art circles that some of them were compelled to eke out a living under the most frugal and humiliating circumstances. So stubbornly persistent, in fact, was official France in its refusal to acknowledge the contribution of this influential group that when the will of Gustave Caillebotte, himself a minor impressionists who died in 1893, named the Luxembourg Museum as the recipient of his magnificient collection of paintings by his friends, twenty-three of sixty-seven canvases were refused.[7]

Considering the absence of an impressionist exhibit in 1885 Munch might well have spent his three weeks in Paris with little opportunity to see contemporary French art—except as conservatively displayed in the *Salon*—had it not been for Paul Durand-Ruel. This art dealer, whose services to the impressionists had been much more in the nature of a patron than a businessman, had already in 1873 begun assembling a catalogue of contemporary French art, illustrated with his own holdings, in which he linked the Barbizon painters and the impressionists. Prior to that and for more than a decade thereafter he had been purchasing the works of these artists with little prospect of immediate sale, so that by the early 1880s his enthusiasm and generosity had brought him precariously close to bankruptcy. By 1884, he confessed much later, he had owed more than a million francs and often had been forced to tell his painters he had nothing at all to give them. Then, as a bright promise of impending recovery, came an invitation from the American Art Association asking him to organize a major exhibit in New York City, and to make this as representative as at all possible he now added to his already sizeable and authoritative holdings a careful selection of the most recent works of the impressionists.

So when Munch arrived in Paris the Durand-Ruel Gallery had on hand a collection of contemporary French art never to be duplicated by any dealer—hundreds of paintings, watercolors, sketches, and graphics, many from the Barbizon group but the far greater share by the impressionists, and this time Manet as well. With the preparatory orientation Munch must have received from his benefactor, Frits Thaulow, and very likely, also from Christian Krohg, it is simply inconceivable that he would have bypassed the Durand-Ruel Gallery. Therefore, despite the absence of works by the newer, progressive artists in various official exhibits he had ample opportunity to study in detail and at some leisure an assemblage of art works at one time uniquely contemporary and informatively retrospective. This notwithstanding, both his early biographers, Jens Thiis and Pola Gauguin, perhaps in a subconscious desire to claim absolute originality on the part of their artist, tend to minimize the importance of such experiences, Thiis to the extent of totally ignoring Munch's first Paris visit. Gauguin, however, does allow that the young artist's first exposure to that undisputed center of modern art was of some importance, but only indirectly. The total freedom he saw in the works of others, Gauguin says, served to bolster his own confidence in what he was already doing and his determination to obey nothing but his own creative instinct and inspiration.[8]

While this is far too limited an assessment of that unique experience in Munch's early career the logic of Gauguin's reasoning is quite clear, for already in his canvas *Morning*—shown in the 1884 Autumn Exhibit—Munch had deliberately departed from accepted standards of painterly expression and amply demonstrated his self-confidence and determination. Therefore it must have been a great joy for him to discover as he viewed the works on display in the back rooms at Durand-Ruel's that he was already on the right track. It is true that his impressionist leanings immediately thereafter appeared less consciously motivated than they would be following his second and much more extensive stay in Paris. Yet even a casual examination of the works produced later that year reveals changes in his approach and technique sufficiently radical to prove that his brief exposure to the city had indeed affected him and contributed to his artistic development.

No doubt eager to reap the benefit of his Paris experiences while still fresh in mind he must have asked a friend and fellow artist to pose for him as soon as he returned home, for already in that year's Autumn Exhibit he was ready to present his full-length *Portrait of Jensen-Hjell* (Plate 8), so far his most ambitious work. That a painting as brazenly different would be a critical failure was almost a foregone conclusion, and it was viewed and discussed with a mixture of disbelief, scorn, ridicule, and downright anger. *Aftenposten*'s critic, enraged by a single feature—the omission of the distinct rendering of an eye in favor of a bright spot of reflected light—bristled, "This is impressionism at its extreme, art in caricature."[9] By then French critics had slowly begun to mellow toward the impressionists, while to their Norwegian counterparts this particular approach to art still implied only the most negative characteristics: a capricious compositional plan or more likely no plan at all, uneven, unattractively fragmented brushwork, shocking juxtaposition of colors, and of course the most blatant disregard for all technical skill and conventional mode of artistic refinement.

In the Munch painting, no one seemed to have discovered, or at any rate appreciated, the bold, carefully balanced placing of the figure, centered, freestanding and nearly shadowless, lifted by the luminescent, broken parallelogram of the floor and brought forward from the darker, more evenly painted surfaces of the abutting walls. On the other hand, that the model had assumed a decidedly derisive pose was infuriatingly clear to all, and he was, in fact, viewed not as an individual but a representative of the entire hated Bohème movement. This antagonism may in reality have pleased Munch, for it was the result of a deliberate and ingenious painterly structure highlighted by the emphasis of a steep diagonal line forcing the viewer's eye from the floor along a slanting axis—the walking cane and the closure of the haphazardly gaping coat—directly to that single notorious spot of light so playfully reflected from one of the lenses of the model's haughtily poised pince-nez.

Ingrid Langaard makes a most plausible case for Munch having become intrigued by Manet's *The Philosopher* during that first visit to Paris, and there are some rather striking similarities between the Munch portrait and that of Manet, first and foremost in the arrogant pose, then in the strong contrasts between light and shadow.[10] But in the Munch painting the brushwork is demonstratively fragmented, the contours fluid, and the total effect, at least on a present-day viewer, more immediate. It is, in fact, as though Munch has wanted to translate an openly admitted influence by Manet into a more contemporary idiom, just as Manet himself did with Goya and Valesquez twenty years earlier.[11]

Other Munch works from the mid-eighties contain features characteristic of the more avowed impressionists. There are family portraits of groups and individuals in casual, unposed attitudes reminiscent of Cézanne's early portraiture. Interior compositions probe the effect of spatial fragmentation, foreshortening of figures, faces variously lit by flickering flames, and he experiments with the rhythmic linear luminescence of drifting smoke. Then there are women out-of-doors, their hats or scarves or dresses bursting like spring blossoms onto the unprimed canvas, and landscapes radiant with bright, primary colors (Plate 19). In fact, it is precisely his strong predilection for the use of primary, unmixed colors that is the most consistent and enduring impressionist feature in Munch's works.

Whatever else his fleeting visit to Paris that spring of 1885 may have accomplished it made him keenly conscious of a need for a more extensive, carefully planned stay, and he was determined to return already the same fall. Sporadic illness and a chronic lack of funds, however, delayed this project for a full four years. In reality, this circumstance may have been a fortuitous turn of events, for in that extended period of time, working in surroundings where his own creative genius towered above that of anyone else—as readily acknowledged by the more perceptive of his contemporaries—he had no other recourse than to develop a style and an approach of his own. Thus, challenged and inspired by the new trends he had observed in Paris he went on to produce some of the most memorable canvases of his entire career and, intent on bringing the art of painting a step beyond its traditional confines, attempted to convey visual manifestations of thoughts and emotions rising from the depth of his own inner experiences. This resulted in works such as *Puberty* (Plate 33) and *The Day Thereafter* (Plate 34), the deeply introspective *Portrait of Hans Jaeger* (Plate 17), the first paintings from Åsgårdstrand, his beloved summer village on the east shore of the Oslofjord, and the initial version of *Sick Girl* (Plate 12), as well as its more meticulously executed variant, *Springtime* (Plate 16). No other single subject would so persistently pursue Munch throughout his career as the never-healing emotional wound left by his sister's illness and death. There are six known versions of *Sick Girl*—not including *Springtime*—all identical in size, structure, and basic composition. However, painted over a time span of nearly fifty years each canvas differs from the preceding in such particulars as impasto, color juxtaposition, and other less conspicuous details, the later versions becoming gradually more sophisticated, controlled, hence less emotionally motivated than those preceding them.

Munch's external impetus for *Sick Girl* may have come from Krohg's canvas of the same title (Plate 13) painted in 1881-82 when he was providing free instruction to Munch and his friends in their studio off Karl Johan's Gate. But Krohg's painting is really a totally different picture, composed by an artist observing his subject from the outside with a keen eye for naturalistic detail. No doubt Krohg also senses deep compassion, but does not attempt to bring this element onto the canvas. Munch on the other hand, pours his own agony onto it in agitated sweeps of the palette knife and nervously broken brush strokes, then slashes the thickly built-up surface with deep intersecting lines. Years later Munch said of *Sick Girl:* "It is perhaps my most important work and at any rate my breakthrough in terms of expressionism. My subsequent art is entirely based on it."[12]

Kristiania critics, though grudgingly beginning to admit that Munch betrayed talent, stubbornly refused to concede that his particular approach to art constituted a viable form of creative expression. Instead, they continued chiding him, maintaining that his works were unforgivably sloppy, unfinished, that he had not taken the necessary time to master the basic techniques and therefore owed it to himself and his nation, to tone down his temperament and cultivate his talent in a proper manner. Of course, considering critical reaction to the first impressionist exhibit in Paris in 1874 and subsequent French reluctance to acknowledge that group, it is hardly surprising that the inexperienced viewers and semiprofessional critics in parochial Kristiania failed to discover the greatness of the works before them. For when Munch at the Autumn Exhibit of 1886 unveiled four new paintings, including *Sick Girl,* he was not only confronting his viewers with a painterly approach never before seen in those latitudes but also introducing to the world of art a completely new, as yet unnamed movement. In retrospect, it is not at all difficult to assess the significance of such works at that particular time, but to contemporaries they appeared as incomprehensible anomalies, doubly disturbing because they actually evoked the admiration of certain artists, among them some individuals otherwise considered reasonable. Yet the critics, incapable of plumbing the depths of such creations, resorted to invectives and ridicule: "Edvard Munch is best served by having his pictures bypassed in silence," one all-knowing authority declared, indignantly adding, "With these paintings the entire level of the exhibit has been lowered"—a judgment emphatically seconded by another: "Here it is no longer a question of nature, only bizarre madness, delirious moods, and feverish hallucinations." One reviewer, linking *Sick Girl* with "deviant French art," gleefully told his readers that he had never approached the picture without finding someone standing there laughing at it. "Let a work of art be as distinctively individual, as different from anyone else's accomplishment as at all possible," he went on, "what good is it if it is devoid of all spiritual content?"[13]

These critics, frustrated by their own incomprehension and seeing only the iconoclast, not the pioneer, failed to detect the surge of emotion—the true "spiritual content"—that throbbed in each canvas and made of the occasion a revolutionary event. Oskar Kokoschka, writing much later of Munch as a pioneer, observes that turning points in history are, as a rule, overlooked by contemporaries.[14] An analysis of the concurrent activities of those most frequently sharing with Munch the distinction of having introduced the expressionist movement tends to confirm that his contribution of the 1886 Autumn Exhibit in Norway marked exactly such a turning point:

Edvard Munch's expressionist pictures are singular phenomena in Scandinavian art, and even among antecedents in European art there are no corresponding features to be found. In the years 1885-86 Van Gogh was still producing pictures in the realist vein, such as the socially oriented *Potato Eaters*... Paul Gauguin was in Pont-Aven in 1886 attracting the attention of his fellow artists with his liberal views. But he was still under the influence of the impressionists, especially Pissarro, and his art showed no tendency toward anything revolutionary.[15]

6

Strindberg Returns to Drama

In the spring of 1886, a little less than three years after his initial departure from Sweden when he had solemnly declared, "I have not only lost all interest in the theatre, but I will travel great distances just to avoid hearing about it,"[1] Strindberg returned to playwriting.

In the intervening period, his enormous creative energy harnessed exclusively for prose writing, he had produced a score of volumes, among these the controversial *Married,* I and II, and his important autobiographical novel, *The Son of A Servant.* In reality he had never really abandoned the drama, says the Swedish critic Martin Lamm, but had found the form stale, in need of renewal, and had been searching for different avenues of dramatic expression. Finally, combining what he had read in Zola's *Naturalism in the Theatre* and in books dealing with the power of hypnotic suggestion, he seemed to have found the proper direction. It was then "that he was able to see new possibilities in naturalistic drama and set in motion plans that undoubtedly had long been brewing in his mind.[2]

The works that resulted would at long last provide Strindberg with an avidly desired, appreciative, but rather esoteric continental audience, and it was through such new-found supporters and friends that he and Munch would finally meet. But before that would come to pass Strindberg was to endure the break-up of his marriage, the prolonged anguish of the divorce proceedings and the virtual terminal separation from his children, a libel suit threatening him with a prison term, and to top it off, perpetually unpredictable, steadily deteriorating financial circumstances, and frequent physical health problems compounded by a mounting dread of approaching madness.

His return to the drama in 1886 may initially have been motivated not so much by the directions he thought he had found as by more mundane issues closer to home. Still residing in Grez, by then no longer the "blessed place" it had seemed to be on his return from the Atlantic coast, he had been working at an unbelievably intense pace to complete on the one hand his voluminous *The Son of A Servant,* on the other the introductory part of his socio-cultural study, *Among French Peasants.* With the latter manuscript finished and on its way to

Copenhagen where, through the intervention of Edvard Brandes, it was to be published as a serial in the daily, *Politiken,* he took time out to assess his precarious state of affairs in a letter to his Danish mentor:

> I am tired! Tired! I go around with a six-shooter in my hip pocket. But then I think, Calm down. Let us see how things turn out. I have been reading too much lately: psychology, morals, psychiatry, sociology, economics, so much that my head is in a jumble.[3]

To a Swedish friend he had suggested a few days earlier that his creative career might have come to an end, or if not entirely so, that he would at least be forced to "pick up old threads and wind these for a while."[4] Old threads? Certainly a far better solution than the use of a six-shooter. So why not write another play? Of all his activities that was really his favorite, giving him "so much pleasure that I found life to be a pure blessing while the writing was going on."[5] Besides, he believed it might offer prospects of more immediate financial return. For a suitable subject he needed to look no farther than at the milieu in which he was living. He had written about artists before and with notable success. So while still in Grez, "locked in for lack of money,"[6] he began thinking of a new play, although nothing was sorted out and committed to manuscript until he had left France and taken up residence in Switzerland—the German-speaking part this time—from where he could look back at his association with artists in Grez and Paris with a degree of detachment. The central subject was not new. Dealing with the relationship between husband and wife it was in part another attack on Ibsen's *A Doll's House,* which he never tired of satirizing. The play, initially called *Maurauders,* then after some changes retitled *Comrades,* treats the husband-wife conflict in more tangible terms—the marital partners are also competing artists—and with greater partisanship than in *A Doll's House*—to Strindberg an entirely fair development:

> That I have presented a stingy and dishonest woman is no more unjust than the shameful attack on man by Ibsen and his sisters. But it happens that woman already by nature is stingy and instinctively villanous . . .[7]

His decision to portray the principal characters as artists in competition is interpreted by Gunnar Ollén as a possible manifestation of Strindberg's lingering bitterness at the outcome of the premiere performance of *Sir Bengt's Wife,* when he, the playwright, failed, while his wife Siri, acting in the title role, triumphed.[8] As for the relationship between them during the time the new play was in the making, it was near the breaking point, aggravated by precarious material circumstances, Siri's negative reaction to the second part of *Married,* and a series of emotional issues rooted in Strindberg's excessively suspicious nature. So despite his own frequent reassurances to the contrary—mostly in letters to his brothers—there is ample evidence to conclude that his marriage, never exactly serene, at this stage was floundering in the most severely troubled waters.[9]

In the forthcoming plays the issue was to be much broader than the relationship between husband and wife, or the emancipation of woman as presented by Ibsen and then countered by Strindberg. Rather, it was the age-old conflict between the male and the female species, the entire battle of the sexes with its insatiable female vampires and, to Strindberg, the ominous specter of an impending matriarchy. This was by no means a new feature in European creative life. In *The Son of A Servant,* Strindberg traces it all the way back to Shakespeare's *King Lear,* and in his own century it was considered by Baudelaire, Mallarmé and Huysmans, and, just as Strindberg was beginning his new series of plays, by Paul Lafargue. Many painters, too—before Munch—favored subjects expressing an apprehension of the role of woman, in the 1870s and '80s particularly Gustave Moreau and Odilon Redon. But in the field of the drama it was Strindberg who carried the conflict into a raging "Sexual Warfare on the Stage."[10] Declared and fought in preliminary skirmishes in *Comrades,* then breaking out with devastating force in the next play, it roared on without interruption for at least four years, then receded somewhat only to flare up again at intervals until Strindberg's last days.

To write a piece for the theatre is really a lot easier than writing novels, Strindberg had claimed in a letter to Gustaf af Geijerstam—"provided one knows the trick."[11] This was in January, 1887. The Strindbergs had moved again, now from the peasant proletariat setting of Gersau, huddled under the jagged Alps by Lake Lucerne, to the much gentler shore of Lake Constance, to occupy an aristocratic country house near the island city of Lindau. There, invigorated by the change and his inspiring new surroundings—not least the virile display of masculinity and military precision put on daily by a regiment of Bavarian recruits and their drill masters in an exercise field nearby—he began toward the end of January to write what was to become a monument in modern theatre, *The Father.* Completing it in record time about three weeks later, he proved not only that he knew the trick, but that he just as unquestionably was thoroughly familiar with the subject at hand.

In this second in his series of new plays he was no doubt eager to put to practical use some of what he had learned from Zola and others in his voracious readings. That he already the same year arranged for a French translation of *The Father* and sent it off to Zola certainly bears this out, although in the accompanying letter he referred to *"la formule expérimentale"*[12] rather than specifically to a naturalistic pattern. And whatever his intention at the outset, in the course of the intensely inspired creative process he must have responded far more to instinct than to any conscious requirement imposed upon him by a formula prescribed by someone else. Whatever he extracted from secondary sources served only to strengthen the mold into which he cast his own experiences as husband and father and his thoughts and purposes as a creative artist. So admirably did he blend these diverse ingredients that the inner reality and independence of the play remains unshaken by the turmoil of actual events behind it. Therefore, it is not as a stage representation of a portion of the playwright's private life that this remarkable work has gained its place in theatre repertoires throughout the world, but as a highly imaginative drama giving viable expression to certain tragic aspects of the human condition, its shuddering action always "close enough to universality to affect every reader and spectator, with either fascinated engagement or horrified withdrawal from such frank revelation of the truth."[13]

In his letter to Zola, Strindberg describes his play as following a formula implicitly advocated by "the master," stressing the inner action at the cost of "theatrical trickery," reducing the decor to a minimum, and preserving the unity of action. *The Father* also shows a Zola influence in relying on a subject pattern similar to that of *Thérèse Raquin,* outlined in Strindberg's essay, *On Modern Drama and Modern Theatre:* to seize a single grand and strong motif, "here the murder of the one partner so that the other may gain the freedom of choosing once more."[14] But there are features in *The Father* pointing toward much more radical theatre than that of Zola: deliberate distortions and exaggerations, and underneath all its eruptive anguish a faint throb of nostalgic lyricism, elements entirely alien to the naturalistic approach but central in the expressionist movement, whether in words or in pictures. This may well explain why one of the most worn books in Edvard Munch's collection is his paperback copy of *The Father.*

The wave of enthusiasm on which Strindberg had once more launched his career as a playwright did not long sustain its flow when his efforts, far from easing his lot, only compounded the complexity of his life. For now followed a difficult search for a fearless publisher—Bonnier having found *The Father* too drastic—and an equally bold theatre director. Moreover, his marriage now moved toward its inevitable breakup. While in the brief periods when he was separated from his family—during visits to Copenhagen and Vienna—his longing for Siri made him miserable beyond words, he was no sooner with her than he behaved as "an unreasonable child . . . literally seeking out opportunities for quarrel."[15] In this precarious state of affairs the entire family moved again, to within sight of Sweden, taking up residence in Copenhagen where Strindberg's contacts were good. *The Father,* published in September, 1887, by Hans Österling in provincial Hälsingborg in Sweden and then translated into Danish, had caught the interest of Hans Riber Hunderup, actor and theatrical entrepreneur, then director of Copenhagen's Casino Theatre. It was there, in an establishment catering to audiences accustomed to much lighter fare, that this modern tragedy was given its première on November 14, 1887. Copenhagen critics, flattered that "the most disputed author of Scandinavia"[16] had chosen their city not only as his arena but as his place of residence as well, and no doubt influenced by the interest the Brandes brothers showed in Strindberg, wrote favorable reviews of the play. The audience, on the other hand, though mollified by a light comedy sharing the playbill, was evidently less receptive to the extraordinary activities on the stage. Strindberg himself, in a later letter to none other than Friedrich Nietzsche, recalls the immediate reaction, perhaps embellishing his account with some distortions and exaggerations as in the play itself:

> One old lady died of fright during the performance, another gave birth to a child, and at the sight of the strait-jacket three fourths of the audience rose *en masse* and stalked out howling.[17]

Eleven performances later the Casino went bankrupt, so Strindberg reaped no financial benefit from the venture, nor did he receive any royalties from his Hälsingborg publisher. Still greater disappointments were awaiting him. In January the following year a Stockholm performance of *The Father* was a failure; next, his hope of an entry into the Parisian theatre world through Zola and André Antoine's *Théâtre-Libre,* which had opened shortly after the completion of the new play, came to nothing. His burning desire for such exposure, however, remained very much alive and was a strong motivating force in the writing of his subsequent plays, especially *Lady Julie,* composed late in the summer of 1888 and prefaced with an essay now as famous as the play itself and considered to be his dramatic manifesto. This analysis of his own play—and by implication his statement of purpose as a playwright—is to no small extent inspired by Antoine, though the French theatre pioneer is not mentioned by name, nor is Zola. Yet that *Théâtre-Libre* must have been his model for "a *little* stage and a *little* auditorium" seems self-evident, and his demands for reform, though many certainly his own, tend to second those already put into effect by Antoine, whose ideas and efforts were part of Strindberg's daily fare in conversations and correspondence during his stay in Copenhagen. More ambivalent in this document is his attitude toward Zola who, in a recent letter of comments on *The Father,* had bemoaned the absence of factual information on each character's background and the lack of other features that might have contributed to a more complete identification. Strindberg, however, in *Lady Julie* more determined than ever to present a section of reality, now obviously disagrees with Zola on the proper method of transferring such reality to the stage:

> My own minor characters seem abstract to some people because everyday people are to a certain extent abstract in performing their work; that is to say, not individualized . . .[18]

And therefore even the main characters in *Lady Julie* are treated with a degree of abstraction. To be sure, in the course of the play much is revealed about backgrounds and motivations, but in their total behavior the characters are not all that fixed, definite, predictable. They are, says Strindberg, intentionally "characterless" to indicate that they are modern, "living in a time of transition... vacillating, tattered mixtures of old and new."[19]

Again, these are features more radical than what may reasonably be placed in the category of naturalistic theatre. The deliberate consideration of the effect of hereditary and environmental factors on the workings of the human psyche is traditional with the movement, but Strindberg's emphasis on less clearly defined but perhaps equally compelling stimuli—sound, rhythm, fragrances, the season, the time of day, and of the month—and of course his bold use of the power of hypnotic suggestion, belong to the theatre of the future.

Lady Julie, portraying through the means of a dialogue unveiling some of the darkest chambers of the human mind the gradual but willing sexual surrender of a member of the aristocracy to her virile, socially ambitious manservant—once more the relentless battle of the sexes—was not the type of play likely to gain entrance into the repertoire of the bourgeois theatre in Scandinavia at this time. Not even in Copenhagen where he had met with so much understanding and support did Strindberg succeed in having it presented in a public performance, and a letter from Antoine, proving to be little more than a courtesy note, shattered his hope of a Paris staging. In the wake of these disappointments he began in earnest to work for the establishment of a Scandinavian Experimental Theatre, planning to make use of available facilities, amateurs, and unemployed dramatic personnel. These plans, he says in a letter written in November, 1888, constitute "the general solution to all my social, economic, artistic, and domestic problems."[20] His principal supporters in the venture were Herman Bang, author of a sensational novel, *Haabløse Slaegter* [Generations without Hope], published in 1880, the actress-writer, Nathalia Larsen, and Siri, with whom he lived in a tenuous state of armistice now made more tolerable by this enterprise which promised to satisfy her desire to return to the stage. Her comeback was to be in *Lady Julie,* but the sudden interference of the public censor reduced the performance to a private showing—taking place on March 14, 1889—thus denying her much of the anticipated pleasure. The grim attitude of her husband did not enhance the moment:

> Siri Strindberg played the title role against the young Viggo Schiwe with 150 people in the audience. The playwright stood half concealed behind a door, his face pale and contorted with jealousy.[21]

The performance of *Lady Julie,* originally intended to be part of the official opening of the Scandinavian Experimental Theatre on March 9, was postponed for five days. On the main occasion it was replaced by *Pariah,* a free stage adaptation of a short story by a young Swede with whom Strindberg had entered into correspondence, Ola Hansson, whose hyper-erotic *Sensitiva amorosa,* published in 1887, had caused a controversy not unlike that generated by Bang's *Haabløse Slaegter* in Copenhagen and Hans Jaeger's Bohème novel in Kristiania.

The performances, which included *Creditors* and *The Stronger*—featuring Siri in its only speaking role—in addition to *Pariah,* were on the whole well received. "My theatre succeeded yesterday!" Strindberg writes to his brother, Axel, "Therefore I consider myself 'rescued'..."[22] And for one of his actors, the otherwise so unlucky Hans Riber Hunderup, under whose leadership the Casino Theatre had gone bankrupt, it might have meant a rescue as well, for his acting in *Pariah* was by one critic characterized as "an art so unique and fine that anything better has seldom been seen on the Danish stage."[23] Unfortunately, this new venture was to prove no more durable than his previous one.

A French critic, René Fleury—pseudonym for Lucien Muhlfeld—impressed with Strindberg's Copenhagen activities, had that summer prepared a lengthy article entitled "A Scandinavian Théâtre-Libre," exceptionally favorable in its appraisal of Strindberg as a playwright and naturalist, and of his bold attempt at creating a modern theatre in the North.[24] It must have come as the most astonishing news to Fleury that his article, published in the September issue of *Revue d'Art Dramatique,* would turn out to be the Scandinavian Experimental Theatre's obituary. But so it was, for those promising presentations that March signified, for a composite of reasons—financial and domestic troubles, for the most part—at once both the overture and the finale of this worthy but not particularly well managed enterprise. Such immediate impermanence, however, was by no means the ultimate result of Strindberg's activities in Copenhagen. His chief investment—his only true capital, he described it—was his creative work, the dramas composed for, or first performed by, the Experimental Theatre, an opus constituting a major and lasting contribution to the world of drama. Moreover, despite the rather discouraging setback experienced in his first striving for such an independent, intimate theatre, he never really lost interest in the project, although years would pass until he once more took deliberate steps toward its implementation.

Also of lasting importance were the contacts he had made. Those with Zola and Antoine would in due time put him within reach of that long-cherished goal, a Parisian audience. That with Ola Hansson, whose interests were largely German-oriented, would soon open up new avenues of exposure and influence, primarily through the Berlin avant-garde, in whose inner and also more peripheral circles he would enter into relationships with individuals who more profoundly than any others would determine the future course of his life.

Meanwhile, his immediate failure making a further stay in the Danish capital both fruitless and embarassing, Strindberg at long last decided to return to Sweden. It was a step he had been considering for some time, and already in September of 1888, before his theatre failure, his departure seemed imminent, but that may well be related to an unpleasant affair involving a young woman on the estate where he was living. When that ill wind had blown over and he became absorbed in the theatre project he settled down again, but in the spring, all ties to Denmark broken, he was ready to leave. "My intentions to return home are this time more certain than ever before," he writes to his publisher, adding as a sigh of despair, "If I only knew where I would live.[25] While he might have had some apprehension about the extent of his welcome in certain places there can actually have been little doubt in his mind where he would prefer to live. In his persistent longing for Sweden he had always conjured up the picture of the one place on earth where he had experienced the greatest measure of his frugally allotted happiness: the Stockholm archipelago. Late in April, even before the winter had fully released its icy grip on these far-flung tentacles of the Baltic, Strindberg arrived in Sandhamn to seek solace for his tortured soul:

> . . . the impression the archipelago scenery has made on me is ten times what it was the last time I saw it . . .
>
> People are glad to have me back and want to recapture me for the land I love to the point of ecstacy.[26]

In the extreme solitude of this setting, still hoping against hope for a reconciliation with Siri, he waited out the course of events, initially sending her some nostalgically pleading letters trying to prevail on her to join him:

> It's so beautiful here that I become rather emotional. It's so unbelievably glorious to be back in one's own country, and to you this area ought to be particularly attractive, because it resembles what we used to call Finland out at Kymmendö . . .
>
> I have been heartsick for fourteen days! I have plagued you, poor Siri, forgive me. Only do come with the children! If you do feel that I'm a good father to your children bind me to you with a little friendliness. And if you want to bend me then be a woman, and I shall bend as a man ought to before a woman. As a human being you are not my superior, but as a woman you are, for happily there are two sexes which fortunately differ greatly from each other.[27]

But within days his mood would change, he would become belligerent, vindictive, and soon it must have become clear to him that this time there was no road leading back.

7

Significant Munch Canvases of the 1880s

In the winter and spring of 1888-89, Edvard Munch began to assemble as much of his total opus as he could lay his hands on—and considering how little he had been able to sell the collection became rather representative, numbering 110 separate items—for the purpose of doing what no other Norwegian artist had ever dared do: present a retrospective exhibit.

Prior to this, in the hope of realizing his plans for studying in Paris, he had applied for a state grant and may have thought the exhibit might serve a twofold purpose: first, providing those making the final grant decision with a detailed view of his production, next, enabling potential buyers to pick and choose in comfort and leisure. These may well have been thought of in reverse order, for although the Board of Norwegian Artists had strongly endorsed his application he had little reason to be overly confident. He was after all no favorite of the establishment. Critics and public alike considered his pictures arrogantly different and disgustingly unpleasing, and to make matters worse he was seen regularly in the company of those decadent Bohèmes whose lives seemed totally devoted to debauchery and who wrote books so flagrantly indecent that no self-respecting reader would even touch them. So bad were these books, in fact—and did not Munch's pictures in many ways resemble them?—that one of these so-called writers had already served a prison term for his literary indecency and another paid a sizable fine.

Mindful of these public attitudes Munch may have mounted his exhibit primarily as a sales effort to forestall another delay in his travel plan in case the state should decide against him. As it turned out he did receive the grant while most of his paintings remained unsold, a development which may have left him with ambivalent feelings, for he was actually never anxious and more often quite reluctant to sell his works. This accounts for the fortunate circumstance that most of his early paintings, with the exception of a few destroyed in a fire, are readily accessible in two of Norway's principal museums, the National Gallery in Oslo and the Rasmus Meyer Collection in Bergen, while the bulk of his later works is found in the Munch Museum in Oslo.[1]

Included in the retrospective—of which no catalogue remains extant—were of course nearly all the works shown at the Autumn Exhibits where he had been represented annually since 1883. His crucial *Sick Girl,* ridiculed at its first showing, was this time totally ignored, as were *Puberty* and *The Day Thereafter.* To supplement his paintings he had included sketches and drawings which should have enabled perceptive viewers to pursue his creative course not only from the inception of each idea to the finished canvas but from one canvas to the next. For already that early there is in all his experimentation and effort a continuity of purpose which today seems so eminently clear and convincingly logical. However, the few critics who bothered to see the exhibit—Jens Thiis, who was there, claims it was deliberately ignored—apparently detected no such clues nor did they see any painting worthy of special mention. Instead their reviews amounted to little more than rhetorical narratives belaboring their own negative impressions and omitting any attempt at analytical observation of individual works. The most detailed account was given by *Dagbladet's* critic who, though staying away from the exhibit proper, made his appearance "on demand" after it had officially closed. Considered well informed and modern this reluctant connoisseur detected "touches of genius" but failed to discover anything he would judge mature, complete, and felt instead that Munch revealed "a pathological weakness in his self-development and an indifference toward form and composition, so much more regrettable in the works of an artist of such talent."[2]

A measure of the continuity and development in Munch's art during the approximately five years covered by the retrospective becomes apparent with the juxtaposition of two early works with two major compositions of similar contents completed shortly before the exhibit: *Morning* (Plate 10) viewed with *Springtime* (Plate 16) and *Portrait of Jensen-Hjell* (Plate 8) placed opposite *Portrait of Hans Jaeger* (Plate 17).

Local critics, steeped in realism and therefore favoring an accurate rendition of scenes from everyday life, had had no difficulty finding Munch's debut work—the girl making up the morning fire in her stove—both acceptable and reasonably well done, while his artist friends were much more generous in their praise, Krohg going so far as to call it "superb." Only a year later, however, when showing *Morning,* in so many ways similar to his debut work, Munch lost all the critics and not a few of his friends. His own cousin, Gustav Wentzel, the most meticulously realistic of all Norwegian realists, is reported to have said, "Edvard, you paint like a pig!"—prompting Munch's sullen retort: "We can't all keep painting fingernails and warts!"

So it appears that Munch, approaching twenty-one, had already decided to set out on his own solitary path, though initially carrying with him such social realist props as the workaday model in her wrinkled housedress, common face and rough hands, hair long and unkept, bed with simple linen and shoes underneath, plain night stand with water carafe and glass, and a room with bare walls. In the same 1884 Autumn Exhibit, Krohg had presented his *Sleeping Mother with Child* (Plate 6), composed around items nearly identical to those in Munch's *Morning* but executed with greater attention to detail and with the important addendum of the child in the cradle to give the painting its unmistakable imprint of social realism through the inference of unwed motherhood.

Morning, Munch's first attempt at juxtaposing light and shadow in distinctly separate surfaces vibrant with fresh colors, is an exuberant expression of painterly joy. The deep blue of the model's simple outfit is reflected on the wall in a lighter rectangle which, with the shimmering white pouring in through the window and onto the bulging bedding and sections of the wall, frames the robust tones of face, neck, arms, and a foot. But the person around whom all this visual interplay is happening plays no role beyond what can be externally and visually manifested. In this respect she differs in function as much from Krohg's model with her implicit pronouncement of social injustice as from Munch's own central figures in *Springtime,* then his most recent work. For in that canvas his consummate artistry—compositional technique, color usage, psychological insight—is directed toward the sole purpose of conveying to the viewer not only what is happening physiologically to the central character in this tragedy—death is already there in the wan face turning sway from the life-giving sources, the sun—but to those left behind as symbolized in the taut pose of the mother whose hands stop knitting and body turns rigid as her eyes, away from the viewer, seek those of the girl.

As different as these two pictures are in content they share a remarkable number of features. The newer painting pictures a simple room, not quite as bare as in *Morning,* a window with white curtains, a table with water carafe and glass, just as in the earlier work. The division of the canvas into clearly delineated surfaces of light and shadow, though more carefully calculated in *Springtime,* is evident in *Morning* as well. The color schemes, too, are rather similar, the earlier painting distinctly recalled in the window wall of the newer with its shimmer of bright blue in the diaphonous white of the curtain and the colder, glossier tone of the wainscoting, this crisp interplay now highlighted by the iridescent green foliage of the potted plants.

Yet this window wall, fully as bright as any single section of *Morning,* reflects none of the exuberance of the earlier painting, for its brightness has no penetrating quality. It is simply a rigid, translucent wall to the dark interior where the shadows, falling deeply, icily, hang oppressively over the figures to form a stark contrast with the regenerative sunshine and gently wafting springtime breeze coming in through the window.

In the evenly sunny *Morning* shadows are little more than slightly muted tones of prevailing brightness, such as in a diagonal of reddish-brown in the model's cascading hair and a deepening of the dominant blue in her outfit, along its back and in streaks and patches throughout her draped skirt—"vibration of tone," a critic had called a similar technique when observed in paintings shown in the first impressionist exhibit. In *Springtime,* however, the use of such contrasting values, much more deliberate and conspicuous, leaves little doubt as to its expressive intent. Applied so that more than one half of the canvas is shrouded in a dismal, confining gloom pierced only by the pillow's chalky whiteness and the drained pallor of the girl's hands and face, this contrast between light and shadow becomes a pronounced symbol of life and death.

The *Portrait of Jensen-Hjell,* when first shown in 1885 angrily denounced as "impressionism at its extreme" and ostensibly rejected for its compositional technique, was in reality the victim of the prevailing antagonism toward the Bohèmes. A year before critics had dismissed the model in *Morning* as nothing but "a seamstress no educated person would want on his walls." Yet had they had a choice in the matter their preference would no doubt have been to look at that plebeian seamstress rather than the seedy, disreputable Bohemian, Jensen-Hjell. Therefore, when Munch in his 1889 retrospective chose to present as one of his major new works a *Portrait of Hans Jaeger,* high mogul of the Bohème movement, he must have done so as a direct challenge to bourgeois society. It was on that premise many critics viewed the painting, one in a left-handed compliment noting, "He has succeeded in giving striking interpretations of certain unattractive personalities,"[3] another, calling the Jaeger portrait live, spirited, and effective, bemoaned that these quality features had been wasted on such an unworthy subject.[4] There were, however, a few sufficiently non-partisan to attempt to come to terms with Munch as an artist and not a social outcast or rebel. One, writing in *Dagbladet,* was much less conditional in his appraisal than those of his colleagues who had merely detected some talent. Going so far as to call Munch a colorist of the first order and an artist who in his portraiture achieves a strength and dimension rarely seen,[5] he must have been referring to the Jaeger painting—perhaps also that of Jensen-Hjell which was shown again—for the admirably controlled color scheme in this newest portrait is unmistakably the product of a master, the portrait's strength and dimension deriving from Munch's persuasive visualizing of his own profoundly introspective analysis of his subject.

To the thoughtful viewer the presence of these two portraits in the small makeshift gallery must have appeared particularly meaningful: on one wall Jensen-Hjell in his energetic, extrovert, haughtily derisive pose symbolizing the aggressive period in the lives of the Bohèmes, on another Jaeger, buttoned to the chin, hunched up, listless, drained, showing the futility of it all. Or perhaps not quite so, for that playful reflection from Jensen-Hjell's pince-nez seems recapitulated in the depth of Jaeger's eyes as they peer, unwavering, at the viewer, counteracting the lifelessness of his drooping hand.

The color scheme in the Jaeger portrait, featuring a variety of nuances of blue and its chromatic affiliates, has much in common with *Morning,* while the structure is strikingly similar to that of the Jensen-Hjell portrait, only with sharper outlines and a deliberate rather than a hectic impasto. Again, a deep diagonal rises from the lower right corner, this time beginning with the edge of the table and continuing, as in the Jensen-Hjell portrait, along the closure of the coat, in the newer painting as introvertly buttoned-up as it was flamboyantly agape in the earlier. This prominent diagonal feature forms with the dark clearly painted horizontal ridge of the back of the sofa an angle on which Jaeger's face, blotchily flesh-colored, has been superimposed. Face and drooping hand, in the same perpendicular, slightly to the left of the center plane combine to suggest a stabilizing axis flanked on each side by such erect foreground items as the front frame of the sofa and the table leg, while the curtain in the left background provides a parallel movement brought about by the streaked impasto in opaque, off-white colors laid on so as to give the impression of a downward flow according to the law of gravity. As a counterpoint to this predominance of perpendiculars in the left half of the picture the right features an elongated rectangle extending horizontally from the upper edge of the canvas all the way to the curtain, catching the shimmering light and reflecting it in subtler shades of the deep blue emanating from the model's coat. The exposed section of the upholstered back of the sofa forms with the model's limp arm a triangle tending to emphasize his slumped pose, hence also the spirit of futility and resignation exuding from the entire picture.

Here, as in the Jensen-Hjell portrait, it is interesting to speculate on a possible influence from Manet dating from that memorable Paris visit in 1885. Either one of two Manet works, his Zacharie Astruc portrait from 1864 and that of Stéphane Mallarmé (Plate 18) from 1873, is as reasonable a source of inspiration for the compositional approach in the Jaeger portrait as *The Philosopher* may have been in that of Jensen-Hjell. In fact, the Jaeger pose is nearly identical to that of Mallarmé, and the personal relationship between Jaeger and Munch has much in common with that between Mallarmé and Manet.

It would appear that Munch's basic technique had changed relatively little in that period of time, not strange considering its dramatic change following his exposure to Paris in 1885. This was shown both in the Jensen-Hjell portrait, completed immediately after his return, and more demonstratively in *Sick Girl,* a canvas already then so advanced in its treatment of color, both in impasto and values, that viewers, totally confused at such a novel approach, simply resorted to ridicule. That Munch's extraordinary concept of color and its creative dynamics was an intrinsic component of his talent had been demonstrated in *Morning.* Yet it was a talent to be developed and controlled in the course of the next few years, then applied in an ever more purposeful way, as ultimately shown both in the Jaeger portrait and in *Springtime.*

A similar development characterizes his buildup of the picture surface. Clearly a conscious concern in *Morning* it became more deliberate in the Jensen-Hjell portrait and subsequent works,[6] until in *Portrait of Hans Jaeger* all pictorial elements rest firmly on a balanced structure nearly geometric in design yet integrated in the total articulation of the picture with such subtlety and logic that its presence becomes apparent only upon close analysis. This is exactly what distinguishes these pictures from their predecessors. They demonstrate the artist's complete mastery of all technical problems and show the range of expressive means at his disposal. Hence, free from all extraneous obstacles he can devote his entire creative energy to the attainment of his principal artistic goal: to convey in pictures the emotional impact of certain moments, events, experienced by the hypersensitive individual attempting to endure the complex and most often bitterly depressing reality of his own existence.

That Edvard Munch, successful recipient of a study stipend in 1889, was already a fully mature artist appears, at least in retrospect, borne out by the works he had shown in his first major exhibit. But that he was also open to new impressions and impulses was made equally clear in a series of paintings completed late that summer and in the early fall, prior to his utilization of the stipend but following another hurried trip to Paris. This came about when the jury of the Board of Norwegian Artists, no doubt pressured by such articulate and insistent public figures as Thaulow and Krohg, agreed that a Munch work would be included in the Norwegian section of the *Exposition Universelle,* opening in Paris in May of that year in honor of the centennial of the French Revolution. The painting chosen was *Morning,* now five years old and apparently no longer offensive to the public taste. How it happened that Munch was allowed to deliver his canvas in person no one seems to know, but the fact that Thaulow headed the Norwegian arrangements committee in Paris no doubt had something to do with it.

Again with only three weeks at his disposal he was obviously not about to waste his precious time on letter writing, so there are no records of his activities. However, with the exposition as his immediate goal and having waited a full four years for this new opportunity to see the arts of France, he can have done little else than try to absorb as much as possible of old and new trends on view right there on the exposition grounds. The special *Salon* of the event, devoted only to officially recognized artists, was far from revolutionary, but it did include works by Monet and Pissarro, at long last considered respectable, while Manet, dead for five years, was well represented in the retrospective section. The presence of a single painting by Cézanne was the result of a ploy of cultural blackmail. The noted collector, Victor Chocquet, had agreed to supply the *Salon* with some much-needed furnishings from his own splendid house on the express condition that his Cézanne canvas, *The House of the Hanged One,* be included in the show. So the impressionists had succeeded in gaining at least limited access to this very special display, although the works selected from their vast repertoire were all of such early dates—Manet's mostly from the 1860s, those of the others from 1871 and 1873—that they could hardly be considered representative of newer trends in French art. Someone intent on discovering these would have to search for them elsewhere than in the Palace of the Fine Arts, more specifically in the refreshment area located strategically nearby, in Café Volpini, where Gauguin and his friends from Pont-Aven had mounted a private exhibit of works by "Impressionists and Synthetists," including Gauguin's own seventeen canvases, an even larger number by Emile Bernard, a small selection by Emile Schuffenecker and Louis Anquetin, and single works by Charles Laval, Léon Fauché, and Daniel de Monfreid.

Of all the painters represented at the exposition, Pissarro and Gauguin have been particularly important in Munch's development—Pissarro already from that brief Paris visit in 1885, Gauguin most likely not until his more extended stay which would begin in the fall of 1889. Actually, he had known of Gauguin for some time, ever since the Frenchman, while still a relatively obscure artist even in his homeland, was represented in the Norwegian Autumn Exhibit that had marked Munch's debut in 1883. More importantly, Gauguin happened to be Frits Thaulow's brother-in-law. Therefore, there can be little doubt that Munch was quite conversant with the extraordinary activities of this uniquely cosmopolitan artist, which in turn makes it inconceivable that the young Norwegian, once more in Paris, partially under the sponsorship of Frits Thaulow, would not have spent considerable time familiarizing himself with the show at Volpini's. Even so, there is no notable sign of a Gauguin influence in the works he had time to complete between his two trips to Paris in 1889, while the Pissarro exposure left its unmistakable imprint. At that time, however, another influence, possibly more decisive than any exerted upon him from without, made its first impact on his paintings, adding a feature significant enough to become a lasting leit-motif in his works, or perhaps better a composite of such motifs, all part of the same visual and emotional experience: his discovery of the caressive contours of the summer village, Åsgårdstrand. Rising gently from the shore, low white houses and rose-speckled picket fences line its softly curving lanes under tall spreading chestnut trees, while the rippling waves of the fjord lazily lap against an undulant, boulder-strewn shoreline. Only the jutting pier, a link to the outside world, poses a threat, but only rarely, for it also marks the artist's route of escape from his self-imposed solitude. In his older days, fond of reminiscing about his summers in Åsgårdstrand, the only place he had ever dared love, Munch described his own emotional involvement with the village:

> Have you walked along that shoreline and listened to the sea? Have you ever noticed how the evening light dissolves into night? I know of no place on earth that has such beautiful lingering twilight... Isn't it sad that I've painted everything there is to paint down there? To walk about in the village is like walking among my own pictures.[7]

This nostalgic joy, so very much like Strindberg's when he writes of the Stockholm archipelago, has its distinct parallels in the affection the impressionists felt for certain locales. It is not quite the same as the spirit of comradship that prevailed among their predecessors in Barbizon or Grez, or among themsleves in Argenteuil or their followers in Pont-Aven, for the importance of these places seemed to derive primarily from the cultivation of communal activities and a friendly competition in rendering the familiar landscape. Rather, it is that soothing feeling of having found, perhaps after long search, a place to unwind, to experience the peace that comes from a sense of perfect intimacy between the self and the setting. In Cézanne this comes across so convincingly in his landscapes from the Midi where in the distance Mount St. Victoire looms safe as a sailor's lighthouse. To Sisley, and even more Pissarro, Louveciennes provided such a secure shelter, and it is therefore particularly interesting that Munch's first extended stay in Åsgårdstrand should follow immediately upon his second exposure to the paintings of Pissarro. Encouraged by the Krohgs who spent summers in the country nearby, he had already prior to his departure for Paris rented a small house in the outskirts of the village, which—besides a very likely shortage of funds—may explain the brevity of his Paris visit. Committed to a vacation with his family[8]—their first ever—he must have decided not to disappoint anyone by remaining abroad longer than seemed absolutely necessary. Moreover, the excitement generated by everything he had seen must have filled him with so many new ideas that he could hardly resist the urge to get back to his easel.

Included in the exposition *Salon* were two Pissarro paintings, both identified only by the vague title *Road.* One may have been *The Road to Rocquencourt,* painted after the artist's bittersweet return to Louvecienne following his London exile during the Franco-Prussian War.[9] Subtly bright and superbly simple in structure it has been called "a hymn to homecoming," and the other *The Road to Versailles in Louveciennes.*

That very summer Munch completed a canvas, *Evening Chat,* Ingrid Langaard cautiously considers influenced by *The Road to Versailles in Louveciennes.*[10] Actually, there are so many points of similarity in structure and content between these two that it would be improper to consider Munch's work independent in conception and execution.

In Pissarro's canvas two women, one with a child, stand chatting by a flower-covered fence beyond which, vibrantly articulated in light and shadow, a road slices diagonally into the center to vanish in the foliage of trees and bushes in the background. Along the road a couple with a child move away from the viewer, their diminutive size contributing with the disappearing road to the spatial perspective of the picture. Visible through the foliage and more prominently in the upper right, in an unobstructed surface corresponding in size to that occupied by the foreground figures, is a blue, glossy summer sky. The predominance of verticals—the edge of the two-story house to the left, the figures, tree trunks, and fence posts—is counterbalanced by the diagonals of the road and the fence running alongside it, and by the short section of the fence jutting out from the left wall, the low, pastel-colored farm houses on the opposite side, and by the overall division of the canvas into two approximately equal parts, earth and sky, which provide the necessary horizontal features.

With some relatively slight variations necessitated by landscape differences a similar structural analysis would come very close to a description of the basic compositional approach in Munch's painting as well. Here there are two foreground figures posed on the steps of a veranda, while two others, heads barely visible, vanish into the distance. The diagonal, steeper but far less prominent than in the Pissarro painting, is a hastily sketched path of parallel streaks disappearing behind the horizontal railing of the veranda but by implication leading all the way to the sea, whose deep blue surface dominates the upper right of the canvas, leaving only a narrow strip of sky to mark the horizon.

Against Pissarro's meticulous brushwork, careful articulation of detail, and colors radiant with the intensity of high noon, Munch's impasto is bold, his drawing blunt, oriented toward larger surfaces, and his colors deeper, less contrasting in tone to suggest that lingering twilight he would later so fondly recall.

This particular departure from Pissarro in a canvas otherwise so highly reminiscent of the impressionist may well be an indication that he had become intrigued by the pictures shown at Café Volpini, at this stage perhaps those by Bernard fully as much as Gauguin's, for it was Bernard, with Anquetin, who had devised the approach called *Cloisonnisme:*

> The painter traces his drawing in closed lines between which he puts varied hues, the juxtaposition of which will provide the sensation of the general coloration intended, the drawing emphasizing the color and color emphasizing the design. The painter's procedure is something like painting in compartments, analogous to the *cloisonné*... [11]

From some rather definite hints of an interest in this method in *Evening Chat,* Munch applies it with considerable care in his next painting, *Inger on the Beach* (Plate 19). His most important single effort from the summer of 1889 and one of two canvases shown in the following Autumn Exhibit, it is a work of such consummate lyric quality that the entire canvas seems to exude the soft music of the Norwegian summer night.

It shows his sister—twenty-one that year—wearing a long white dress and seated on a boulder on the shore below their summer house. Her profile is projected against the surface of the fjord whose grayish-blue is gradually yielding to a rosy stain from an invisible, setting sun. The principal color scheme, a triad of russet, white, and blue, is clearly stated in a diagonal row of boulders rising steeply from the lower right corner past the model to a point in the center, beyond the water's edge, in receding nuances of red and blue variously affected by the dominant white. Each boulder, carefully drawn—"analogous to the cloisonné"—displays its own self-contained shade of the two colors, from the granite giant in the foreground whose red is bleached by the outpouring of white, to the cobalt blue of the next line, whose color fades in rhythmic sequences until dissolved in the faintly blue fjord. The lyricism of the canvas is further enhanced by the reedy quality of a row of fragile stakes of net hangers extending, as in a Japanese scroll, diagonally from the upper left toward the center, disclosing in the distance a mystic, nearly invisible boat with three people ready to pull the nets.

That few critics detected anything of merit in *Inger on the Beach*—at that time shown with the title *Evening*—does of course come as no surprise. *Aftenposten,* then as always speaking for the conservative element, provided a reasonably accurate summary of the negative reaction evoked by this remarkably beautiful canvas:

> Even more difficult is it to discover anything creditable in Mr. Edvard Munch's *Evening,* representing a woman... sitting on some huge boulders by the seashore. To determine the contents one must of course proceed to the opposite side of the room, but even at that distance it is difficult to... place things in proper order. It may be assumed that the intended light must bear the blame for the sketchy, disembodied indecisiveness in which the portrayal moves and which reaches its climax in the seated woman, a bodily creature devoid of life and expression...
>
> All in all, the picture appears to us to possess so little artistic merit that its presence at the exhibit can hardly be defended.[12]

But by the time this review appeared an exuberantly happy Munch had arrived in Paris with two fellow artists, eager to enter Bonnat's studio. Of course his faithful aunt kept him informed of developments at home, sending him clippings of good and bad criticism and in her own decisively terse way passing judgement on the writers: "Reviews from *Aftenposten* and *Dagbladet* are enclosed. Our subscription to *Aftenposten* has been cancelled."[13]

8

Strindberg as Painter

In 1889-90, at the height of his marital crisis and while in the archipelago waiting out the course of events in his divorce proceedings, Strindberg worked on the novel *I havsbandet* [In the Outer Skerries]. Dealing with man in nature and man against nature, inspired equally by Nietzsche and Zola, it is a brooding saga of a superman told in the most minute scientific terms, with certain landscape descriptions providing a measure of relief. In the present context these are the features that fascinate, for they are so visual in conception that several of Strindberg's contemporary Swedish artists professed their direct indebtednesss to his descriptive power as demonstrated in that particular work—and its predecessor, the light-hearted *Hemsöborna* [The People of Hemsö]—in their own approach to the seaside landscape. Among his greatest admirers were Karl Nordström and Richard Bergh, in the final analysis perhaps the most faithful of all Strindberg's artist friends and unequivocal in their enthusiasm for his newest work of fiction.[1]

That these painters reacted so positively to this novel is not at all surprising, for it contains a series of penetrating, varied, and imaginative pictures of the landscape Strindberg loved "to the point of ecstacy." Already on the opening pages he presents the archipelago in a broad sweep encompassing the coast and the islands far out to the open sea, then, gradually focusing on more clearly defined sights, he finally produces a canvas nearly abstract in its concentration on color radiance and variations:

> The sun had now descended to the horizon, and the waves broke, dark purple at the base, deep green on the sloping edges, and when the crests rose to their greatest height they shone grassy green, and the foam splashed and hissed reddish, champagne-colored, in the sun . . .[2]

But the landscape, an inner experience as much as an external manifestation of form and color, is not always that exuberant. Its quality of beauty shifts with the prevailing mood of the viewer, and as the sea itself rises and falls in slow, glossy swells or crashing breakers, so the spirit of the main character undulates in a similarly unpredictable flow:

> But nature, with which he had always sought to communicate, now appeared dead to him, for the intermediary, man, was missing. The sea, which he worshipped and craved as the only grand feature in this land with its frugal, dwarfish summer wildness, now began to seem confining in the same degree that his own self seemed to expand. This blue, turpentine-green, gray circle closed in on him like a prison compound, and the monotonous little landscape evoked the same anguish as that of a prison cell with its total lack of new impressions.[3]

Despite its powerful surge of emotion, *In the Outer Skerries* contains little that is directly new in Strindberg's literary approach. Its darkly hovering destiny was present in *The Father* and *Lady Julie,* as were other, more specific Zola-Nietzsche features, and more deeply and exclusively inspired by Nietzsche was the novelette, *Tschandala.* Even nature description in the new novel, while of central importance and rich in flashes of genius and inspiration, is by no means consistently impressive—ranging, in fact, from a series of sweeping portrayals of the fatalistic grandeur of the sea and the sky to the most intricately pedantic and often dull exhibits of scientific minutiae.

This strange mixture of the studied and the brilliant, the pedantic and the lofty, has its root, as so much else in Strindberg's production, in the starkly contrasting elements making up his own complex intellectual-emotional fiber. In periods of crisis the pendulum would swing particularly widely, and there can be little doubt that the writing of *In the Outer Skerries,* in progress while his personal tragedy raced toward its inevitable conclusion, bears the mark of that severe crisis. But as in the past he must have succeeded through determined will and concentration in harnessing his anguish into an outpouring of creative energy. This is not to say that the novel was written in a single rush of inspiration as was the case with *The Father.* Requiring the better part of a year and a half from inception to completion it seemed to prove Strindberg's own claim that it was a lot easier to write for the theatre than to write novels. The final chapters reached the publisher in September, 1890, and the book was on the market in time for the Christmas trade—for Strindberg a season that would bring with it the melancholy task of buying gifts for a last gathering with his children, for in mid-December a preliminary hearing was scheduled in his divorce case.

A month later a deposition was filed, assigning custody of the children to Siri, and in March an interlocutory decree was signed. To compound these difficulties a slander suit was filed against him by one of Siri's friends.[4]

Remaining throughout these trying times in the wintry solitude of the archipelago he began to turn his attention to the visual arts by sketching the familiar scenes around him, just as he had done twenty years earlier when he had failed to interest publishers and theatre people in his major literary effort, *Master Olof.* At that time he had had no intention of becoming a professional who would exhibit and sell, he states in *The Son of A Servant.* All he wanted to do was to try his hand at something more tangible than mere words. It must have been a notion inspired by the company he then kept, that strange lot of men fictionalized in *The Red Room,* among them a former gooseherd, a farm hand, a blacksmith, and a discharged enlisted man. All so different from himself in background and upbringing they were nevertheless so educated in their own way, filled with intellectual curiosity and creative sincerity to the extent that most other people, traditionally nurtured and educated, seemed shallow by comparison. With one of these artists[5] he had been sketching in and around Stockholm, learning to see and appreciate a setting, a landscape, for its creative potential. Then, when summer came and he joined his friends in the archipelago, as he had done the year before, he had discovered with his sharpened vision that the landscape had a breath-taking, primeval grandeur, and with an intense craving to reproduce it he had roamed the scrubby island in stormy weather or calm, climbing rocks and trees to gain perspective and scanning the sea, the skerries, and the vast, ever changing sky. Filled with these images he would return to his lodging to draw or paint. But in his eagerness to record his powerful impressions he might suddenly find his newly acquired facility with charcoal sticks and brushes wholly inadequate and feel compelled to resort to his principal medium. Hence, his new passion had an immediate and direct effect on his writing as well. What he did commit to the sketch pad or the canvas at that time turned out to be discouragingly repetitious and unimaginative—"one anomaly after the other," he called it in a letter to a friend, over and over again the same sea "with the coast in the foreground, windswept pines; farther out some naked rocks . . . Sunset or moonlight, never bright daylight."[6] Years later, attempting to assess what he had wanted to accomplish as a painter in those early days, he formulated these thoughts:

> One should paint one's inner emotions and not keep copying sticks and stones which in themselves are insignificant and attain proper meaning only by passing through and being molded by the individual's perception. Therefore, one should not paint out-of-doors but at home, from memory and with imagination.[7]

This statement, from *The Son of A Servant,* written in 1885-86, is not really an accurate indication of the young Strindberg's attitude toward painting, for when he first started sketching he did his very best to produce faithful representations of his surroundings, and none of these early works reflect the emotional quality that would so totally dominate his maturer efforts. To arrive at such advanced ideas of the primary function of the visual arts he would first need to acquire greater experience in and exposure to the field.

His friendship with Per Ekström may have contributed to his own painterly technique, that with Ernst Josephson,[8] whose canvases from the 1880s convey a deeply troubled soul, to his emotional approach to the subject. More significant in this respect, however, was his period of exile from 1883 to 1889, especially his stay in France, where he had his eyes opened to the expressive potential inherent in visual representation. In Grez and Paris, surrounded by searching artists, he must have had almost unlimited opportunity to probe the subject in its widest perspective and at the same time examine a great many works in progress. And in exhibits, private and public, he saw paintings of the most varied periods and approaches, among them the thought-provoking canvases of Puvis de Chavannes whose *The Poor Fisherman* (Plate 29) made a particularly deep and lasting impression on him. From all of this he must have concluded that in the visual arts, at least, realist-naturalist concerns were issues of the past, that it was no longer a question of depicting "sticks and stones" but of unveiling one's own soul.

It was inevitable that these experiences and exposures should be reflected in Strindberg's writings at that time. Already in *The Father* and *Miss Julie* there is a greater tendency to emphasize the emotional element by visual means than had been the case in earlier dramas, and in *I havsbandet,* as has been shown, nature descriptions definitely serve to convey a character's specific mood. Even so, a complete rejection of the "sticks and stones" method in his writings was still a long way off, while his efforts in the visual arts immediately show the effect of such influences. That it should be so is readily explained by his tendency to surmount a crisis by a radical change of concentration. It has been shown how in the early 1870s, disheartened by the apathy of theatres and publishers toward his *Master Olof,* he had turned to painting. Then, following his marriage to Siri von Essen, he had gone back to playwriting until in 1883, still without success in the field, he had again abandoned the drama vowing that he would travel great distance just to avoid hearing about it, and true to his word had rushed all the way to France, where for three years he had poured out his energy in prose writing. And now, in the aftermath of his divorce, anguished by the separation from his children and apprehensive about the outcome of the pending slander suit, he once more felt the need for a change of focus and again turned to the visual arts. First he did some casual sketching. Then, in the company of Robert Thegerström,[9] a successful painter whose skill and accomplishments may have intimidated and momentarily sidetracked him, Strindberg took up sculpting, initially completing a bust of Thegerström but thereafter promptly turning his attention to the model he had wanted to portray in the first place, Thegerström's "wondrously beautiful wife" Elin.[10]

While none of these works remains extant there are five plaster of Paris copies of a statuette representing a boy weeping, of which Strindberg has this to say:

> Once I got the idea to mold in clay in antique manner a boy worshiping. He stood there with his arms raised high, but I felt betrayed by him and in a fit of despair let my hand fall on the head of the unfortunate boy. But look! A metamorphosis of which Ovid would not have dreamed. The Grecian hairdo, flattened from the blow, becomes a Scottish tam covering his face. The head and neck are pressed down between his shoulders, his arms are lowered so that

> the hands remain level with the eyes under the tam. He legs buckle, the knees come together, and the entire model has been transformed into a nine-year-old boy weeping and hiding his tears in his hands.[11]

This "happening"—in Strindberg's recollection given added significance by its implied portrayal of his own boy—marks the foreshadowing of his "art by chance or accident," a painting procedure whereby he would rely on instant and subconsciously inspired notions and allow the creative process to take its own natural course. When asked toward the end of his life how he went about composing his literary works he said, after a moment's hesitation, that the process seemed to start with a fermentation, a pleasant fever which quickly rose to a state of ecstacy or intoxication. "Now and then I believe myself to be a sort of medium," he went on, "because everything works so easily, only half consciously, with moderately little calculation."[12] This rather abstract stream-of-consciousness technique is certainly not applicable to his tightly composed dramas of the late 1880s and early 1890s, but it is clearly present in his most ambitious paintings. It was in the fall of 1891, no longer with the Thegerströms and while working on a fairytale drama intended as a Christmas gift to his children,[13] that he ventured into painting again, at first dividing his time between that and writing, but with the coming of spring he pursued it with a zeal and a determination surpassing any he had previously exerted in that direction. Certainly more deeply troubled than he had ever been in his youth but also more skilled in the medium he had chosen, he finally felt he succeeded in doing what he had failed to do earlier: convincingly project his emotions onto the canvas. That summer, 1892, having completed a total of thirty paintings, he chose eight for an exhibit in a private establishment in Stockholm, hoping for sales to ease his enormous financial burden. Pressing him at that particular time were payments for child support and also a fine imposed upon him as a result of the slander suit.

In this modest show there was little variety. As in the past, Strindberg's pictures all represented various aspects of the seaside landscape, his brooding pigments applied with a palette knife in broad splashes or long arcs and sometimes in turbulent spiral motions, always very thickly, then built up even further, one color on the top of the other, from darker toward lighter hues, often resulting in a relief pattern. Space proportions tend to favor the sky, as in Dutch landscapes, and its turbulence whips the sea into a frenzy that gives the horizon the appearance of a serrated range of mountian tops. The sky, invariably more skilfully done, is more convincing than is the sea or any section of land visible, which may in fact account for its persistent predominance.

One of the works shown was *White Sailing Mark* (Plate 22), a relatively large painting—18 by 24 inches—and a perfect example of his technique. It is held in somber, grayish-green colors against which the chalky whiteness of an impetuous sky provides scant relief. This sky, gushing onto a strip of the stormy surface of the sea and the hostile protrusion of a rock in a broad mass of diagonal streaks gives the painting its dynamic quality, while its central feature, the rigidly unyielding sailing mark, suggests its symbolic contents.

The hectic impasto in Strindberg's paintings could bring about forms not originally part of his conscious plan. His interest in chance creation, however—"at first one sees nothing but a chaos of colors, then it begins to look like something"[14]—demands a close scrutiny of all his pictures. Thus in one version of *White Sailing Mark*—now in Stockholm's National Museum—such probing seems to yield under the opaque veil of the clouds the torso of man posed slightly off center and leaning parallel with the sailing mark, which in that version is swaying in the storm. If this is accidental it is really rather remarkable, for it tends to support, perhaps even overstate, the symbolic significance of the sailing mark: Strindberg himself stubbornly defying the turbulence of his life.

Two major books and a number of articles have been written on Strindberg as a painter, but because of his dominant position in literature it is extremely difficult to arrive at an unbiased evaluation of his contribution in this or any other non-literary field. There is ample evidence to support the claim that his literary art, entirely aside from its profound significance in its own right, directly influenced painters and sculptors. Whether his talent in painting was sufficient to earn him a place in the annals of European art independent of his position in his principal field—as Göran Söderström unequivocally claims[15]—is really a moot question. The most meaningful statement on the subject may be that by Jean Cassou in his contribution to a volume devoted to various aspects of Strindberg's paintings. While it may be interesting to speculate, Cassou says, on whether Strindberg with his premonitions of an abstract art form actually contributed to its development, it is far more fruitful to concentrate on his paintings within the framework of his own multifaceted creative world:

> Here we do not place ourselves in the history of painting but in that microcosm that bears the name Strindberg. August Strindberg's genius cannot be compared to anything else, any more than can his appearance and his destiny. Then came the moment when this singular August Strindberg felt the need to paint. That is to say, he felt that in painting he had at his disposal another means by which he might express his own inalienable personality.[16]

Viewed in this perspective his ventures in the visual arts in the early 1890s may be seen as a foreshadowing of his Inferno experiences and his post-Inferno writings, both devoted to an exploration of the most varied aspects of the human condition, always in search of answers to unanswerable questions. Therefore, his sincere attempts at probing his own expressive potential in visual images are motivated by the very same inner force that compelled him to seek to unravel the mystery of the universe through an analysis of the components of the basic elements, a fixed idea ultimately driving him into a futile pursuit of the formula for the production of gold. In the same way that his scientific studies and research and articulate writing on specific aspects of the subject reveal not only a definite aptitude for the sciences but often an astonishingly extensive knowledge in certain areas,[17] so his efforts in painting prove beyond doubt that he possessed both talent and a considerable measure of expressive facility. What was missing, however, was the carefully structured and guided study necessary to attain a professional status in either field. Had he continued his science studies in Uppsala beyond the preparatory level, or taken proper instruction in the field of drawing and painting—as did even his independently-minded friends in the early 1870s—he might well have become an outstanding scientist or painter. However, always lacking the basic, laboriously acquired knowledge and technique that give professionals direction and confidence to pursue work of a sustained creative quality Strindberg never quite made it into those ranks and was frequently stymied to the point of despair by his own inadequacy. Perhaps not as immediately noticeable in his scientific work this flaw is conspicuous in many of his paintings where a sometimes excessively bold sweep of the knife and its resulting impression of turbulence may not always reflect the depth of his troubled soul but rather something no more profound than the painter's frustration at his own technical deficiency.

None of this is intended to detract from or deny the instant impact many of Strindberg's paintings tend to make on the thoughtful viewer. Rather, it is meant as a warning against measuring these works by standards applicable to those having deliberately and consistently prepared themselves for the pursuit of expressive perfection in pictures. Strindberg's paintings are more fairly observed for their overall compositional impression and their unmistakable dynamics than for technical skill or structural details. Yet when he exhibited his paintings in 1892 he did in fact present himself as a professional leaving himself open to professional judgment, as he had no doubt anticipated, and there were highly diverging opinions on the merit of the show. Polar opposites, in fact, for only two reviews appeared, one, by an amateur and friend, extremely favorable, saying that the paintings revealed "not only a fine poetic perception but in many cases a surprising technical facility." The other, however—by a professional critic—was so caustic it might have competed with *Aftenposten*'s most vitriolic assessment of Munch's works. Beginning with a lengthy simile between Strindberg and the artist in Henri Murger's *Scénes de la vie de Bohème,* who hauls his masterpiece from gallery to gallery, unsuccessfully, because no one can agree on what it seems to represent, the critic goes on to say:

> I'm inclined to believe that that rascal Strindberg, when putting these small "studies" into gold frames and hoisting them for exhibit as "paintings" did so with only one purpose in mind: to poke fun at the public...

> Whether *Snow Storm at Sea* is meant to be a dirty sheet hanging up to dry or a new method of painting barn doors is impossible to tell. So also whether *Pack Ice* is a plateful of margarine sandwiches or a platter of calf's feet with brain sauce.
>
> *Sailing Mark* might well be an old butter churn ready for donation to the Nordic Museum, while *Storm Mark* might be a still life based on a motif from the storage shed of the department of sanitation.[18]

The exhibit did nothing to enhance Strindberg's position artistically, and financially the result was equally disheartening, for there were no sales. Actually, a month after it had closed someone did buy a painting, but the trifling amount paid for it did little to bring about a settlement in Strindberg's accounts. Because he was now determined to leave Sweden again, this was a matter of considerable urgency for without a settlement he feared he might not be let out of the country.

That spring and summer he had not limited his activities to painting. In the hope of launching another experimental theatre, this time in the Djursholm suburb of Stockhom, he had written, in addition to the full-length play, *Himmelrikets nycklar* [The Keys to the Kingdom], six one-acts, among them, *Leka med elden* [Playing with Fire], an amusing comedy inspired by his summer infatuation with Elin Thegerström, and the bitterly retrospective, *Bandet* [The Bond], a dramatization of his own divorce proceedings. While *Himmelrikets nycklar* had to wait nearly forty years for its first performance,[19] the one-acts were premiered in relatively rapid sequence, not in Stockholm where the experimental theatre failed to materialize at that time, but in various establishments in Berlin, where Strindberg's star, in ascendance since *Die freie Bühne*'s staging of *The Father* in 1890, would shine brightly for a full decade.

Much credit for Strindberg's strong position in the Berlin avant-garde must go to Ola Hansson, the young Swedish exile whose short story, *Pariah,* Strindberg had used as the basis for one of the plays written for the Scandinavian Experimental Theatre in Copenhagen. Hansson was living in Berlin with his German-born wife, the writer Laura Mohr, whose pen name was the more Scandinavian-sounding Laura Marholm. These two, learning of the hardships Strindberg was suffering in Sweden, now put all wheels in motion to bring about his departure and subsequent entry into their own circle in Berlin, and even provided from various sources a sum of money to help release him from obligations he had referred to in a letter:

> The trick is to get away from here... I have debts which I cannot leave behind without the newspapers beginning to search for me... That I have fellow countrymen, friends, and relatives does not help, for all such sources have been exhausted during these three horrible years I've spent at home.[20]

An article by Hansson in the Berlin periodical, *Zukunft,* led to a collection of money on Strindberg's behalf, a temporarily embarassing development which nevertheless solved his immediate problem, and by the end of September he was packing his belongings. His hope of seeing the children before he left was shattered when a cholera epidemic in Russia threatened to cut off the steamer connection across the Baltic so he was obliged to advance his departure by several days. All he could do was to bid them farewell in a mournful yet not entirely pessimistic letter:

> As I've been having a great many worries and adversities all this year your future has seemed less than bright to me, but now it seems headed for something better.
>
> Live well, dear children, keep peace among yourselves and continue to do well in school and at home.
>
> Write to me and remember that I am working for you and that my success will be your gain.[21]

By the time the three had read this note their father had already been rushing through Stockholm "like a wind to vanish without trace." On the first of October he arrived in Berlin to be met at the station by the Hanssons, the Swedish-born Finnish writer, Adolf Paul, and one of the most extraordinary personages in all of Berlin, Stanislaw Przybyszewski, Polish poet, pianist, art critic, and dedicated Satanist, whose unorthodox attitudes and opinions would have considerable effect on Strindberg as well as Munch.

Three days after his arrival, Strindberg declares that his boldest expectations have been surpassed, and in less than a week, his melancholy having evaporated in the combined warmth of an Indian summer and the adulation of friends and supporters, he sends off this exuberantly confident note to a member of his local coterie:

> Seeing that you strange birds actually rejoice in my success, let us meet tomorrow, Tuesday, at 12 noon in your place. When Strindberg gets money Paul and Przybyszewski do too, and at Müggelschloss Priapus will be dancing *The Dead Russian* to the accompaniment of three pianos.
>
> The sun is shining, Blumenthal writes in the *Stock Courier,* and the bull will be making money. It's a joy to be alive![22]

9

Munch's Second Retrospective

As Strindberg's departure from Sweden for his first exile had coincided with Munch's debut at the Norwegian Autumn Exhibit of 1883, so his departure for Berlin came about nearly simultaneously with an equally significant event in Munch's life, his second retrospective exhibit in Kristiania, which also marked his first major meeting with the public following his three years of study in France.

Despite his conscious maturity as an artist, and perhaps mindful of advice and admonitions from people at home, he had approached his first extended stay in Paris with an open mind and the eagerness of a student appreciative of the opportunity. It did not occur to him to complain, then or later, about the orthodox instruction offered him in the studio of Bonnat, where so many Scandinavians had preceeded him—from Norway, Erik Werenskjold and Harriet Backer, from Denmark, Peter Krøyer, and from Sweden, Gustaf Cederström and Prince Eugen. All of these, though much more progressive than their master, earnestly expressed their indebtedness to him for the technical facility they had acquired, and Munch was no exception. He proudly displayed his sketches with Bonnat's markings and freely quoted his comments. Being Bonnat's student included the rare privilege of once a week seeing the master's impressive collection of art from the Renaissance to the mid-1800s.[1] Munch's respect for Caravaggio's expressive power and the dark mysticism of Zurbaran and Ribera may derive from these gallery visits with Bonnat as the lecturer, so also his admiration for the uncompromising portrayal of human emotion in Goya's graphics.

But Munch did not remain long under the tutelage of Bonnat. As one of his more famous predecessors in the studio, Toulouse-Lautrec, he took his leave after four months to set out on a course of his own, studying in the Louvre and the *Salons,* in private galleries throughout the Left Bank where the symbolists were said to be in control, and those in Montmartre, supposedly dominated by the decadents. Actually, aside from their nominal separation by the generously spanned Seine river there was no meaningful way of distinguishing between these groups or movements which held fluctuating and frequently overlapping memberships. Their basic principle was the same: a rejection of the scientific, objective approach to art in favor of a visual, literary, or musical expression of the mystic realm of the creative idea, dreams and imagination in place of the tangible, prosaic, everyday world. "Although any label is vain," one of their followers said, "we feel compelled, for the exact information of those interested, to remind them that *decadent* is pronounced *symbolist.*"[2]

The paragon of both movements was Richard Wagner whose extravagant attempts at merging, synthesizing the three basic forms of creative expression approached the artistic ideal. In visual arts they looked with ecstatic admiration at the works of Gustave Moreau and Odilon Redon whose glistening, often mystic canvases suggested "the combination of the sensual spirit and the sorrowful flesh and . . . all the violent splendours of the late Roman Empire."[3] In more calmly contemplative moments the nostalgic, classically oriented simplicity of Puvis de Chavannes held their rapt attention.

In poetry, Baudelaire was the antecedent of the symbolists and decadents, and *Les Fleurs des Mal* was in everyone's possession, but with the coming of Mallarmé in 1887 and Verlaine in 1899 the movements got their own court poets. Already in 1884, however, a fanatic follower of their ideas had appeared in fiction in Huysmans' *A Rebours,* whose character—for there is really only one—Jean des Esseintes,[4] leads a life of absolute self-indulgence, removed from labor and responsibility, forever in search of "new scents, larger flowers, untried pleasures." His house, behind its austere facade, displays an otherworldly opulence linked to the existing world through the presence of paintings by Moreau. Within these premises Des Esseintes experiments with a variety of vices, though never with much energy or determination, for from the very outset he possesses no will and finally presides in grand solitude at an elaborate ritual celebrating his own impotence.[5]

To the extent that a viable distinction can be made between symbolists and decadents it may in one respect be made in terms of the latter group's predilection for a cult of love—often bisexual—impotence, and death rooted in strong misogynist tendencies, against the former's decided bent toward religious mysticism as shown in its love for incense-laden rituals of Roman Catholic or vaguely conceived oriental origins, but even more for the strange spiritual world of Emmanuel Swedenborg, better known to the symbolists through Balzac's *Seraphitus-Seraphita* than the mystic's own writings.

That Munch's stay in Paris in a most unique way happened to prepare him for his meeting with the Berlin avant-garde should be apparent from these observations on the activities and notions of the two groups then most prominent in radical cultural circles in the French capital, although there is little indication from his limited correspondence and diary notes that he learned much about their philosophies—except as inferences drawn from their visual manifestations. Better and more comprehensively than in individual galleries these were displayed in the *Salons des Indépendants,* an annual survey of all contemporary trends. It was there that he also saw the works of another group, the neoimpressionists. Having emerged from the ranks of the impressionists these artists rejected their mother group's instinctive and instantaneous approach to painting and practiced instead the prismatic decomposition of colors which were then fused again with the aid of the spectator's eye. Such optical mixture had also played an important role in the works of the impressionists and was even experimented with by Delacroix, but the neoimpressionists, having studied the color theories of Eugéne Chevreul,[6] advocated a deliberate, purely scientific application of such principles. Chief among their exponents were Georges Seurat, Paul Signac, and from the old guard, Pissarro, now accompanied by his son, Lucien.

In the very first Independent he visited, that of 1890, Munch saw paintings by all of these as well as Redon, Moreau, Puvis de Chavannes, Van Gogh, Bernard, Bonnard, and Toulouse-Lautrec. No doubt he had seen works by most of these elsewhere as well, and by Gauguin, who was not represented in the Independent but was regularly on view at Goupil's and Durand-Ruel's.

On his arrival in Paris in 1889 Munch had first taken lodging with other Scandinavians in Neuilly, but already before the change of the year he had moved with two friends, the Norwegian sculptor, Valentin Kielland, and the Danish poet, Emanuel Goldstein, to St. Cloud, then a rural idyll on the shore of the Seine. It was there he made this diary observation:

> It is no longer a question of painting interiors with people reading and women knitting. It must be living human beings who breathe and feel and suffer and love. I will paint a series of such pictures. People must comprehend the sanctity of it all and remove their hats as in a church.[7]

So similar to Strindberg's rejection of "sticks and stones" in favor of an emotional approach to the arts, this is, of course, a verbalization of what he had been trying to do in *Sick Girl, Springtime, Puberty* and *The Day Thereafter*— his thoughts now reinforced by the cultural climate surrounding him.

During his three first years in France his preoccupation with sickness and death seemed to sink below the surface of his consciousness. Instead, working in a state of perpetual exuberance at what he saw and learned he produced canvases of a brightness so consistently shimmering it would never again be equalled in his career. Only once in these years did that melancholy strain reappear in a work, called back by a deeply personal experience in early December, 1889, when Valentin Kielland received a note from Munch's aunt in which he was asked "... if Edvard is not sick, to let him have the enclosed letter which regrettably informs him of his father's death."[8]

From this came his profoundly nostalgic canvas, *Night,* characterized by Ingrid Langaard as a self-portrait. So it is, not because the background shows vaguely the silhouette of a person seated by the window, but because the entire canvas suggests the portrayal of the artist's inner self as he tries to come to terms with the sad news. "It must have been very dark up there," he writes home in response to the letter. "I had so been looking forward to seeing all of you again. It will be strange to come home."[9] In that quietly mournful frame of mind recalling certain indelible images of his father—evenings at home with the fading light seeping in through the window and the father resting in his chair, or seeing him alone in his study reading the Bible—he began committing his thoughts to the canvas, first framing in two luminous areas, the window and its reflection on the floor, then in broad, contemplative brush strokes of dark blue modulating toward mauve stressing the introspective quality of the subject. With its nearly total absence of new elements the painting exudes a feeling of the familiar, resembling, in fact, many of his earlier interiors from home. There is only one single new feature, representing, perhaps, the event directly responsible for the composition: the symbolist presence of a cross in the window reflection.

Inspired by the river right outside his window Munch painted several scenes showing the Seine—it is present also in *Night* in the multicolored lights seen through the window—in all these experimentally varying his approach from an emphasis on fragmented brushwork in early impressionist style, as he might have seen it in parts of the major retrospectives of Monet and Pissarro held separately that spring of 1890, to a carefully delineated division of the canvas into generous spaces of specific colors inspired by the Cloisonné style of Bernard and Anquetin, both well represented in the Independent the same spring.

Early in May, plagued by homesickness, he left Paris—missing a major Scandinavian event in the performance of *Ghosts* at *Théâtre-Libre,* the first staging of an Ibsen play in the French capital. Arriving home with few paintings but hundreds of sketches and a storehouse of impressions he settled in his soothingly familiar Åsgårdstrand and quickly recaptured the creative rhythm that had been interrupted by his busy schedule of seeing Paris and absorbing the city's unique atmosphere.

At the Autumn Exhibit that year he showed ten paintings, none well received. That Monet and Pissarro also happened to be represented made him an easy prey for the critics who compared the hometown impressionist with the Frenchmen, doing this with merciless ridicule of benefit to none of the parties. One, having discovered quite correctly a similarity in brushwork and structure between Munch's *Music at Karl Johan Street* (Plate 24) and one of Pissarro's works, dubbed him "Norway's Bizarro."[10]

On his way back to France in the fall of 1890 Munch suffered an attack of rheumatic fever and was kept bedridden in LeHavre for several weeks, but around New Year's he was able to travel to Nice. There the exotic Mediterranean landscape and its sunny brightness not only contributed to his complete recovery but affected him as strongly and positively as North Africa had once affected Delacroix and the Midi, Gauguin and Van Gogh. "I was sick for three days after the trip down here," he reports in a letter home, but then goes on to describe how the marvelous summery weather seems to have cured him more quickly than could all the world's doctors have done. "You have no idea how beautiful it is here," he writes "the ocean nearby and the sky always blue." In his exuberance he encloses a few rose petals.[11]

His Riviera paintings from 1891-92 reveal a particular concern for structural detail, in itself nothing new in Munch's approach. At this time, however, the idea seems far more deliberate and advanced than earlier, suggesting that the crisply scientific manner, the classical attention to form so prominent in the works of Seurat, Signac, and their followers, had made its impact upon him. In brushwork and color, on the other hand, most of his paintings from this period are more reflective of the traditional impressionist approach than of the dotted, pointillistic technique of these innovators, and in one particular canvas, the dazzling *Promenade des Anglais,* painted in strong contrasting colors of raw sienna and cerulean blue in clearly defined spaces, he displays his fondness of the Cloissonné method.

On his way home in the spring of 1891 he spent a month in Paris, seeing first of all the current Independent, that year featuring ten paintings by Van Gogh who had died the preceding summer. The profound grief felt in progressive art circles was beautifully expressed in an article by the writer, Octave Mirbeau:

> At the exhibition of the Independents, among some happy experiments and, above all, many banalities and even more frauds, sparkle the canvases of the greatly lamented Van Gogh. In front of them, before the black veil of mourning that surrounds them and singles them out for the crowd of indifferent visitors, one is overcome by great sadness to think that this magnificently gifted painter, this instinctive, supersensitive, visionary artist is no longer among us.[12]

Among the many sincere mourners was Munch who had first seen Van Gogh's works in the Independent the preceding year and in the Dutchman's strongly emotional approach to his subjects instinctively felt a kinship with him, an impression that could only have been deepened by the retrospective which, though rather sparse, contained some of the artist's anguished landscapes from Auvers. On his return to Norway Munch produced two canvases, a figure study and a street scene in the rain, highly reminiscent of certain works by Van Gogh.[13] Later, in a series of sunny landscapes and starry firmaments he must again have recalled Van Gogh's glistening palette.

Also memorialized in that year's exhibit was the originator of the Independent, Albert Dubois-Pillet, a neoimpressionist who died in August, 1890. Then, a few days after the exhibit's opening, it turned out that it would also be a memorial to Georges Seurat, the most active promoter of the Van Gogh retrospective, who died very suddenly as a consequence of a throat infection contracted during the preparatory work.

An event of some importance taking place in February, 1891, prior to Munch's arrival in Paris, was the auction sale Gauguin arranged to raise money for his journey to Tahiti. Generating considerable interest, it did much to establish Gauguin's reputation beyond the limited circle that had long recognized his genius. Somewhat later the avant-garde community with Mallarmé in the lead staged a farewell banquet for him. Munch, in Paris at the time but totally unknown, was of course not among the guests, but two of his fellow Scandinavians were, Mogens Ballin and J.F. Willumsen, countrymen of Gauguin's estranged wife. It was in Pont-Aven Gauguin had noticed Willumsen and his pictures of Breton women and, "despite his dislike for Danes," became interested in him and gave him much of his time. Gauguin even drew a portrait of Willumsen.[14]

Immediately before leaving Paris that spring Munch painted his decidedly neoimpressionist *Rue Lafayette* (Plate 25), a bird's-eye view from his hotel window. Executed not in pointillist dots but crisp streaks of primary colors it is characterized by a firm geometric structure of decisive perpendiculars and horizontals pierced by highly elongated diagonals giving the canvas a deep and rigidly accurate perspective.

Back home in the summer and fall he produced some of his most typical works from this period. Among these were two more scenes from Karl Johan Street, *Rainy Day* and *Summer Day,* deliberate atmospheric studies in the manner of Monet, each canvas showing the identical scene varied only by the weather, which also dictates the painterly approach. Smooth, even brush strokes in glossy surfaces mark the rain-soaked street, while the row of houses seems to lose contours and merge into a blurred, continuously receding shape. In the sunshine, however, the same scene is marked by the razor-sharp projection of the houses against a street painted in bright dots and streaks irregularly juxtaposed and long, gently convex, flowing brush strokes to mark the drifting clouds. Black umbrellas angrily tugged by the wind in one canvas become gaily swinging parasols in the other, and a somber, tightly buttoned procession of people in one opens up into a leisurely strolling group of promenaders in the other.

While the presentation of identical scenes under different atmospheric conditions seems, as suggested, inspired by Monet, Munch's painterly approach in *Summer Day at Karl Johan Street* appears influenced by Seurat as well, a supposition vigorously denied by Ingrid Langaard. To prove her point she submits in color and natural size a juxtaposition of a small section of the Munch canvas and one from *La Grande Jatte,* Seurat's most famous work, showing that Munch, though using commas and dots in pure colors, does not employ Seurat's rhythmically devised pattern of placing these on the canvas but instead a freely swirling color fragmentation.[15] This notwithstanding, Munch's basic technique is still very similar to Seurat's and a study of Seurat's preliminary sketches shows his initial conception to be much less scientifically motivated, freer in color and structure than the finished product which constitutes a transfer of the inspiration onto a deliberately controlled level of creativity. Munch, though by nature incapable of proceeding that far in the conscious utilization of subject and inspiration, preferring, as did Van Gogh, "to use the execution in little dots merely as an experiment in texture,"[16] shows in this particular canvas a remarkably deliberate technique both in structure and brushwork, and with Seurat's works and destiny no doubt very much on his mind that spring it seems only reasonable that it was *his* method he had studied and molded into a technique more suitable to his own temperament.

In the Autumn Exhibit of 1891—the last in which Munch participated—he was represented with three paintings, two of these from Nice, and though critics either continued their sullen disapproval or simply ignored him he did score a partial success when the National Gallery purchased his *Night in Nice,* thereby modestly starting its now world-famous Munch collection.

Twice Munch received renewal of his state grant, both times under severe criticism. His second request, calling attention to the fact that he had spent a substantial time of the preceding year bedridden with rheumatic fever, prompted none other than Bjørnson to write a scathing letter to *Dagbladet* bemoaning the use of the artist grant as a compensation for the sick, saying it ought to be given only to those physically capable of making full use of it.[17] Munch, recalling this thoughtlessness on the part of Bjørnson, once said, "He actually lived long enough to write something stupid about me."[18]

Back in France from the fall of 1891 to the following spring, Munch remained in Paris long enough to have seen the first group exhibit by young impressionists and symbolists, opening in December in the gallery of Le Barc de Boutteville. The artists, actually members of an emerging group calling itself the Nabis—the Prophets—included at that time the two Cloisonné masters, (Emile Bernard and Louis Anquetin), Maurice Denis, Pierre Bonnard, and with them a much more diversified genius, Toulouse-Lautrec. They had advance press support in the newly established *La Revue Blanche,* whose progressive publishers, the Natanson brothers, vied with the actor-director, Lugné-Poë, in promoting this group as well as other progressive trends in the arts, an enthusiasm that would soon be extended to the Scandinavians to the benefit of both Munch and Strindberg.

The immediate effect on Munch of his exposure to the artists represented in this exhibit can be found in the paintings completed on the Riviera that winter and spring. Most lastingly, however, he was influenced by Toulouse-Lautrec whose affiliation with the Nabis was rather nominal. In Munch this influence appears unmistakably in a series of paintings of people in search of diversion—on the dance floor, in cafés and shops, in a trance at the roulette table—and later in his portraiture and his graphic works.

On the threshold of his departure from Norway in 1889 Munch had produced his extraordinarily moving canvas, *Springtime,* and prior to that the hauntingly expressive *Sick Girl,* then *Puberty* and *The Day Thereafter,* all inspired and conditioned by more or less precisely defined experiences. In contrast, his efforts during his first two years in France—with the notable exception of *Night*—were all directed toward subjects detached from significant existential circumstances, each serving, it seems, to build up his creative repertoire. When viewed in that light such works as his various scenes along the Seine and the Riviera, his Parisian street scenes and those from Kristiania, as well as his interiors from cafés and casinos, are all exercises aimed at developing his talent toward virtuosity—"to reach the summit," as he says in one of his notes[19]—bold experiments in color and form but intentionally devoid of emotional implications. Then, as his stay in France approached its end in the spring of 1892, and while continuing to fashion his formal paintings in the same detached manner, he began to revert to subjects of greater emotional content, initially by filling makeshift sketch books with drawings either echoing experiences of the past or recording more recent episodes,[20] but gradually—even reluctantly, to judge from the time elapsing between sketching and painting—committing some of these subjects to the canvas. His notes, written in a style both uniquely his own and so definitely influenced by the company he kept,[21] would often describe thoughts and experiences motivating the creative process.

The first of these more elaborate ventures back into the emotional domain appears to be the series entitled *The Kiss.* The first sketches date from 1890, the paintings from 1892, the first version most likely completed in May of that year, immediately prior to his departure from Paris, where he had just seen the exhibit of the new Societé National, where his benefactor, Frits Thaulow, had been represented. Far more important for Munch, however, was the presence of works by Puvis de Chavannes, Rafaëlli, Max Liebermann, and Whistler.

In some ways 1891-92 had been a Whistler season in Paris. In November the French government had purchased his *Arrangement in Grey and Black No. 1*—"Whistler's Mother"—shortly after the city of Glasgow had invested one thousand guineas in his *Portrait of Thomas Carlyle.* He was awarded the French Legion of Honor, and in March-April of 1892—while Munch was in Paris—Goupil's, capitalizing on all of this, mounted a major Whistler retrospective which included among forty-three works the two recent sales and also *The Blue Wave* and *Old Battersea Bridge*[22]

Munch's preliminary sketch for *The Kiss*—a few dynamic lines only, some of them erased to alter the pose—shows a nude couple in an all-consuming embrace, as in Munch's notes of this experience:

> She was warm and I felt her body close to mine. We kissed long—it was absolutely still in the lofty studio.
>
> I put my cheek to hers and stroked her hair. Her cheek was burning. I felt a hot tear on my hand.[23]

In contrast to the sketch the first of the three painted versions presents a rather elaborate compositional scheme. The couple, now fully clothed, occupies the right third of the canvas, while in a similar space on the left a French door—its lace curtain pulled to the side—provides the balance. Through the door can be seen people moving along a boulevard and in the house opposite a few lit windows. The principal color, a nocturnal blue as in Whistler's *Old Battersea Bridge*—moving from its darkest shade in the couple toward a much lighter, opaque tone in the curtain, then back again to a darker nuance in a tree visible through the window—is contrasted by only two other, subtly unobtrusive colors. In the cheeks of the lovers is a tinge of russet recapitulated in a similar pigment marking a window high up on the wall of the building across the boulevard, and in a more prominent row of windows on its first floor is a subdued yellow tone.

The two subsequent versions, painted the same year but most likely after the artist's return to Norway, may be considered sequences to the first and forming with this a unified composition of a triptych of the act of love. In the first version the outside world is still very much present, playing a pictorial role equivalent to that of the lovers, while in the second (Plate 28) all extraneous matter has been eliminated in favor of an exclusive concentration on the figures. Now projected against the window's center post and intersecting crossbar the lovers seem crucified by their own passion. Finally, clothed again, they stand in the aftermath of the consummated act still in embrace by the window, now only a broad, white ribbon on the left edge of the canvas diffusing its muted light as a soft veil enveloping the figures.

It has been pointed out how Munch tended to favor certain landscape features in his summer village, Åsgårdstrand—the undulant shoreline, the spreading chestnut trees, the jutting pier—sometimes simply for their painterly appeal, but often as symbolic leitmotifs. With the three versions of *The Kiss* other such leitmotifs, already used in previous works but more ambiguously, come into play. One, the figure of the cross, present in its traditional application as a symbol of death in *Night,* functions more subtly and on an entirely different level in *The Kiss.* Referring to the act of love it becomes a symbol of the sacrifice of the self on the altar of erotic ecstacy. At this stage in Munch's life the relationship between the sexes is free of misogynist implications, but soon, through the influence of Strindberg, the sacrificial aspect will always be the burden of man, while woman rises triumphant.

The window, too, is a leitmotif. Seen first in *Morning* where its sole function is to flood the canvas with that white shimmering light, it is present again in *Sick Girl* and more prominently in *Springtime.* In both cases, while retaining its original function, the window has become a significant symbol as well, in these canvases life versus death, but more often the external world against the inner world of inspiration, emotion, as in *The Kiss.*

Munch returned to Norway on May 30, 1892, and spent a few weeks at home preparing for his forthcoming retrospective—"these great bon marchés of the arts," as he called the exhibits.[24] There were paintings to be gotten out of storage, a few to be obtained from present owners. Many would have to come down from the walls at home, and not a few of those brought back from France still needed finishing touches. He had, moreover, several sketches pressing him for transfer to the canvas, among these some pointing directly toward aspects of his creative-emotional preoccupations in the years to follow. One subject, a young man posed by a shoreline not unlike that in Puvis de Chavannes' *The Poor Fisherman* (Plate 29) but in reality the stony beach below his own summer house, already existed in three separate versions: a sketch in India ink, a pastel, and a formal drawing prepared as frontispiece for Emanuel Goldstein's collection of poetry, *Alruner* [Mandrakes; 1892]. In Munch's notes written in France are these observations:

> I walked along the shore one evening, alone. There were sighs and whispers among the stones—gray elongated clouds above the horizon. Everything was vacuous, another world—a landscape of death. Then suddenly there was life over by the pier—a man and woman, and another man, oars over his shoulder, and the boat out there, ready...
>
> It looks like her! I felt a sting in my breast. Was she here now? She's supposed to be far away—and yet it is her walk...? God, God in heaven have mercy, let it not be...
>
> Those two—they're going out to the island. In the bright summer night they'll be strolling among the trees, arm in arm...[25]

First shown in the drawings, this experience led after his return to Åsgårdstrand that summer to the painting *Melancholy,*[26] depicting all the landscape features he had so fondly recalled while in Paris—the shore, the mysterious stones, the elongated clouds above a vaguely defined horizon—and in the foreground the figure, facing away from the pier. As in *The Poor Fisherman* the entire composition is horizontal—the streaky clouds of mauve and yellow caressing a long, low headland painted in dark green, the pier in a linear projection out to a slender orange boat. Only the shoreline, gently diagonal, provides a nominal contrast, and even that in its undulant course features a rhythmic sequence of horizontals. In Munch's production this is the first in a series of paintings attempting to visualize the emotion of jealousy, the most famous of which would be completed after his arrival in Berlin where more direct and complex relationships would intensify his feelings.

Of another simple sketch (Plate 31) showing a head barely above the surface of the water and high above that a white swan, Munch has this to say:

> She was a swan. With her long, white, fine neck she was slowly gliding along the surface of the water... which reflected her perfect lines and the clouds of the sky.
>
> I lived down there in the deep... fumbling in the mire, remembering a time when I lived up there...[27]

The resulting painting, a distorted self-portrait, must be intended as a visual expression of rejected love as suggested by the image of the swan, a classical symbol of love and eroticism brought back into prominence by the romantics and again the symbolists and decadents, as shown in part by their enthusiasm for Wagner's *Parsifal* and *Lohengrin.* Actually, such specific use of an established symbol is rare in Munch's art. Instead, he tends to express his metaphoric ideas through an adaptation of much more ordinary visual features, imposing upon these his own interpretation and transmitting this to his viewers through the total mood and content of his creation. For this reason the symbolic aspect of *A Swan* is less original than such features in other paintings from the 1890s, and his use of such an image must be an influence from his exposure to specific works while in Paris, most likely the ambiguous symbols employed by Moreau and Redon. A self-portrait completed a year later reveals a closely related structure, showing his own face surmounted by another object, the mask of a woman (Plate 49), and in portraits produced later in the decade a similar juxtaposition of the model's likeness with an object acquiring a momentary symbolic significance would become a fairly normal procedure in his interpretation of the subject portrayed, as in his lithographed likeness of Strindberg (Plate 1).

Another sketch, showing a man posed on a pier and looking out over the fjord and the islands, would lead to a significant painting in 1892. Munch's notes on the preceding experiences are rather specific:

> I walked along the road with two friends. Then the sun went down. All of a sudden the sky became blood. I stopped, leaned against the railing, weary to death. Over the dark blue fjord and the city lay clouds dripping with blood. My friends went on, I remained behind, trembling, with an open wound in my breast and sensed a surging cry throughout nature.[28]

In the first painted version, *Despair,*[29] the representation closely follows the descriptive notes, an acute diagonal projection of the railing and the churning, threatening cloud formations providing the most prominent features. While his friends vanish in the distance the main figure, dramatically foreshortened, turns away from the viewer and the blood-red sky. Through a combination of structure, strong contrasting colors evoking no pleasure, the dynamics of the clouds, and the gap between the foreground figure and his uncomprehending friends, the entire canvas exudes a darkly ominous mood, though rather subdued when compared to the following year's visual expression of the same experience, *The Shriek* (Plate 42).

Included in the 1892 retrospective were fifty paintings, among them most of the works discussed in this and preceding chapters. Also shown were *Puberty* and *The Day Thereafter,* quite astonishing considering that the original versions, from 1885-86, had been lost in a fire in 1891. However, so essential to an understanding of his artistic purpose did Munch consider these works to be that he repainted them expressly for this exhibit.[30]

Puberty (Plate 33) may be his first deliberate attempt at going beyond direct appearances by intensifying the expressive potential of a living model, for it is inconceivable that the young person posing for this particular work could have displayed an inner anguish as profound as that exuding from the canvas. It is a visual representation of the inexpressible fear of entering adulthood, of reaching sexual maturity, articulated in color and structure and with a compassion perhaps deeper than many would expect of a man. The model's gauntly yellow flesh tones, the starkly plain wall and the greenish-white bed give the viewer an instant chill turning into a shudder at the sight of the huge, darkly foreboding shape hovering on the wall—a monstrus fetus rather than a reasonable rendition of the shadow of the frail creature portrayed. Within her cell-like space she sits tautly on the edge of her bed, legs tightly pressed together, arms instinctively attempting to cover her nudity, eyes wide-set, livid with fear. Every muscle, every fiber of her body ready for flight, she is inescapably imprisoned in the fate inherent in her lot as a woman.

It is not unreasonable to consider *The Day Thereafter* (Plate 34) a sequel to *Puberty.* Created in the same vein, inspired not by any social or moral concern but by the same deep awareness of a biologically motivated destiny this painting may be interpreted as the justification of the child-woman's dire apprehension. Even a casual glance at the setting is sufficient to reveal the same spatial confinement: the wall, the bed, even a similar hovering shadow, although now a phallus. A closer scrutiny shows the face in both paintings to be the same, only with a mature beauty added in *The Day Thereafter.* Jens Thiis's characterization of the latter as "a visual manifestation of human compassion," bears repeating. The painting is, however, much more than that. With *Puberty, The Kiss, Melancholy,* and *A Swan* it is a testimony of Munch's view of woman at that particular time in his career, as yet allowing no room for the vampire.

Predictably, Munch's retrospective was no success. A substantial number of the works had already received their usual treatment by the critics, either on the occasion of his 1889 retrospective or in the three Autumn Exhibits in which he had taken part since then, and a renewed showing prompted no recantations, nor did the new works bring him any converts. *Aftenposten*'s critic, apparently enraged by the painting discussed in the present chapter under the title *Melancholy* but in the retrospective called *Evening Mood,* resorts to vulgarities in his description:

> He paints his notorious orange boat... now placing in the foreground something that most closely resembles smoked hams and blood sausages—a veritable butcher shop! Painting with blood-stained fingers he calls it *Evening Mood.*[31]

Two other Scandinavians, both then better known than Munch, happened to be exhibiting in Kristiania the same month. One was Adelsteen Normann, a Norwegian genre painter strategically residing in Berlin where, capitalizing on the prevailing Prussian sentiment for matters Nordic, he had made a name for himself as depicter of landscapes from rugged West Norway. The other was J.F. Willumsen, Gauguin's Danish acquaintance, now back in the north from Pont-Aven and Paris. He and Munch, who met for the first time during those autumn days, could have taken comfort in their mutual failure with the critics, for the quotation from *Aftenposten*'s review of Munch's *Evening Mood* was a paragraph from a more extensive account of "the wonderful creations of these two champions of the most modern trends in the world of art." Following that acid introduction the critic went on to say:

> On most viewers these two exhibits have no other effect than to evoke their laughter. Yet there have been those who have taken all of it seriously and solemnly declared that these "art-of-the-future" absurdities make sense. Of course! For there is no earthly beauty or truth that cannot be twisted into its own caricature, and there is no madness or inanity in this world that some fool or other won't eagerly admire.[32]

Apparently, one such "fool" eagerly admiring what Munch had to show was Adelsteen Normann, who in the Norwegian Art Society was showing landscapes from the Fjord Country, most of them painted on order for his Berlin clients and in Norway admired equally by patriotic critics and appreciative hotel owners. That this unimaginative painter steeped in the rigidly conservative establishment of the Prussian capital would be the first person to promote a Munch exhibit outside Norway defies explanation. Yet, for whatever reason, when Normann returned to Berlin he suggested to the board of the Association of Berlin Artists that they sponsor an exhibit of the works of this totally unknown Norwegian, to which the board agreed. That is how it happened that Munch, with his entire retrospective exhibit as well as a few brand new canvases in the baggage car, on October 20, 1892, set out for Berlin, no doubt hoping for a much more informed appraisal of his art.

It is possible to read some of his parting thoughts into the newest of his major works shown at the retrospective, the eerie *Evening at Karl Johan Street* (Plate 27)—so immediately different in its impact it made critics and public alike question the artist's sanity. With this extraordinary canvas Munch may have wanted to accomplish two separate purposes, first of all to proclaim through this strikingly new interpretation of a thoroughly familiar scene the end of his impressionist leanings. The juxtaposition of one of his earlier Karl Johan's street paintings, *Summer Day* (Plate 26), with the new interpretation makes this point very clear. In the newer painting Munch's approach is not unlike that of the so-called Nabis. Not because his *Evening at Karl Johan Street* directly resembles any of the paintings he may have seen in the group's Le Barc de Boutteville exhibit that year—for his total presentation is much more extreme—but because their artistic ideals would so closely express his own:

> To the Nabis a picture had merit only when it possessed "style," that is to say, when the artist had succeeded in changing the shape of the objects he was looking at and imposing on them contours or a color that expressed his own personality. Resemblance was of small importance, or rather resemblance was the enemy. What counted . . . was the "mental image" imagined by the artist, the distortion brought about by the bending of a line or the exaggeration of a tint.[33]

Munch's second purpose may have been to issue an indictment against his fellow citizens who had greeted all his efforts with hostile resistence or blatant ridicule, those inflexible, unimaginative men and women Ibsen in *An Enemy of the People* had called "the compact majority." It is doubtful that anyone else by visual means has so poignantly conveyed the meaning of that phrase, and this Munch accomplished without compromising his primary purpose, to create a work of art.

Building up a structure of diagonals—a row of houses, the street, the sidewalk—radiating sharply from the center of the picture toward its frontal focus, he slices through the surging crowd, dissecting it and baring its soul by bringing some of its members up close, their vacuous stares eye to eye with the viewer. He intensifies this spectral portrayal of randomly chosen individuals with a color scheme of bright, glaring pigments contrasting dissonantly with the deep blue of the summer night, thereby succeeding in plunging the entire canvas into a shuddering representation of the horror of conformity—against which one solitary individual moves without apparent concern.

Munch's departure from Norway in the fall of 1892 marked the beginning of an extended exile—he too, as Strindberg before him, seeking a creative environment more appreciative of his talent. Yet he can not have viewed his experiences at home in a wholly negative perspective, for every spring he packed up his easel and paints and set course for the home shore, more specifically Åsgårdstrand, where the caressive landscape provided balm for his often wounded spirit. Not so with Kristiania. Although on occasion he might speak nostalgically about Karl Johan Street it was only reluctantly that he mingled with the hometown crowd, always remembering "your scorn and your vicious attempts at shaking my balance." A futile effort, indeed, for no one would ever make him change his determination to portray life precisely as he saw it. "Whether a picture resembles nature means nothing. To explain a picture is impossible. It's exactly because an artist has no other way of explaining a subject that he paints it... People must comprehend the sanctity of it all..."[34]

10

Strindberg and Munch Meet

Ever since the 1850s, but more specifically after the city had become the capital of the German Reich in 1871, Berlin had been a center of activities for young Scandinavians bent on widening their horizons. This was not so much a preference for Berlin over Paris or Rome but a natural gravitation toward that part of the Continent for which these artists and intellectuals were educationally and linguistically best prepared. For the serious student the universities of Leipzig and Berlin exerted considerable drawing power, so also the music conservatory in Leipzig and somewhat later its sister institution in Berlin. Among painters the migration to Germany had started out in the direction of Dresden, while Johan Christian Dahl was still there. However, when a group of young Norwegians, following in the footsteps of Adolf Tidemand, August Cappelen, and Hans Gude, had established themselves in Duesseldorf, other Scandinavians quickly followed suit, the Swedes in particular, once these three had taken part in an Inter-Scandinavian Exhibit in the Stockholm Academy in 1850:

> In Tidemand's vivid scenes of everyday life, in Gude's and Cappelen's powerful and moody landscapes they seemed to read their own future. Duesseldorf loomed as a highly attractive goal, and a general migration was planned among academy students.[1]

Gradually, France began to draw—first Paris, then the Fontainebleau villages—but many still remained in Germany, in the last quarter of the century more frequently in Munich, then considered very progressive. Yet when all these aspiring artists and intellectuals had finished their formal education and wanted to establish themselves professionally—or at least sample a cosmopolitan life devoted to intellectual-creative pursuits—they often chose an extended stay in the new German capital. By the 1880s, however, when Strindberg had embarked on his first extended journey abroad—to Grez and Paris—Berlin had entered a period of temporary decline as a center for Scandinavian progressives, so it was natural that he would go elsewhere. More important, however, was the fact that he was primarily Francophile in his leanings and that in Grez and Paris he had friends and supporters eager to welcome him.

Munch, too, had friends in Paris, but his preference for France in 1889 had been based exclusively on his conviction that the rigid German approach in art, which he felt had stifled the creative originality of many, among them Krohg and Werenskjold, was far behind the times and that Paris was the only place where he personally would find it possible to grow and develop as an artist.

When it came to a second exile for these two, however, they were drawn to Berlin for rather similar reasons, not so much to meet friends—of which there would actually be many more than either had anticipated—as to respond to special professional opportunities that beckoned. In Munch's case it was the forthcoming exhibit, in Strindberg's several indications of potential success. The recent staging of two of his plays in Berlin theatres had been very favorably received, several of his works had been translated into German and further translations were in progress. Most seductive, however, were the intriguing pronouncements by Ola Hansson, who no doubt felt that Strindberg's presence in his particular circle would be a matter of considerable added prestige. In July, 1892, following a series of similarly encouraging letters, Ola Hansson painted this irresistibly rosy picture of Strindberg's opportunities in the German capital:

> There is a colony of writers here, which may not necessarily interest you. Then there is Friedrichshagen, center of the "Independents" headed by my good friend Bruno Wille, founder and director of the *Freie Volksbühne.* Otherwise Berlin is so intimate that you'd be able to choose your own company as you might wish. Finally, I'd like you to know that your arrival here will be greeted with pride and joy. Here in Germany you have a greater measure of sympathy and better chances than you could ever imagine.[2]

Then, having received Strindberg's cabled response that he would come, Hansson wrote further:

> Fill your pockets with all your manuscripts, the six pieces for the theatre (here there is a complete lack of theatre novelties)... everything you have. Money will be available as soon as the manuscripts have been delivered.[3]

To Strindberg, burdened with unperformed, unpublished, and untranslated material and in constant need of money, these must have been promising prospects, indeed, and for a month or so after his arrival things seemed to be going his way. Having settled in Friedrichshagen, near the Hanssons, he had first paraphrazed the name into *Friedrichsruh* to emphasize his newly found peace of mind. "Are you satisifed with the world, and do things go according to your wishes?" he asks in a letter to a friend, adding for his own account. "For the moment destiny seems to have tired of persecuting me."[4] Only a few days later, however, in a letter to Adolf Paul, he changed the name of the place again, now calling it *Friedrichshölle,* partly because he was suffering from a gigantic hangover but mostly because he was beginning to feel exploited by the Hanssons.

Those early days in November of 1892 were important to the Scandinavian community in Berlin and would later be recalled as crucial in the development of German art. Strindberg, however, busy with his own publishing and theatrical projects—primarily the proposed staging of *Lady Julie* in Paris—and a love affair with a young Norwegian, seems to have missed entirely the sensational goings-on in *Architektenhaus,* where Munch's exhibit had opened with pomp and circumstance on November 5, only to be closed a week later, out of "high respect for the arts and honest artistic endeavor."[5]

None of this is mentioned in Strindberg's correspondence, and on November 16, referring to a proposed book on himself to be edited by Ola Hansson, he suggests that Richard Bergh be asked to provide a suitable portrait, indicating that he was as yet unaware of Munch's presence in Berlin. Shortly thereafter, with the Berlin press in the midst of a heated polemic about the Munch exhibit, he could hardly have avoided learning of it. At that time, however, anxious to extricate himself from his involvement with the Norwegian woman, he had hurriedly left for Weimar, intending to continue to Dresden and Munich and possibly Vienna and Prague, but getting no further than to the Goethe-Schiller city. There he remained for two weeks, most of the time, because of a severe shortage of funds, in extreme misery, suffering "as in a torture chamber."[6] For a brief interlude this sorry state of affairs changed for the better through the presence of a beautiful young actress. Without the slightest consideration for the feelings of her doting husband, the Finnish poet Karl August Tavaststjerna, a devoted and obviously long-suffering Strindberg admirer, he sought her favors, exuberantly describing the situation to Paul: "*Neue Liebe!* Full declaration of love in the presence of her male partner. Jealousy. *Alles!*"[7] But when the Tavaststjernas had left and he was once more on his own, his misery returned and he had to cable friends in Berlin for help. Adolf Paul and Przybyszewski succeeded in collecting enough money to bail him out of his Weimar hotel, and he was soon back in more congenial surroundings.

Immediately thereafter he must have met Edvard Munch, for a December 10 notice in *Dagbladet,* a Kristiania paper pursuing Munch's career with a modest amount of interest, reports that the painter has rented a studio in Berlin and is in the process of painting a portrait of August Strindberg. Thereafter, for an entire year, Munch's name occurs with a high degree of frequency in Strindberg's correspondence, while Munch's—both the published portion and the archive material—is almost totally devoid of references to Strindberg. But then Munch is rather frugal with the amount of information he provides in his letters, a situation his brother, Andreas, trying to become better informed on his activities in Berlin, bemoans:

> Write in some more detail how you've been getting along this winter—about the people you've been associating with. It would be so interesting, but you haven't said a word about this in your letters.[8]

And there would have been a great deal to tell, to clarify, for what his family was able to find out from the local press was for the most part so negatively slanted that it was not only distressing to read but frequently unreliable. The report *Aftenposten*'s correspondent filed on the Berlin reaction to Munch's "fifty-five wild caprices," is a good case in point. Citing a series of press reviews tending to confirm *Aftenposten*'s well-known opinions the article concludes that the Berliners, just as Munch's own hometown people, simply do not comprehend or appreciate his madness and therefore stand before his creations laughing.[9] Munch had already warned his family of this, saying that the exhibit had generated a great deal of fury in the ranks of the Old Guard, that the Berlin press had scolded him frightfully, although a couple of critics had reacted with considerable understanding. "Of course you'll be reading only the bad reviews," he adds, "the right-wing papers will see to that."[10]

Even prior to the opening of his exhibit Munch must have discovered that Berlin, despite the presence of an articulate avant-garde, in many respects was a rigidly conservative metropolis. On the eve of his arrival, having discussed various procedures with Adelsteen Normann, he wrote home asking for his frock coat—"an important piece of clothing down here. Send it as cheaply as possible. It's reasonable to assume that I'll be invited out once my exhibit gets underway."[11] Obviously not prepared for the kind of reception his works would receive he fully expected to be treated as a distinguished visiting artist and was perfectly willing to conform to local etiquette. The ensuing furor must therefore have come as quite a surprise to him. Whether initially disappointed or not, once he had caught his breath he felt rather flattered having become the crucial pawn in a bitter chess game between the liberal and the conservative elements in the Association of Berlin Artists, the former led by Max Liebermann and Walter Leistikow, the latter by the official Imperial Battle Painter, Anton von Werner. The consequence was the now famous Berlin Secession which split apart the German capital's art community, not in support of or opposition to the works of Edvard Munch but in a drive by the progressives aimed at drawing a clear line of distinction between a liberal and a conservative approach to painting. In reality, the Berlin Secession, following behind that of Munich but preceding similar events in other major centers of the Reich, was a delayed reaction to issues having surfaced much earlier in Paris, where the *Salon des Indépedants* had been the most tangible result, and in Stockholm where it had led to the formation of the Opponents group.

Aftenposten's correspondent, reporting back to Norway on this cultural battle and gleefully asserting that Munch's pictures were hardly significant enough to have set such passions in motion, was really quite wrong in his assessment. Regardless of the relative merit of Munch's works at that time, it was, indeed, their presence that provided the spark igniting an already explosive situation. Gerhard Mazur, in a recent volume on Berlin, places *"Der*

Fall Munch" [The Munch Case] in a broader historical perspective. First pointing out that the scandal of the exhibit itself and the ensuing uproar prompted the Kaiser to deliver his speech on "the art of the gutter," Mazur explains that the imperial irritation was rooted in the view that the secessionists were cultural traitors tending by their action to negate the official optimistic stance that the Kaiser was leading his people toward a great and glorious future. All this could be dismissed as the laughable and ludicrous notions of an egomaniac and his supporters, Mazur goes on to say, had it not established a precedent for a later generation whose interpretation of cultural treason lead to the "maniacal deeds of the Nazi period," among whose lesser evils were "the burning of 'decadent' books, the removal of 'decadent' art from museums, the ban on painting."[12]

As for Edvard Munch, unwitting instigator of the turmoil, though bruised by harsh criticism, he considered the total effect of what had taken place to be in his favor, as he was quick to point out in a letter to those at home:

> I could hardly have received better advertizing... People came long distances to see the exhibit... I've never had such enjoyable days. It's incredible that anything as innocent as art can create such furor. You asked whether it has made me nervous. I've gained six pounds and have never felt better.[13]

When Strindberg had returned from Weimer the Munch case was no longer front-page news, but he still must have heard a great deal about it—from the artist himself as he posed for him, but also from his own friends and followers as he resumed his daily routine, which included extended stays in an Armenian *Weinstube* he had discovered and renamed *Zum schwarzen Ferkel* [The Black Pig]. Originally of a reputation as indifferent as its clientele the place soared in popularity as soon as it became known that Strindberg had made it his headquarters. From then on it tended to be on the itinerary of most of the members of the permanent or transient avant-garde, and it was not long before the grateful owner was able to remove the rusty chains supporting the black wine sack that had inspired Strindberg in his renaming of the inn, replacing them with a set in pure silver. Here is the way one of the habitués described the *Ferkel:*

> The entire *Weinstube* consisted of two small rooms separated by a narrow serving counter overflowing with bottles containing all sorts of drinks. The entire area was so limited it could barely accomodate twenty persons. And by six o'clock in the evening, once Strindberg had begun frequenting the place, it was impossible to find a vacant square inch.[14]

Stanislaw Przybyszewski, the fiery and multi-talented Pole who wrote these words, was a part-time art critic who must have followed the Munch controversy with particularly keen interest. It was therefore quite likely he who brought Strindberg and Munch together and perhaps also suggested the portrait—which Munch must have completed in record time, for it was ready to be shown in his next Berlin exhibit (Plate 38). As for the opening date of this event, Norwegian sources indicate December 27, but to judge from Strindberg's correspondence this would have to be in error, for on the day before Christmas—certainly not the ideal season for Munch's type of pictures—this triumphant note appears in a Strindberg letter to a friend: "Today Munch opens his exhibit once more to strike a new blow for the Scandinavian Renaissance."[15]

For Strindberg to call the combined contribution of the Scandinavian community in Berlin in those days a Renaissance was not as presumptuous as it might seem. Within a little more than a week of that writing Hermann Sudermann, distinguished German playwright, would be paying tribute to the entire group by declaring, "From the North the light has reached us."[16] Before the end of January—it was now 1893—Strindberg himself would have had several plays performed at the *Residenztheater* in Berlin—and one even in Paris where at long last *Lady Julie* was headed for its French premiere at *Théâtre-Libre.* This event, though preceded by several flattering articles on Strindberg in the Paris press, did not turn out to be much of a success. In fact, it prompted the sort of critical comments Munch had become so accustomed to: ". . . madness . . . Derived from French sources . . . evoking laughter"[17]—to which Strindberg himself wryly observed, "Now I've been panned in Paris! The realization of a dream from my youth!"[18]

Strindberg and Munch were not the only ones within the *Ferkel* circle emitting the kind of light Sudermann had alluded to. There was Holger Drachmann, for one, a Danish poet and painter whose very appearance—he was tall, blond, and with chiseled features—might send an ethnocentric German into a trance. There were Gunnar Heiberg, Norwegian playwright and iconoclast, and his countryman, Knut Hamsun, whose debut novel, *Hunger,* had been received with equal acclaim in Scandinavia and Germany and who had just then completed his *Mysteries.* Of painters there were Christian Krohg and Severin Segelcke, Norwegians, both in the process of doing Strindberg's portrait—that by Segelcke ultimately chosen as the frontispiece for the long-awaited Strindberg book—and Axel Gallén-Kallela, the Finn, who produced a particularly sensitive likeness of Munch. Later the circle would be expanded to include for shorter or longer periods the Norwegian poets Arne Garborg and Sigbjørn Obstfelder, their countryman, the sculptor Gustav Vigeland, the Finnish composer, Jean Sibelius, and there were of course always the charter members, Ola Hansson, Adolf Paul, and—although not exactly a Scandinavian—Przybyszewski. Principal participants among the Germans were the poets Richard Dehmel and Max Dauthenday, the writer and theatre entrepreneur, Otto Erich Hartleben, two physicians, Carl Ludwig Schleich and Max Asch, and on rare occasions the painter Hermann Schlittgen.

Munch's second Berlin exhibit, following the first by five weeks during which the paintings had been shown in a number of art centers throughout the Reich, was mounted in a private gallery in the heart of the city, a huge Norwegian flag without the union insignia[19] marking the spot. There was reasonable press coverage of the event. Thus *Berliner Tageblatt,* expressing its pleasure that the citizens would have another opportunity to evaluate the controversial works, pointed out that a few paintings had been added, among them a portrait of "the Norwegian [*sic*] poet Strindberg."[20] This time the exhibit remained on view for four weeks but earned Munch few laurels and no sales. However, attendance was good, and by sharing the nominal entrance fee with the promoter he was able to clear 1,000 marks.

Jens Thiis, in Berlin at the time and a frequent visitor to the exhibit, was standing in front of the Strindberg portrait one day when two men entered the room:

> Munch and Strindberg. Munch introduced me. I had read enough by the great Swedish poet to admire him, and this was a great experience. He made a very favorable impression on me. There was a certain grandiosely Swedish stylishness about his manner, so different from Munch's straightforward Norwegian ways, but the two seemed to get along well together, and already during this first period in Berlin there must have been quite an exchange of ideas between them.[21]

In this exhibit *Sick Girl* and *Springtime,* always Munch's own favorite canvases, shared the place of honor with his Strindberg portrait, a clear indication of his respect for his fellow Scandinavian and his pride in having had him as his model. The portrait, now in Stockholm's National Museum, is a somewhat stylized yet powerful representation which a critic in *Berliner Tageblatt* described as unfinished, though adequate to convey the impression of a most unique personality:

> It is as though he had been caught unaware in his study and skillfully captured in a characteristic moment. Head and torso emerge vividly from the warm background, disclosing an impetuous temperament and a certain touch of superiority and bitter agitation.[22]

Strindberg himself, far from pleased, is reported by Adolf Paul to have said:

> I don't give a damn about likeness! It was supposed to be a stylized portrait of a poet. Like those of Goethe. Munch ought to have known as much![23]

It is likely that he looked askance at other items in the exhibit as well. After all, in the immediate aftermath of his divorce and in one of his most pronounced misogynist phases, he must have viewed some of the erotic works with downright revulsion. In Munch's favor, however, was the fact that Strindberg just then happened to be deeply engrossed in painting again. Thus, scrutinizing these pictures with professional interest and a greater degree of objectivity than would otherwise have been the case, he may well have recalled how he himself had once decided that to paint meant the visualizing of one's own inner emotions and not the copying of "sticks and stones." In that frame of mind he could not have failed to appreciate Munch's creative effort, for in the principal canvases all superficial attention to realism had been eliminated in favor of an intensive concentration on the expressive intent. There can be little doubt that Strindberg, hypersensitive and impressionable, experienced with Munch his profound grief in *Sick Girl* and *Springtime* and the inescapable anguish of the last stage of the event portrayed in the most recent work in that series, *Death in the Sickroom.* At the sight of *The Kiss* and *Melancholy*—one representing the sacrifice of the self on the alter of love, the other the inconstancy of the female heart—he may have felt simultaneously nostalgic regret and scornful resentment, while in the throbbing turbulence engulfing the solitary dejected figure in *Despair* he may have glanced into his own emotional wilderness.

The exchange of ideas between the two must have had its beginning in the difference between their respective points of view on woman, Strindberg's as relentlessly negative as Munch's then was compassionate and positive, even adoring. While there is no indication in their own documents or correspondences, or in observations by mutual friends, to suggest that these two associated on any other than a fully equal level, it is nevertheless quite evident from the sudden changes of tenor in Munch's paintings at this juncture which of them held sway. Only a few weeks had passed since their initial meeting when Munch, writing home to tell that his Berlin exhibit was closing—by his own choice that time—says, "You can well imagine how bored I am with my paintings!"[24] As a matter of fact, it is quite impossible to imagine any such thing. So much a part of him were Munch's paintings that he felt downright dismembered when they were not within reach.[25] Therefore, this outspoken indifference marks such a radical departure from his long-established attitude that had made him speak of "the sanctity of it all" and of people removing their hats "as in a church," that it must have been prompted by a very sudden and drastic change of mind in regard to the validity of a key section of his contribution, that dealing with his interpretation of the relationship between man and woman. Had Strindberg, older, more experienced and persuasive, that easily succeeded in enlisting Munch to wield his exceptional talent on the male side in the ongoing battle of the sexes, or had other people and experiences affected his outlook?

11

Frida Uhl and Dagny Juell

Following the premiere of a Sudermann play at the *Residenztheater* early in January of 1893, a carriage brought a young woman to one of Berlin's most sophisticated neighborhoods where she entered the brightly lit home of the Julius Elias family, just as the hostess bid three gentlemen goodbye. One was the painter, Hermann Schlittgen, the other,

> an elegant man, spirited, blond, face narrow and pale with wonderful blue eyes, one who is shy in his daily life but in his art dares all: Edvard Munch, the painter I had long ago wanted to meet as ardently as I wanted to live.

Yet even the presence of this much-admired person was completely overshadowed by the magic exerted upon the young woman by the third gentleman, half hidden behind the others:

> A dark rain cape over his shoulders. Like a huge gray rock does he stand there. Stone gray is his cape, stone gray the hair. As though chiseled from gray stone is his powerful head, eyes gray and searching, gray his hollow cheeks... Mr. August Strindberg.[1]

The moonstruck hero-worshipper was Frida Uhl, by the grace of her father, Friedrich Uhl, editor-in-chief of *Wiener Zeitung,* sent to Berlin to serve as cultural correspondent for his influential but conservative Vienna daily. That evening, according to her memoirs—not characterized by absolute integrity but in regard to these particular events in general agreement with other, more reliable documents—she was introduced to Strindberg twice and succeeded, without really trying, she claims, in changing his mind about leaving the party.

That a full month would pass until Strindberg himself made any reference to Frida Uhl in his correspondence may seem surprising until one considers his schedule of events that January. There were letters to be written to translators and publishers, play producers, and influential friends. He had direct conferences with such people, attended dinners and receptions leading to formal and informal meetings with scores of dignitaries, admirers, and those simply curious about this controversial man from the North. Not that he complained. To him it was all new and intoxicating, for although he had in the past been subject to occasional demonstrations of support and admiration this early part of his Berlin stay represented the most sustained period of public recognition in his entire career and did a great deal to bolster his self-confidence. "The year of 93, following *l'année terrible* of 92, seems to mark a turning point in my tragicomic life," he writes to Birger Mörner, then editing the projected Strindberg book. Explaining this further he refers to the successful staging of *Creditors,* claiming that he is so certain of similar success with his two newest plays, *The Bond* and *Playing with Fire,* "that I consider myself 'rescued,' even financially." He adds this observation: "Curiously amiable nation, this, that bows down to foreign talent, sincerely, without resistance or the slightest touch of envy."[2] On February 8, again writing to Mörner, he closes on this unexpected and exalted note: "Perhaps you will soon be hearing even more glorious news about me." That this impending glory is in the nature of a personal rather than an artistic conquest is made unmistakably clear by the addition of a quote from—of all places *A Doll's House*! It is with Nora's wistful parting words to Helmer on the perfect marriage that Strindberg hints of what may be in store for him: *"Det vidunderlige"*[The most wonderful thing]![3]

This new situation, when subjected to his own creative manipulation in *The Cloister,* an autobiographical novel based on his Berlin experiences but written five years later, acquires a structural logic obviously not part of the original sequence of events. In the main, however, *The Cloister* does not radically depart from the reality which can be extracted from Strindberg's letters and from observations made by members of his circle.

In the early part of the novel a psychological conflict arises in the wake of Strindberg's anticipation of his first rendezvous with Frida, twenty-three years his junior:

> ...as he now tried to imagine the Miss X of yesterday, he saw not her, but his own elder sister, a fairly short, dark, female type. As a result, anything of an erotic nature—if such there had been—was eliminated, and his only memory was of a good female friend.[4]

There are indications in his first communications to Frida—hurriedly written notes carried by messenger across Berlin to her place of residence—that he may indeed have intended, at least initially, to cultivate her as an attractive friend rather than a lover let alone a wife. The letter to Mörner, on the other hand, written the very same day as the first of these notes, tends to contradict this, as do subsequent notes beginning to pass between Strindberg and Frida from mid-February on. The psychological conflict hinted at in the quote above, however, may be genuine enough, for it resembles very closely the imaginings recorded in another autobiographical novel, *Le Playdoyer d'un Fou* [The

Confessions of a Fool], when he recalls his first meetings with Siri von Essen, except that then it was his mother rather than his sister he had envisioned. In this neurotic attitude Gunnar Brandell sees one of the explanations for Strindberg's problem with the opposite sex. Through the evoking of such disturbing visions his erotic experiences became "one of the most consistent means of awakening his guilt."[5] Instinctive though this may have been, in the case of his first meeting with Frida—if the quote from *The Cloister* is to be taken at face value—that stymying guilt feeling seems deliberately called up *in advance,* perhaps as a protective shield against his own vulnerability, conscious as he was that his involvement would inevitably develop far beyond the stage of a man toward "a good female friend."

That it was his sister he had imagined this time suggests a subconscious reaction to his close association with Munch and his familiarity with the items in the Berlin exhibit which contained no less than six major works featuring Munch's sisters. Four of them represent Inger: a close-up portrait at age sixteen, another, full-length, at twenty-one featuring a taut, apprehensively protective pose not unlike that in *Puberty,* then the caressively lyric *Evening* (Inger on the Beach), and the Pissarro-inspired *Evening Chat.* Through such persistent preoccupation with the physical features of his sister Munch too seems to be building up a shield against erotic involvements that would, in his view, lead to nothing but guilt and shame.

In spite of such conscious or subconscious efforts to remain aloof, both Munch and Strindberg experienced during those early months of 1893 a rather strange alliance with one and the same woman whose presence in their midst threatened not only the tenuous equilibrium of these two but of other members of the Ferkel circle as well. Although in Strindberg's correspondence the first hint of such complications in his daily routine dates from mid-March, observations in *The Cloister* indicate that these disturbances may have had their beginnings as early as in January. At that time the Danish[6] painter had been staying away from the Cloister—the name given *Zum schwarzen Ferkel* in the novel—because he was entertaining a young lady from Norway and was said to be reluctant to bring her within sight of the Swede—Strindberg—for fear he would turn her head. As matters developed it appeared that his fear—if he really had felt any—had been well founded. When at long last he did bring her—having learned of Strindberg's forthcoming engagement to Frida Uhl and presumably secure in his assumption that the Swede was unlikely to take interest in any other woman—he soon found out that Strindberg, far from being disinterested, lavished upon the extraordinary newcomer all the pent-up passion the formal circumstances of his courtship to Frida had compelled him to repress. The young Norwegian, a long-time admirer of the bold Swede, quickly responded to his overtures:

> In less than an hour she had broken with her friend of many year's standing—whose prophesy had thus come true—and she was now allied with the Swede, who only half an hour before had been kissing his bride-to-be goodbye.[7]

Strindberg's rapidly mounting passion, however, was accompanied by a pronounced and steadily increasing feeling of guilt alluded to in letters to Frida written in mid-March. "Bad conscience, poor press notices in Stockholm, and restlessness drive me to *Zum schwarzen Ferkel,*" he says, and "I am anxious about myself" because "I am so weak when you are not here."[8] In this frame of mind he began looking at the "other" woman through eyes gradually blinded by a hatred generated by his own guilt and dependence and soon found her "ugly and badly dressed, and there were moments when the idea that he might be taken for her wooer made him feel ashamed."[9]

In reality, this biased view of the novel's Laïs—Dagny Juell, daughter of a physician at Kongsvinger and niece of Norway's prime minister at the time—was definitely not shared by others. Jens Thiis, in the *Ferkel* circle for a period of time in 1893 and that summer visiting with the Juell family at Kongsvinger—while they were also entertaining Przybyszewski who was to marry Dagny later that year—calls her "uniquely captivating" and her sisters, Ragnhild and Astri, "piquant . . . and beautiful."[10] More interesting in the present context, however, is that Frida Uhl, who had learned of the relationship that had developed between the young Norwegian and Strindberg during her own absence, describes her in uncommonly flattering terms:

> A beautiful figure. Tall and sophisticated. Dressed in dignified, colorless gray. Curly blonde hair above her brows. Down below protrudes a fine Grecian nose. Her lips are narrow and sensual, her teeth white. Her most beautiful features are the aristocratic hands, the well groomed feet, and her lack of weight.[11]

Przybyszewski—his viewpoint of course far from unbiased—stresses Dagny's intellectual-creative qualities, saying that whatever was latent in his own soul she succeeded in bringing out: "She was my highest intellectual and aesthetic enjoyment."[12]

It is difficult to determine whether Strindberg's persistent hatred for Dagny—for his determined effort at discrediting her must have been rooted in nothing less—was based entirely on the guilt feeling his relationship with her had generated or on a combination of that and possible personal defeats he may have suffered in the course of that relationship. Przybyszewski, writing about it many years later, says:

> Strindberg . . . became engaged to Frida Uhl . . . While she traveled to Vienna to inform her parents of this conquest he fell so in love with Miss Juell, a Norwegian who just then had come to Berlin to study music, that he, forgetting his engagement to Miss Uhl, offered to

> marry Miss Juell. When she then made him aware of the fact that he might have been her father he was filled with a furious hatred toward the woman who in this way had insulted him.[13]

For whatever reason, Strindberg pursues Dagny in his correspondence for a period of more than a year, calling her Aspasia from the Greek courtesan, expounding upon her flagrant promiscuity to individuals as widely apart in interest in this matter as on the one extreme Bengt Lidforss, young Swedish scientist and Strindberg disciple who had met Dagny in Lund, fallen hopelessly in love with her, and then followed her to Berlin only to become one of her rejected lovers, and on the other Georg Brandes. He, totally unaware of her existence and never having expressed the slightest interest in Strindberg's erotic escapades, learned, no doubt to his own astonishment, that this allegedly insatiable woman had allowed herself to be mounted by "four different nationalities within thirty days," Sweden having been ably represented by Strindberg himself who had simply done his duty and retired from the field.[14] At the writing of that letter these events were already more than a year in the past, but Strindberg's hatred remained undiminished. Or it may have been on the increase, for insult had been added to injury when a young Lund scientist, Helge Bäckström, married to Dagny's sister, Ragnhild, had reviewed a collection of Strindberg's scientific writings issued in German under the title *Antibarbarus* and characterized the volume as "78 pages of misunderstandings, erroneous information, and too hastily drawn conclusions."[15] It was no doubt in an effort at discrediting Bäckström's scientific objectivity in the eyes of Brandes that Strindberg had volunteered the crude information on his own and other men's alleged adventures with his critic's sister-in-law. This accomplished nothing, however, for Brandes's response, as might have been expected, contained no reference whatsoever to that irrelevant section of Strindberg's letter.

Few nineteenth-century Scandinavian women not directly engaged in one of the creative fields have received the retrospective attention accorded to Dagny Juell. From statements such as those in Strindberg's letters, *The Cloister,* and *Inferno,* it would be easy to conclude that this remarkable woman from the provincial aristrocracy of Norway was for all intents and purposes a mere sex object, or worse a nymphomaniac seeking to satisfy her ravenous appetite by circulating freely among the members of the male-dominated group frequenting the *Ferkel.* Such conclusions, however, would provide an unfair and sadly truncated view of a woman whose influence is manifestly present in some of the more imposing creative efforts coming out of that particular group.

Although it is difficult to separate fact from fiction in the diverse writings dealing directly or indirectly with Dagny Juell there is ample evidence to suggest that she was someone of far greater significance than Strindberg in his bitter recollections was willing to admit. As regards his prejudice, it is again Frida Uhl who seems to provide the most perceptive analysis of it. She, fully justified in denouncing Dagny and deliberately preconditioned toward that end by Strindberg himself, chose instead to look beyond the immediate problem and as a result found herself in a state of puzzled admiration and secret compassion:

> From her colorless summer outfit a dark shadow has fallen upon us. It weighs him down like a nightmare, and I cannot chase it away. I cannot help wondering about the reverse side of the picture of this woman, who in reality seems so different from the way he, the man, sees her.[16]

Similarly ambivalent are nearly all attempts at measuring Dagny by common standards, which suggests that her personality and unique qualities, while leaving no one unaffected, varied in its impact from one individual to the next. Julius Meier-Graefe, distinguished German art critic and on this issue perhaps as neutral as any person might be, saw her, incongruously, as "a Madonna from the trecento, with a laugh that drove men crazy,"[17] while the Norwegian critic, Jappe Nilssen, Munch's close friend[18]—and a victim of that madness—found her singularly regal and achingly desirable: "Wherever she happened to be she was in command. She was beautiful, agonizingly beautiful, and had dazzlingly white, slender, nervous hands."[19] Even Strindberg, having first roundly denounced her, seemed suddenly reignited by the recollection of her charm as he tried to describe her attributes to Frida—though claiming he was merely reporting how Munch, hopelessly bedazzled, was attempting to portray her on the canvas (Plate 37): "A thoroughly modern type, delicate and refined, a spiritual rather than a physical seducer"—pompously adding, "a vampire of the soul yearning for the sublime."[20]

Dagny Juell, bold, progressive—indeed a modern type—was a product not only of the prevailing drive for the emancipation of woman but just as much the broader quest for individual freedom as expressed in the life style of the Bohèmes. In Berlin to prepare for a career as a concert pianist she was equally interested in literature and the visual arts and must have found it both relatively easy and highly challenging to create a place for herself within the *Ferkel* circle—easy because of her own free social manner, challenging because so many of these men, professed radicals, deliberately cultivated a reactionary view on the position of women. To Strindberg, their chief spokesman, the emancipation movement posed the ominous threat of "the dismissal of man, the reverting of the male to a state of dire need, and the creation of a female class of Androgynes."[21] This specter, at the root of his unshakable hatred for Ibsen, he had fought in *Married* I and II, implying that it was one of the principal sources of conflict in his own marital struggle. The same misogynist attitude had inspired several of his plays, and to no small extent it accounted for his Europe-wide fame. Therefore, not only convinced of its validity but directly committed to the pursuit of that same cause he liked to refer to himself as a woman hater—in *The Cloister* doing it repeatedly and with no small measure of pride. At the same time he described his incongruously proper courtship of Frida Uhl, a situation having forced him into the humiliating position of assuming a role entirely out of character, confusing even to himself:

> What a tangled thicket is the human soul! Who could disentangle it? From hatred to contempt, over to respect and admiration and then back again, a leap to one side and then two forward. Good and evil, sublime and ridiculous...[22]

And with the deepening of that relationship and his growing dependence on Frida's presence he begins to fear this woman who so unexpectedly has succeeded in scaling his barricades: "She had his soul in the pocket of her dress; she could fling it into the river, or the gutter, and this added hatred to his feelings for her."[23] At that crucial time she has to go to Munich and Vienna, her absence driving Strindberg back to the *Ferkel* and his instant involvement with Dagny. In its aftermath comes his prolonged and vicious verbal assault on this new type of enemy, the vampire of the soul. The entire experience, though by all indications less than satisfying, must nevertheless have served to restore some of his fighting spirit and reaffirm, in the face of his submissive attitude toward Frida, his continued belief in male supremacy.

While Dagny Juell's role in the dramatic life of August Strindberg was relatively episodic it was absolutely crucial in Edvard Munch's, for she is the only woman whose influence is directly and repeatedly reflected in his works,[24] most demonstratively in the series of paintings entitled *The Frieze of Life,* conceived of already in the late 1880s but not begun in earnest until the summer of 1892, intended to portray in sequence "the course of life, the beginning of love, the dance of life, love at its zenith and in its waning stages—and then death."[25] Perhaps equally crucial is it that Munch's friendship—or love affair—with Dagny coincided with his nearly daily association with Strindberg, who in *The Cloister* portrays Munch as a rejected lover. Such interpretation of Munch's reaction to the rapidly developing relationship between Dagny and Strindberg is difficult to accept in light of his paintings and his continued and apparently unchanged attitude of friendship toward both. As a matter of fact, while he was no doubt happy to spend some time again with the young woman he had met in Norway the summer before, he can have had no intention of binding himself to the extent that his relationship with her would interfere with his creative pursuit. Therefore, he kept her to himself only for as long as he felt a need for the kind of intimacy their relationship provided, then deliberately and by no means fearfully brought her to the *Ferkel* to expose her to the celebrated, intriguing, and vulnerable August Strindberg.

When Frida has asked Strindberg to describe Dagny as he had seen her featured on an unfinished canvas in Munch's studio and Strindberg had responded with his glowing interpretation of that "thoroughly modern type... a spiritual rather than a physical seducer," Frida had rejoined with a spontaneously enthusiastic, almost envious exclamation: "Imagine to be seen that way by Munch!"[26]

Among his many direct and imagined visions of Dagny the most impressive and significant is the one now entitled *Madonna* (Plate 40), painted in 1893 and presently in the National Gallery in Oslo.[27] Munch himself was always reluctant to attach specific titles to his works, feeling that such clues would limit the extent of the viewer's own visual experience. *Madonna* has therefore been exhibited with various titles, none of them originating with Munch, who may have found *Woman in the Act of Love* or *Conception* to be the most meaningful. Yet his attitude toward womanhood until that time in his life is better expressed in the more elevated title by which the painting is now known, not only because it relates directly to his stated intent of portraying "the sanctity of it all," but because its consummate quality of transfigured beauty speaks so movingly of the timelessness of the existential moment when past, present, and future meet. Many have contributed their interpretations to this painting, beginning with Franz Servaes's analysis in his contribution to the volume, *Das Werk des Edvard Munch,* prepared in 1893 by Przybyszewski and published early the following year. In *Madonna* Servaes sees woman "the instant before the ultimate ecstacy of love with its blissful surrender... approaching her most sacred moment of fulfillment... lifted to a state of unearthly beauty." Far more sensual and unmistakably misogynist is the interpretation by Przybyszewski who sees the painting as a symbol of "woman's total submission through which all her senses contribute to an eroticism of the most intense voluptuousness."[28]

Munch himself made many attempts to put into words the thoughts that had combined with the experience to make this particular painting a durable work of art, but his many unfinished sentences and frequent deletions only prove that his visual representation is as little served by words as a perfect poem is by music. Even so, Munch's simple description seems more meaningful than most critical remarks on the same subject:

> The pale beauty of a Madonna. She senses the instant when new life rushes through her, when the link is tied from thousands of years in the past. Life is born to be born again and to die...[29]

Also completed in 1893, but most likely earlier in the year, since it gives the impression of being a preparatory study for *Madonna,* is the more programmatic and symbolically less subtle picture of woman as the object of man's lust, *The Hands* (Plate 39),[30] another nude protrayal of Dagny, this time upright, haughtily challenging, surrounded by an arabesque of hands greedily reaching for her femininity.

It will be recalled that *Puberty* and *The Day Thereafter,* destroyed in a fire in 1890, had been repainted in time for the Kristiania retrospective of 1892. So well known are these works and so essential in the development of Munch's art that it is rather difficult to imagine each of them in their original versions possibly different in one specific aspect. Unfortunately, except for passing reference in press notices of the Norwegian Autumn Exhibit of 1886—constituting a confirmation of their existence at that early stage—there is nowhere a contemporary description of compositional details or the features of the persons portrayed. Yet it is unlikely that their facial characteristics had much in common with those in the final repainted versions, for these, as a careful parallel scrutiny will readily disclose, represent the very same person pictured in *The Hands* and *Madonna:* Dagny Juell. Considering that *Puberty* and *The Day Thereafter* were given their present appearance sometime in 1892-93 it is not unreasonable to conclude that the friendship between Munch and Dagny had by then developed beyond the point of the Platonic. This in turn suggests that the final repainting signified a good deal more than the mere recreation of a work accidentally lost. By altering the personal characteristics of the individuals portrayed in these earlier conceptions into those of Dagny—adolescent and mature—Munch deliberately removed the paintings from their more or less accidental context as part of his production from the 1880s and placed them logically as introductory statements in his projected *Frieze of Life.* In so doing he at the same time elevated Dagny from the level of a specifically identifiable model to the state of a timeless symbol of love to be featured in a variety of works throughout the series, such as *Jealousy, Woman in Three Stages, The Dance of Life,* and many more. Between these newer creations and their predecessors, however, appears a threshold painting now entitled *Vampire* (Plate 41).

An India ink sketch from 1889 showing a man kneeling before a woman, his head in her lap and her lips caressing his hair, appears to be the germinal idea for the painting. A version no longer extant was committed to the canvas sometime in the course of 1892 and shown in Munch's controversial Berlin exhibit that year under the title *Erotisch.* The painting as it is now known was completed in the spring of 1893 and exhibited in Berlin in December of that year. Entitled *Love and Pain* it was grouped with certain others under the collective designation, *Love,* all forming the introduction to the somewhat nebulous, never quite defined concept, *The Frieze of Life.* It shows man prostrate at woman's breast, seeking simultaneously the protective warmth of the mother and the passionate fire of the lover, a duality stressed and symbolized on the one hand in the all-consuming embrace under the flaming veil of her cascading hair, on the other by the distinct presence of a totally enveloping ovate mass suggestive of the womb.

In Munch's paintings and notes from the Berlin period there is ample evidence that Strindberg had filled the young artist with his ideas and had affected Munch so decisively as to bring about some radical changes in his own interpretations of earlier works and drastically alter his future orientation toward a visual representation of certain aspects of human emotions, in particular those involving the relationship between man and woman. It is in this context that *Vampire* comes to signify a threshold between the old and the new.

Strindberg was not in Berlin during Munch's exhibit in December of 1893. However, he had certainly visited Munch often enough to become familiar with the majority of the works shown. Therefore, when in 1896, prior to Munch's first show in Paris, he was asked by the editor of *La Revue Blanche* to write an evaluation of Munch's art he could safely rely on his earlier observations. Besides, he had it all available in writing, he claimed, in Przybyszewski's analyses in *Das Werk des Edvard Munch.* All he needed to do was simply to retrieve his own "stolen thoughts."[31] Obviously, he considered the wordy Pole to have quoted too freely from remarks he, Strindberg, had been making on Munch's art in their regular gatherings at the *Ferkel,* and no doubt he did so with some justification, for in part Przybyszewski's interpretations clearly echo Strindberg's well-known opinions. Thus when Przybyszewski sees *Love and Pain* as "a broken man and on his neck a biting vampire," the phrase certainly has a Strindbergian ring to it. And so does his continued interpretation of this particular painting:

> In its depth love becomes a stinging pain, a biting vampire, a torment rooted in the knowledge of never, never becoming free of the woman, never, never being able to satisfy the hungering demons within one's soul.[32]

From this rather literary analysis came not only the painting's lasting title, *Vampire*—a negative reference not implicit in Munch's original conception of the subject—but in direct sequence a remarkable change in his approach to the portrayal of other topics of an erotic nature. In a written observation most likely dating from the time of the initial ink drawing suggesting this particular subject, he describes his inspiration as rooted in a suddenly felt need to "press his weary head to the breast of a soft, gentle woman, to inhale her perfume and hear her throbbing heart beat . . . Then she would tenderly stroke his hair."[33] But years later, having adopted the prevailing misogynist interpretation of his art, he recalls the very same emotional experience in a rather different key:

> And he put his head to her breast, feeling the blood surging through her veins. He listened to her heart. And burying his face in her bosom he felt two burning lips against his neck—it sent a chill through him.[34]

No doubt a similar chill went through many of those viewing his paintings that December of 1893, for among the works shown were some of the most profoundly disturbing visions ever committed to the canvas—not allegorical extravaganzas but awesome visual commentaries relying on readily identifiable imagery rooted in basic experiences and in emotions otherwise carefully concealed or even deliberately repressed: the ghastly, nearly monochrome *Fever* recapitulating *Death in the Sickroom,* only stripped of all but its vacuous horror, the nightmarish *Death,* an obvious variation of Max Klinger's ornamental, Böcklin-inspired *Death and the Mother,* the shudderingly Gothic *Death and the Maiden* (Plate 50) with its revealing symbolist frame of fetuses and sperms, and first and last the painting which more than any other would link the *fin de siècle* spirit with a twentieth century ambience, *The Shriek* (Plate 42).

12

Marriage, Painting, and Paris

During his stay in Berlin Strindberg had a great many irons in the fire. From his initial concern with performances and translations he gradually branched out into other activities, painting, for one thing. Most of all, however, he was engrossed in scientific studies—color photography, spectral analysis, astrophysics—his impatience and imaginative bent soon moving him into the area of alchemy. There was really only one of his many talents he deliberately seemed to neglect: creative writing, an ironic fact that justifies the rather astonishing opening phrase in Gunnar Brandell's *Strindberg in Inferno:* "When August Strindberg abandoned writing in 1892..."[1]

His friendships were somehow synchronized with his current sphere of interest. During his first few months in Berlin he was in the daily company of Ola Hansson and his wife, Laura Marholm, but his relationship with these two, to whom he ought to have acknowledged a debt of gratitude, proved to be the most fragile of all, and he quickly seemed to forget that without the enthusiasm of the Hanssons he might not have been able to come to Berlin at all. Gratitude alone, however, is rarely a source of friendship and might in fact rather lead in the opposite direction, in the case of Strindberg not infrequently the natural sequence of events. Besides, he soon felt exploited by the promotional activities of this busy couple, as evidenced by his quick renaming of their part of town calling it *Friedrichshölle.* One source of his irritation at that time was the slowly progressing Strindberg book, over which Ola Hansson, one of its sponsors, seemed to procrastinate. A more direct and decisive reason for his rapid disenchantment, however, can be found in his attitude toward women in general and Laura Marholm in particular. About six weeks after his arrival in Berlin he was through with the Hanssons. Early one morning he took the train into the city and appeared in Przybyszewski's quarters, panting, "I've freed myself!"[2] In a subsequent letter to Birger Mörner he calls his former benefactors *"Gesindel!"*—trash—adding other special terms for Laura Marholm, among them *Leichenfrau.* Later, again writing to Mörner, he comes straight to the point: "I do not love Ola H—n, let alone his wife!"[3]

Frida Uhl, who did not meet Strindberg until he had moved out of the Hansson sphere of interest and therefore could not have known the couple, nevertheless seems correct in her analysis of the relationship between Strindberg and Laura Marholm, a woman who would hawkishly seize any opportunity to promote her own husband's cause and in Strindberg's presence in Berlin saw a situation uniquely suited to that purpose. So she became his principal mentor:

> In her efficiency she was exactly what he needed, but—she was everything he hated. He needed her boundless energy, solidly rooted in practical matters, her Martha qualities . . . She sold his books, brought his plays to the right person. She managed his earnings. But—she slaughtered him that he might live! She did not keep him unburdened of business affairs but allowed him to choke under them . . . And she was forever trying to bend him, force him into a role unsuitable for him.[4]

After Strindberg had broken with the Hanssons all their other friends followed suit, Frida claims, seeking instead of the punch bowl in the Hansson living room the heavy wooden tables and chairs and generous selections of drinks at the Ferkel. Strindberg still remained the focus of attention, occasionally challenged, though never deliberately, by the fiery Przybyszewski, whose manipulation of the keyboard with a limitless repertoire of Chopin and a small selection of Schumann, held the company spellbound.

For his serious scientific studies Strindberg sought the advice of the physician Carl Ludwig Schleich, who in later years wrote a touching account of his friendship with Strindberg, remembering him as a Beethoven-like figure: "His Promethean nature was reflected in his high forehead, radiant with rare intelligence but at the same time a trace of suffering emanating from his piercing grayish-blue eyes." Schleich, a scientist with an expansive horizon, gregariously bold in his mode of life and with a passion for literature, the theatre, visual arts, and the mystic elements in nature, was from the very outset a perfect candidate for friendship with Strindberg, hence he was also one of the few members of the *Ferkel* circle never experiencing a falling-out with the temperamental Swede. "It was my fortune," notes the physician, "to be spared from that attitude of suspicion toward his nearest friends that came over Strindberg, or rather always seethed within him like some supernatural power."[5]

No such fortune was in store for Bengt Lidforss, another friend, whose precociously brilliant career as a botanist Strindberg had followed with interest and admiration since their first meeting in Lund in 1890. Despite his mere twenty years Lidforss was then already a member of the university faculty. Their relationship, severely strained during and immediately after Strindberg's involvement with Dagny Juell, whom Lidforss adored, reached its breaking point with the *Antibarbarus* affair, in which Strindberg suspected the young scientist of having conspired with Helge Bäckström in his denunciation of the merit of Strindberg's research. In a letter to Adolf Paul written in the spring of 1894 he says:

> Lidforss I no longer know. He translated *Antibarbarus*, pretended to be an admiring disciple, etc., and then he is said to have written, shortly thereafter . . . the article in *Dagens Nyheter* in which my book is presented as the product of a deliberate joker, who later became mad.[6]

Soon to share destiny with Lidforss was the recipient of this letter, of whom contemporary opinions appear unanimously negative, an impression not at all modified by an objective reading of his highly vindictive memoirs. Jens Thiis calls Adolf Paul "a dog and a slave . . . a pariah . . . I couldn't stand him,"[7] and Munch, in conversation with Rolf Stenersen, expresses the identical point of view, saying that Strindberg "had hired [*sic*] a repulsive fellow named Paul—used him as a valet and door mat."[8] So also Przybyszewski who passes over him with a few derogatory words: "Following him as a lackey was the Swedo-Finnish writer Adolf Paul who, on the pretext of carrying out Strindberg's business in reality took care of his own."[9] All of this may give the impression that Paul was entirely without individual merit and talent, which is not quite in keeping with fact, for his collection of short stories, *The Ripper* (1892), placed him in the forefront of Swedo-Finnish naturalists. The volume, dealing with highly erotic, sometimes perverse subjects (much like Ola Hansson's *Sensitiva amorosa*), was accorded the same destiny in Finland as Strindberg's *Giftas I* in Sweden and the Bohème novels by Hans Jaeger and Christian Krohg in Norway. It could well be that Strindberg's outrage at this new official interference with literary creativity, made him value Paul's contribution more highly than would otherwise have been the case. At any rate, a conflict between the two soon followed. Initially related to the *Antibarbarus* issue in which Strindberg strongly suspected Paul of having sided with Lidforss, it reached its breaking point with Paul's novel of 1894, *Med det falska och det ärliga ögat* [With the Treacherous and the Honest Eye], a satire on life within the *Ferkel* circle arousing Strindberg's suspicion that its main character was a lightly disguised caricature of *him*.

A far more complex personality than any of the individuals making up Strindberg's Berlin entourage was Stanislaw Przybyszewski who, admiring with equal fervor and devotion Strindberg and Munch, would soon be more passionately drawn to Dagny Juell than either of these had been. Yet to claim that Przybyszewski became a center of attraction at the *Ferkel* through Dagny rather than on his own merit—as does a Swedish commentator[10]—is a denial of the considerable and varied talent of this rare artist. Besides, he had definitely made his contribution long before Dagny appeared on the scene. His own recollections as well as Strindberg's tend to imply that the relationship between Dagny and Stachu—the name by which the Pole's friends knew him—did not develop until Strindberg had lost interest in the young Norwegian. Munch's visual observation, however—as in *Jealousy* (Plate 47)—recorded much closer to the actual time of these goings-on than the retrospective writings of the protagonists, suggest that there certainly was something in the making between these two music enthusiasts already at the time of Dagny's first visit to the *Ferkel.* Moreover, Frida Strindberg's notes on the subject—no doubt based on Strindberg's conversations with her, since she herself was not a direct witness—indicate that most everyone within the circle had seen Dagny and become intrigued, even infatuated, with her long before she made her official entry into their headquarters. The anguish Strindberg suffered later on at the thought of the "Aspasia" affair was therefore rooted in a guilt complex originating with his treachery not only toward Frida but toward two of his closest friends and supporters at that time, Przybyszewski and Lidforss, the latter having arrived on the scene just in time to see his hope of a reunion with Dagny dashed by Strindberg's unexpected interference.

Strange to say, while the relationship between Strindberg and Dagny was in progress—in March of 1893—there seems to have been no break between any of the parties involved. Even Lidforss did not exclude himself from the circle. That he must have felt deeply injured, however, may be inferred from the tone of Strindberg's subsequent letters to him in which Strindberg tends to emphasize Dagny's promiscuity, no doubt for the purpose of reducing Lidforss's sense of loss. Of this his melancholy presence in some of Munch's canvases from those early spring months of 1893 speaks very clearly.

Despite Strindberg's portrayal of Munch as a rejected and pouting lover, these two continued to meet, as Strindberg also kept seeing other artists, posing for some of them, and in his quarters eagerly working at his own easel. When Munch introduced him to Hermann Schlittgen, Strindberg invited the German painter to see his works, which he then did and, to Strindberg's chagrin and irritation, came away unimpressed. The Swede was probably spoiled, Schlittgen suggests in his recollections. After all, he knew so much he thought he also knew how to paint. "He was a bit conceited too," Schlittgen adds.[11]

Of Munch's works from those days Strindberg may have watched with particicular interest the first in the *Jealousy* series and detected people and situations directly familiar to him. What possibly intrigued him the most, however, may not have been so much such points of identification as the evolvement of the painting itself—the witnessing, perhaps for the first time, of a professional artist in the process of committing to the canvas a readily recognizable emotional conflict. It was exactly what he himself had envisioned doing, and from this time on his paintings more and more acquire literary-symbolic titles, such as *Night of Jealousy* (Plate 43) completed that spring. To a limited degree inspired by Munch the painting reflects—so he claims—his reaction to a meeting with Frida at which another of her male friends was present.

Surprisingly, Ingrid Langaard finds that *Night of Jealousy* has "many points of similarity with Munch,"[12] while in reality it resembles nothing Munch ever did. To be sure, the title is undoubtedly derived from Munch, but nothing else points to Munch's influence. Strindberg, despite his obvious talent, remained an amateur as a painter, and his "art by chance or accident" was by its very nature far removed from Munch's approach which was deliberate and direct, each canvas from the outset built on a relatively clear concept of the finished product.

Strindberg, apparently rather pleased with *Night of Jealousy,* presented it to Frida as an engagement gift:

> He takes a few steps back, scans the painting, then looks quizzically at me.
>
> Only slowly does my eye adjust to the details of the gloomy color, fumbling for meaning as in an ominous night. Coal black, chalky white, ocher, dark green, gray, gray, gray. Never have I seen gray that vividly presented.[13]

On the back of the canvas he had written: "To Frida Uhl from the painter (the Symbolist) August Strindberg." His claim to be a symbolist in the visual arts, however, is not supported by any indication of a conscious approach in the manner of symbolist painters, such as in the works of Moreau or Redon, but rests entirely on the titles he happened to give his paintings—these as well as his interpretations of their contents, invariably ex post facto. As for *Night of Jealousy,* it differs relatively little from paintings completed in the Stockholm archipelago prior to his departure for Berlin—in keeping with his own ideas, perhaps, for he had claimed that one should paint from memory; and in this work, by title and explanation supposedly inspired by a Berlin event, it is still his beloved archipelogo he is recalling. Executed with a thick, hectic palette knife impasto it represents a coastal scene with an oppressively gray, turbulent sky in which streaked diagonals suggestive of wind-lashed rain surge toward a sea of whitecapped waves—as in a Turner painting but with none of Turner's structural logic. A splash of green against the top ledge of a rock provides the only color contrast, otherwise the entire painting is, as Frida Uhl had seen it, "relentlessly gray, gray, gray."

A few other works date from the same spring months of 1893, among them *The White Sailing Mark* (its third version), *The Lonely Poisonous Mushroom,* and *Palette with a Solitary Flower on the Shore*—all having once been in the safe keeping of Adolf Paul—and also his single most ambitious effort at that time, *The Wave* (Plate 44), donated to the owner of *Zum schwarzen Ferkel,* Gustav Türke, no doubt in settlement of an account.[14] Said to have remained on display until World War II—and in Türke's days always pointed out with great pride—it was most likely destroyed with the building in an air raid.[15]

Another painting, dated 1894 but assumed to have been begun the year before, entitled *The Green Island* may have been inspired, at least indirectly, by a visit to Berlin's National Gallery, an occasion described by Frida:

> We have come to See Böcklin. The gallery had recently acquired his *Pieta*, and *The Isle of the Dead* happened to be there for a few weeks. *The Isle of the Dead* is Strindberg's favorite painting. Under a deep blue sky a wall of cypresses stands silent and solemn against the sundrenched white rock rising from the Grecian sea.[16]

Although Arnold Böcklin[17] through his rather belated recognition as an important antecedent to the surrealist movement has in relatively recent days been reinstated as an artist of historical consequence, his star faded out of sight during the first half of the present century, a phenomenon as difficult to explain as its brilliant and surprisingly vivid appearance in the last two decades of the nineteenth century. However, since his popularity at that time was a phenomenon strictly limited to the Germanic regions of Europe its explanation must be sought in a probing of the cultural atmosphere then prevailing in those areas.

Romanticism, though long past its creative zenith, was still a viable force. In painting it echoed the contributions of the landscape mystic Caspar David Friedrich and the Renaissance-Reformation devotees called the Nazarenes, a group eager to develop a German way of painting "by observing 'the way of phantasy' as represented by Michelangelo, 'the way of beauty' as represented by Raphael, and 'the way of nature' as represented by Dürer."[18] Yet the most consummate and deliberate exponent of these tendencies was not a painter but a musician, the same creative genius held up as a paragon by the French symbolists and decadents, Richard Wagner, with his merging of music, drama, and poetry and his predilection for a glamorized rendition of a mythical world of Germanic origin. In the visual arts a similar role was played by Böcklin, whose canvases present a blending of classical and northern myths often paradoxical yet much admired by German critics and patrons. Böcklin's popularity was slow in coming, yet once he had reached his public his position was of unquestioned importance and influence, so much so that Wagner himself thought him an ideal collaborator for the visual aspects of his spectaculars. Böcklin on the other hand—described as a fine musician in his own right—happened to dislike Wagner's music "to the extent of having violent physical reaction to it, claiming it gave him griping pains in his stomach."[19]

Among the highly art conscious members of the *Ferkel* group Böcklin must have been a frequent subject of conversation, more so perhaps with the presence of Christian Krohg and Jens Thiis who saw Böcklin as the true progressive in German art. Munch agreed, saying, "With me he rates higher than nearly all contemporary artists."[20]

That they had all seen what the National Gallery had available of Böcklin's works may be taken for granted, and when Strindberg decided to bring Frida there he must have wanted to share with her some of the ideas that had come to him during previous visits. On this particular occasion he used *The Isle of the Dead* (Plate 30) as the point of departure for a long and imaginative soliloquy, not on art but on the relationship between man and woman and on death, to which Frida responded by saying, "It is your beautiful dream you like, not the canvas." Her observation agreed with his earlier reasoning, when he had said that from every source of inspiration or influence he extracted only what he specifically needed.[21] Of this pragmatic approach his relationship to the art of Böcklin is a good case in point, for his highly selective enthusiasm is in reality directed only at that one canvas, *The Isle of the Dead.* Frida's description of the picture itself is adequate insofar as its immediate appearance is concerned, but she fails to call attention to its otherworldly tranquility, a state not broken but rather heightened by the implied motion of a boat crossing the silent sea, carrying in its prow a casket surmounted by an almost transparent white figure, the soul of the deceased.

Without resorting to extreme or untried painterly means Böcklin here succeeds in conveying a genuine quality of the mystic, rooted in his meticulously realistic rendering of separate details whose composite function it is to create a deliberately stylized, super-realistic totality suspended in time and unidentifiable in place. With this work, so pure in composition and so free of the extraneous narrative elements that tend to distract in so many of his other pictures, Böcklin may be said to have bridged the romanticism of Friedrich and the symbolism of Moreau and Redon, and with the latter two pointed the way toward much more radical developments in the world of art.

Strindberg, always eager to be counted in the ranks of the avant-garde, was in reality surprisingly conservative in his own art preferences—as was Frida who had written a devastatingly negative review of a German impressionist exhibit.[22] He must therefore have felt particularly attracted to the orderliness, the decorative, symmetric beauty, and the tableau-like subject presentation characteristic of this canvas—not the least because Böcklin's strict adherence to such traditional rules of painting in no way detracted from his basic purpose: to express himself in a nostalgically lyric metaphor. Into this melancholy canvas Strindberg found it easy to read a meaning of his own:

> Death is only the gateway into a new form of existence for man, who in the Isle of the Dead finds peace and deliverance from the dualism and darkness of his own earthly soul. Beyond the cypresses on the white rocky isle live the blessed, delivered from the animal and the animalistic, from the flesh and the fleshly.[23]

His fondness for the painting or his own interpretation of it apparently never changed; for in *The Ghost Sonata,* when he wanted to portray the transfigured state of total deliverance brought about by death, in contrast to "this world of eternal change and disappointment and never-ending pain,"[24] he did so by transforming the background into a distant view of *The Isle of the Dead.*

Strindberg's courtship of Frida met with many obstacles, including extreme resistance on the part of her family. However, when a Vienna newspaper announced the engagement of the two—rather prematurely—Friedrich Uhl relented, but not until he had received a letter of apology from Strindberg, who in the same letter formally asked for permission to marry Frida. Herr Uhl then promptly dispatched his older daughter, Marie, to Berlin to assist with the wedding preparations and at the same time deliver a relatively substantial sum of money as a dowry. This family representative, married to a distinguished Austrian sculptor, Rudolf Weyr, summarized in a letter to her husband her various impressions of Strindberg and of him and Frida together. She told of his appearance—saying that he looked better than his pictures, most of the time—of his unpredictable temper: "When I'm with him I can't for one moment rid myself of the fear that at any instant he might go mad," and of his activity as a painter:

> He paints fantasy pictures, symbolic pictures. Nearly every other day or every third day a new picture, astonishingly good when one considers that he has had no formal training. It is as if the talents within him do not know how they can best express themselves. But there is not a trace of a healthy, happy desire to create, rather a drive, an uncontrollable passion of the kind that forces a criminal to commit murder.

She goes on to say that there is no way to keep the two apart, that one must therefore do everything possible to get them married without delay. "I'm afraid his love for her is of a rather sensual nature, for spiritually Frida could never satisfy that man, nor could any woman." Frida's love, she reasons, amounts to admiration for his writing and worship of his genius, that she probably wouldn't dare throw her arms around him unless he should specifically permit or demand it. "Heaven only knows how it will turn out in the end!"[25]

As for the marriage itself, it did not take place as promptly as the couple, let alone the bride's sister, had hoped. There were sporadic disagreements and even a decisive break, and besides such personal problems rigid Prussian statutes regarding the remarriage of a divorced person made it impossible to proceed with the wedding plans in Berlin. Off the Frisian coast, however, was the tiny island of Helgoland, recently returned to Germany after nearly a century of British rule. There such regulations were more humane. On a sunny morning late in April the wedding party—the couple and Frida's sister—set out by train on their journey to the Isle of the Happy. Many of Strindberg's friends had gathered on the platform, although Frida seems to remember only two, Adolf Paul and Bengt Lidforss, who presented the bride-to-be with a huge bouquet of roses—for which Strindberg had lent them the money the same morning. Actually, the Tavaststjernas were there, too, and so was Przybyszewski, and it is likely that all these well-wishers may have sensed some relief at this departure and its purpose. With Strindberg safely back in the state of matrimony Tavaststjerna might recapture the attention of his Gabrielle and Paul at long last have some time for his own neglected activities. As for poor Lidforss, only twenty-five, on the verge of chronic alcoholism and with ominous symptoms of venereal disease, he might be nourishing the hope of once more pursuing Dagny Juell. Yet in that respect Przybyszewski, with an invitation to spend the summer in Norway with Dagny and her family, had a substantial head start. So Lidforss, pressured by friends and relatives, would soon be returning to Lund for the doctoral promotion and a summer of rest and recuperation, while Paul was planning on a trip to Finland.

Meanwhile, Strindberg's wedding plans had run into unexpected obstacles, not from the local clergyman in Helgoland who was both understanding and compassionate, but from Swedish authorities in Stockholm who failed to send the required documented proof of Strindberg's divorce. Finally, a week after they had set foot on that desolate rock rising from the North Sea they were ready to proceed. That the ensuing ceremony could have been quite as ludicrous as Frida makes it out to have been seems rather doubtful.[26] On the other hand, with the uncertainty of the long waiting period and everyone's patience tested beyond the breaking point it quite likely was not the solemn occasion it was intended to be. With the event safely in the past Strindberg wrote to Paul:

> After three days of terrible quarrels we were finally married Tuesday evening. And now I have a wife and a home again. All right! Everything is so hushed, so calm and beautiful. Only a faint echo of monetary straits and poor business affairs rings in our ears from Berlin and Stockholm, but the mail reaches us only twice a week.

And as though nothing had really changed he goes on to ask Paul the usual favors, wanting him to sell paintings and arrange for galley proofs of his plays, then inquires about all his friends at the *Ferkel:* Lidforss, Przybyszewski, Munch—and Dagny.[27]

In *The Cloister* these two weeks at Helgoland, "so hushed, so calm and beautiful," are described in more ambiguous terms suggesting a creative vacuum: "I can neither read, think, nor write anymore. Why, I can hardly speak." In that state of affairs the idyll of their insular existence quickly lost its charm:

> The silence between them began to make them feel uneasy and in the midst of a loving embrace each was aware that the other was now sharpening the knife that would sever their bonds.[28]

The honeymoon continued in London, where they had gone in the hope of paving the way for Strindberg's access to British publishers and play producers, but the situation did not improve. Frida, who knew English, carried out the negotiations, and Strindberg, feeling totally left out, retreated into his scientific studies. Then one day he caught her reading the book he had written about his first marriage, *Le Plaidoyer d'un fou* [The Confessions of a Fool], just then published in German, and with that Pandora's box had been opened—because he knew now that "his peace was at an end, and that this woman would never rest until she had killed his honour and forced him to cut short his life."[29]

Initially, it was only his stay that was cut short. Unwilling to learn to like London, a city that seemed to excite Frida, he returned to Germany alone—at first, for lack of money, remaining cooped up in a Hamburg hotel for an unproportionately long time until at long last he was bailed out by Adolf Paul. Thereafter, proceeding to the island of Rügen in the Baltic, he lived among friends in relatively pleasant circumstances for a period of time, always hoping that Frida would decide to join him. But she, too busy to leave London just then, kept postponing her departure, and for Strindberg life once more took a sour turn: "If only this damn summer with its suicidal mania and lack of energy would come to an end!" he lamented in a letter to her.[30] Finally, at a loss for what to do, he accepted an invitation to join his father-in-law at his country estate on the shore of Mondsee near Salzburg, fully expecting that Frida, too, would be coming. Now she did leave London, but a confusing sequence of misunderstandings brought about by letters and telegrams crossing each other en route made Strindberg abruptly leave Mondsee in order to meet her in Berlin, while she, totally unsuspecting, made her appearance at the parental estate:

> Father stands behind his roses in front of the house. His pince-nez hangs far down on his broad nose, almost to his mouth. He eyes me angrily above the rim of his glasses. No greeting, only a question: "Where is your husband?"
>
> Cain could not have become more terrified at the sound of the Lord's voice asking him about his brother.
>
> "With you . . . ?" I stammer.
>
> "If so I shouldn't have asked."[31]

Spending only one brief night at Mondsee, Frida caught the early morning train to make the fastest possible connection to Berlin where, after a separation of two months, the couple was finally reunited. In their recollections they agree that it was an ecstatic event, Strindberg saying, "Two months of torture were forgotten, effaced, as if they had never been,"[32] and Frida noting that "their young happiness was there. We take it for granted"—apprehensively adding that they should never again be apart, not even for half a day, for then "everything will go wrong."[33] Strindberg must have had grave doubts about such togetherness:

> Here a memory from Helgoland popped up, and then one from London, places where they had not been parted for a single minute, and where, for that very reason, things had gone utterly wrong.[34]

But their new-found bliss lasted two full months during which, according to Frida, they had grown so close that they could not stand to be separated, not even for a single hour. In *The Cloister,* on the other hand, the situation continues to be described in less ecstatic terms. Here the inescapable closeness creates a feeling of cramped confinement, a circumstance further threatened by their discovery of Frida's unwanted pregnancy, through which the attic, at first so idyllic, is "transformed into a perpetually untidy sickroom."[35] In that situation they keep slashing at each other with fierce determination, until their bonds, though not yet completely severed, become so weakened that a final break appears imminent, and one morning Frida is suddenly no longer there. For a few days and nights, in a state of severe depression, Strindberg seems to be tossed about as a ship in a raging storm until, directed by a letter from Frida's sister, he is able to rejoin his wife in Brno, capital of Moravia, a city "peculiar for its hatred of Swedes," Strindberg says. "Every year they launch a feast to commemorate the Swedish withdrawal under Torstenson," an event from the Thirty Years War. And now Strindberg claims to be the very first Swede to set foot in Brno since that time, besieged by unfriendliness—and by his own wife. "Indescribably I'm alive," he writes to Adolf Paul shortly after his arrival—"whether in captivity or freedom I don't know, but at any rate I do have a warden!" In utter frustration at the place and his prospects he appends, "How the hell did I get here? And what am I doing?"[36]

The next phase of this tentative mode of existence did little to relieve Strindberg's sense of confinement or apprehension. Totally out of funds he and Frida left Brno for Dornach in Austria, arriving at the imposing Danube estate of her maternal grandparents more as charity cases than welcome guests. Yet they were comfortable enough in the generous manor house where there was ample space to allow each family unit—the host couple, Frida's mother, the newlyweds—their own spacious and separate quarters. That way they did not necessarily meet or communicate much except at principal meal times and for relaxation after evening dinner. On such occasions Strindberg was on his very best behavior, responding with politeness to the retired imperial functionary's inquiries and observations. Although as a mature man and a widely recognized writer, he could not really be expected to remain tolerant of the old man's didactic, condescending attitude. It was a discussion of Nietzsche, whose works the grandfather knew only secondhand through the writings of a philosophy professor, Ludwig Stein, that brought about the inevitable clash:

> And it happened one day when the "Unknown" had taken possession of Strindberg and cosmic relationships cried for a change of atmosphere. He contradicted the old man, calmly but decisively. "Have you read Ludwig Stein?" the old man retorted in triumph, for him a professor's opinions were infallible.
>
> "No, but I've read Nietzsche himself."[37]

Following this confrontation the atmosphere did indeed change, and soon another matter arose to contribute to the deteriorating mood. Some months earlier the issuing of the German edition of *Le Plaidoyer d'un fou,* entitled *Die Beichte eines Toren*—the Pandora's box Frida had happened to open up in London—had brought with it an indictment for indecency from Prussian authorities. After much delay in the pursuit of the case a request had come from Berlin to the police in the Austrian village near the estate to obtain a deposition from Strindberg. Though questioning both the Prussian and the Austrian authorities' rights in the matter he yielded to the pressure of the grandfather who considered the request equal to an imperial edict, and set out on foot to the village to resolve the matter. On the way, however, he met the mailman who brought a long-awaited parcel containing an important item for Strindberg's scientific research, and instead of reporting to the authorities he promptly rushed back to his makeshift laboratory. This rash behavior, to the grandfather nothing short of a deliberate slight of Austrian officialdom, led to the couple's eviction from the main house to a separate cottage on the grounds—in reality a welcome change through which at long last they could be entirely by themselves.

Between scientific experiments and repair work on the cottage Strindberg kept up an intense correspondence—with Adolf Paul, then in Finland, Lidforss in Berlin, and Georges Loiseau, his French translator. It so happened that prospects in France seemed suddenly promising, for through the proposed publishing activities of Albert Langen in Paris he envisioned the issuing of a series of volumes of his works, while Lugnë-Poé appeared quite willing to stage his plays at *Théâtre de l'Oevre.* So from early 1894, with Paris—and Berlin, too—and his potential presence among artists there very much on his mind, Strindberg found it increasingly difficult to enjoy Dornach, and the thought of getting away appears ever more urgent in his correspondence. Already in February, writing to Lidforss about a possible opportunity at Berlin's *Neues Theater,* he unequivocally declares, "I'll be coming to Berlin!" To leave no doubt as to exactly where in Berlin he wants to be meeting his freinds, he asks that his guitar be brought to the *Ferkel,* "so that it'll be there when I arrive," and that his *stammbord* [regular table] be reserved. The remainder of this rare letter is devoted to a detailed stage design for a veritable "theatre of the absurd" to form the setting for a bizarre carnival to celebrate his return. Lidforss is to instruct Przybyszewski's half brother, Anton, "to build a pagoda as an artist's hangout with portraits (not caricatures) of all of us . . . It must be *fin de siècle.* In the pagoda must be hanging a real skeleton of a woman, with the extra tailbones."[38]

It was the end of March before he was able to leave Dornach for Berlin—ostensibly to check on the progress of the printing of *Antibarbarus.* Of the ensuing events none turned out to be as spectacular as the one he had envisioned. On the contrary, judging from his letters to Frida he was having a downright miserable time, but then, with her back in Dornach as bored as he had been and in the last trying months of her pregnancy, he may not have been too eager to share with her the excitement he must have felt at his various Berlin reunions.

That he visited the *Ferkel* is clear from Frida's notes, but he found it an anticlimax, she says. The various members having drifted away it was impossible for him to recapture the spirit of its past:

> The *Ferkel* was no longer the same old animal it had once been. It had changed. If one analyzed the matter carefully it became clear that its historical period was over. It had once given birth to a new life, but now it was dead. And because it was so absolutely dead August Strindberg experienced it as a ghost that would be haunting him for a long time.[39]

In store for him during his brief visit were other, equally haunting experiences, one a visit to the newlyweds. Frida tells of it—as it must have been related to her by Strindberg—and this time her description of Dagny suggests none of the womanly understanding she had previously displayed:

> Aspasia, now Dagny Przybyszewska, held salon in Berlin. The newest literary world, with the short, rotund but highly vivacious, spiritual and highly inventive Otto Julius Bierbaum at the head, associated with her, and as a reaction against sober realism they proclaimed—freely after Strindberg—the great Pan . . .
>
> Aspasia's salon consisted of only one single rented room rather simply furnished . . . There was only one table, and against it stood the place's two chairs under a lamp featuring a faded red shade. Actually, the chairs were out of circulation since they were permanently occupied by the two best friends of the house, Munch and Lidforss, who sat there in silence, drinking . . .
>
> The salon offered a varied program of entertainment. Aspasia danced enchantingly, Przybyszewski played the piano in his own wonderful way . . .
>
> If the room, as a result of the steadily flowing toddy became too crowded for the guests, or even for the hostess (most often for the hostess), then those involved quietly left . . .[40]

From this unhealthy atmosphere, Frida claims, Strindberg was anxious to rescue Munch, whom he admired. So also the foolish Pole who was about to drown himself in alcohol, and even more the foolish Lidforss. But they were lost, she says, "addicted to love," implying that Dagny's favors, especially to

Munch and Lidforss but possibly also Bierbaum, were not limited to solo dances. Now it is the same notion of her unbridled promiscuity so persistently advanced by Strindberg in his correspondence that is echoed by Frida, her biased information on the subject liberally spiced with her own jealousy.

The person within the circle who would be giving the gentlest and perhaps most viable testimony of the spirit of Dagny Przybyszewska was Munch who, having known her longer than had any of the others, was able to see her attitude, her entire mode of life, in a broader, more meaningful perspective:

> Proud and free she moved among us, encouraging and sometimes comforting as only a woman can be, her very presence having a calming and inspiring effect on us. It was as though it gave us new impulses, new ideas, as though the creative spark that was about to die was reignited.[41]

Although Strindberg, still angered at his confrontation with Frida's grandfather, hinted that he might not come back to Dornach—in one letter saying, "Whether we'll meet again I don't know"[42]—he did return, sensitive to Frida's condition and pleas. Now followed a period of frequently idyllic waiting, described by both as their finest months together. For a brief period during this interlude Strindberg again expressed himself in paintings, some echoing earlier subjects, such as the second version of *The Green Island,* showing his familiar rocky coast, only this time with a shore surmounted by pleasantly green foliage and caressed by a calm sea reflecting the bright colors of sky and shore. Presumably inspired by the Dornach landscape is his *Flooding at the Danube,* although the only feature directly identifiable with the setting is the title. Otherwise it is a picture of a greenish-brown expanse of water under a pink and yellow sky, the horizontal emphasis counteracted by a clump of partly submerged trees. Had he consciously or subconsciously been recalling his first meeting with the French impressionists in 1876 when at Durand-Ruel he saw Manet, Monet, and Sisley? In his report to *Dagens Nyheter* that time it was Sisley he concentrated on, attempting to describe one of his summer landscapes "painted in colorless white, faintly red and faintly blue . . . as though covered by snow or rime."[43] But he may well have seen *Flood at Port-Marly* as well, for although this important Sisley canvas is much more clearly defined and purposefully structured than Strindberg's the main feature of both is their juxtaposition of sky and water and the vivid reflections resulting from that colorful interplay.

That the idyll in the rose-covered cottage at Dornach was a fragile phenomenon is shown in two of his paintings from those days, of which the first, entitled *Sweden,* must have been produced in a rage when he first learned of the Swedish reaction to his *Antibarbarus.* In a descriptive inventory prepared prior to his final departure from Austria, when he shipped his Dornach paintings to a friend for safekeeping and possible sales, he describes item number one as "A shit-green landscape with shit-red rocks, a shit-yellow sky and shit-black pine trees. Sweden?" The other, a more ambiguous work entitled *Golgatha,* is a variation on his stormy archipelago theme, closely resembling his earlier *Sailing Mark* pictures, except that in this version that readily identifiable object has been replaced with three precariously slanting masts of a wrecked ship. In the foreground is an accidentally formed shape, by Strindberg said to represent a man in a gray cape—as he himself had been portrayed by Christian Krohg—gazing into the raging inferno:

> By closer scrutiny one discovers that the man on the rock is wearing a slouch hat, as Vodan (Buddha); that the crest of the waves resembles monsters, the clouds demons, and in the center of the sky there is an excellent portrait of Rembrandt. The three masts with their crosstrees look like Golgatha, or three cemetery crosses, and could also be a Trimurti, but that depends on one's individual liking.[44]

Again, Strindberg's visual symbolism is largely a product of his own retrospective analysis, and in his inventory listing, detailing both the erotic contents and its esoteric meaning, he does imply that everyone may not view these works as he does. As for his technique, it has not changed appreciably, although Göran Söderström sees a more deliberate influence from Turner in *Golgatha* than in earlier paintings, which suggests that during their brief stay in London he and Frida may have visited British museums. Such influence, however, does not extend beyond a desire to bring about Turner's dynamics, for in actual creative method one could hardly conceive of a contrast greater than that between Strindberg's "art by chance or accident" and Turner's meticulous, truth-seeking probing of atmosphere, color potentials, and structural details in his preparation for each major canvas.

When not occupied with painting or scientific experiments Strindberg would spend his time with Frida sharing her joy and anticipation at the impending event—by now as agreeable as in similar situations in his previous marriage. They talked of nothing but the child, he says in *The Cloister,* yet when the event did occur and the immediate excitement and sense of relief had abated, rather than making the idyll perfect "it appeared to have brought it to an end."[45] It is really quite remarkable that in letters written during the next few days all reference to the arrival of the new daughter is either very casual or entirely missing. Instead, what seemed to be occupying his mind was, on the negative side, the *Antibarbarus* controversy, on the positive his increasingly bright prospects in Paris. It was at the thought of a full utilization of his opportunity there that his increased, domestic responsibility became a burden, not a joy. Therefore, determined to reap the harvest of his reputation, he was not going to allow anything to stand in the way of his intended departure, not even Frida's complaint that he did not love his new child. In reality, he was guilty only of restraining his emotions, fearful that they would otherwise tie him down. Moreover, uncertain that his marriage would last he held back his affection, mindful of the agony he had suffered as a result of his separation from his and Siri's children.

On June 19, 1894, he wrote to Adolf Paul saying that he would be going to Paris "in a few days," and on the same date contacted a friend from the 1870s, Leopold Littmansson, with whom he had last corresponded three years earlier. Married to a Frenchwoman Littmansson lived in Versailles, conveniently close to Strindberg's intended arena. In his letter, summing up the accomplishments of his immediate past, he swears by his own successes:

> By now I'm really damn great. I have my bust in the Finnish (!) National Museum, I'm represented in two wax cabinets with a head of hair like a whore and messy clothes... I've been booed in Naples and played once in Rome; moreover, I've been panned by Sarcy in Paris.

Then, coming straight to the point, he asks whether Littmansson might be willing to receive him, making the request sound urgent: "Please, respond right away."[46]

This eagerness to leave and his assurances that he is ready to depart at a moment's notice are highly reminiscent of his state of mind ten years earlier when he wanted to join his fellow Scandinavians in France, and also of his correspondence with Ola Hansson in 1892. His departure this time, as before, came much later than planned, for nearly two months passed before he was able to leave Dornach and board a Danube steamer for Linz from where he continued to Paris by train. Having arrived there he repeatedly assures Frida that they will soon be together, but when she responds by saying she is eager to join him he becomes suddenly discouraging, pointing out how difficult and unattractive Paris is for a housewife and mother.

Meanwhile, though having come to Paris as a celebrated author and playwright—as he had to Berlin two years earlier—he showed remarkably little interest in writing and instead turned his attention to painting. Encouraged by Willy Gretor, an enterprising Danish painter in whose home he lived for some time, he produced a series of pictures, some purchased by Gretor who thereby bolstered Strindberg's confidence in his own talent and the sales potential of his works. "I wish I were at Kymmendö!" he exclaims in a letter to Littmansson,"[46] but whether there or not he must have succeeded in creating for himself a microcosm of his beloved archipelago, for all his paintings are simply new variations on that familiar theme.

By mid-September Frida did arrive, having left the child in Dornach. Yet the relationship between them was not what they had hoped for, and after a few rounds of amusement and several moves from homes of friends to hotels of declining quality Frida returned to Austria and her child. Later that fall, writing to Richard Bergh, Strindberg says of his marriage that "it was never taken very seriously, as you probably realized while in Berlin, and it will no doubt be dissolved." He then goes on to comment on life in Paris, where everything was new and exciting and where in certain circles he found himself addressed as *Cher Maître.* All this is well and good, he says, but—and here he may be providing a clue to an understanding of subsequent events—"Paris must only be touched now and then. To stay is dangerous."[48]

13

Munch's Early Graphic Works and Third Retrospective

Munch's life, despite Strindberg's desire to rescue him from it, had been creatively very productive if not economically stabilizing. Following his Berlin exhibit in December-January of 1892-93 he had sent his paintings to Copenhagen, hoping for critical approval and sales. However, his presentation there became a rather secondary event when it happened to coincide with a major show of contemporary art in the same gallery. This exhibition, sponsored by Ballin and Willumsen, was the first assemblage of modern art in the history of Scandinavia and included such items as twenty-nine canvases by Van Gogh, thirty by Gauguin, and representative selections by Bernard, Bonnard, Sérusier, and Vuillard. That Munch received critical attention at all must be ascribed to the sensational outcome of his initial show in Berlin, but even on that premise Copenhagen critics felt disappointed, finding it difficult to understand that Berliners could have reacted that strongly to such relatively insignificant works. One reviewer, detecting a certain ability, concluded that it had already gone so far astray that "there is hardly any hope the talent will ever be developed." All the same, Munch, having become a martyr of the arts, he goes on to say, was a lucky man who could now be touring with his paintings and do good business with them.[1] He ought to have known that martyrdom had never been a particularly profitable state. Even in Germany, where his works had been widely shown with moderate success and never-ending controversy, this martyr had been able to sell only two canvases in the course of an entire year. Therefore he continued to be humiliatingly dependent on money furnished from sparse sources at home, where members of his family, never in doubt of his talent or calling, kept denying themselves all but the bare essentials to allow him the freedom to create. Consequently, nearly every letter he writes contains grateful acknowledgments of these "loans" which he sincerely intends to repay. At long last, having completed one of his two sales, he was actually able to enclose a small amount. Only two days later, however, receiving a letter with a ten *kroner* bill, he writes back, "Thank you so much! It so happened that

I was completely broke. Meanwhile, I'm hoping to return the money soon and add a little more to it."[2]

In December, 1893, marking the end of his first year in Berlin, he opened his second exhibit. Again, it was no sales success, and critical reaction was mixed. Moreover, the sensational aspect that had made people flock to his exhibit the first time and prompted him to write, "I've never had such enjoyable days," was no longer there. Even so, he scored one significant gain through this new exposure, for it gave the impetus to the issuing of the volume *Das Werk des Edvard Munch,* for which Stanislaw Przybyszewski had taken the initiative. This book with its stimulating discussions by well known writers and critics did much to establish Munch's position as a serious artist and pioneer in visual expression. Franz Servaes, whose essay speaks most directly to the issue of Munch as an exponent of current trends, begins by referring to Gauguin's quest for the recapture of the primitive human instinct shown not only in his paintings but his mode of life, and seeing in this a profound expression of the cultural mood of the age. Weary of realist-naturalist approaches artists seek through varying means new paths, new goals, new materials and forms, Servaes continues, the Germans by juxtaposing traditional imagery and contemporary subject reference—Stuck with his centaurs, Hofmann with his children in paradise, Liebermann with his peasant women, Uhde with a peasant Christ—all not greatly different from Gauguin's efforts. Munch's approach, on the other hand, though equally expressive of the cultural mood, the *Zeitgeist,* he considers more deeply and instinctively inspired:

> He does not need to paint peasants or centaurs or children in paradise, nor does he need to go to Tahiti to view and experience the primitive aspects of human nature. He carries his own Tahiti within him, and with the certainty of a sleepwalker he strides through our confusing cultural life, totally unerring, in full possession of his own through and through naive Parsifal nature.[3]

Next, pointing to Munch's Åsgårdstrand pictures with their melancholy figures against the undulant shoreline, he detects a mystic relationship between man and nature, emotional, deeply secretive, and impressively visionary, in comparison with which the realist-naturalist approach to the landscape appears lifeless and inert. Equally evocative is Munch's portraiture, characterized by a similar visionary-emotional penetration of the subject. In the portraits of Jensen-Hjell and Hans Jaeger, Servaes claims, Munch has made a significant contribution to modern art. Even more eloquent is his analysis of the Dagny Przybyszewska portrait, which he views as part of the modern soul, the most noble aspect of modern woman." Stressing its subtle blend of the sophisticated and new with the instinctive and primal, he reads into it the intangible, mystically erotic quality with which Dagny's admirers endowed her as she moved among them, unencumbered, in the *Ferkel* circle. In her attitude

Servaes sees not the vampire but a woman striving for full recognition of her human worth, in her pose and demeanor

> an expression of her insatiable desire for fulfillment, her longing for an ever finer differentiation of her being so that she might live a life in keeping with her own individuality, but at the same time share that individuality with a man and thereby completely unfold the magic of her personality, while fully and intimately enjoying all of this in her own right.[4]

That this analysis is not extracted exclusively from the painting but also from the writer's own familiarity with the subject portrayed, seems self-evident—which is not to imply that Servaes knew Dagny more than only casually. He was an infrequent visitor to the *Ferkel* and did not belong to the group gathering regularly at Przybyszewski's salon. Even on the level of a mere casual acquaintance, however, he could not have failed to become cognizant of the highly charged atmosphere that seemed to surround her, and he may, in fact, as his analysis suggests, have felt drawn into it. Whatever he may personally have thought, his perception of her character closely corresponds with Munch's, not only as expressed in this and other paintings, but as he would later articulate it in the newspaper article already cited. The agreement between Servaes and Munch on this point—and it would of course be endorsed by Przybyszewski—lends considerable weight to a much more favorable interpretation of Dagny's role and contribution than that offered by Strindberg in his Laïs and Aspasia characterizations, let alone his correspondence. Moreover, it suggests that a misogynist reading of Munch's erotic imagery at this time would be invalid. From late 1893 and regularly thereafter, on the other hand, he consistently weaves into the compositional fabric of canvases dealing with such subjects an unmistakably ominous note of despair rooted in an apparent belief in the ultimate destruction of the male species.

It has been pointed out how Munch seemed to reinterpret his *Love and Pain* once he became exposed to the members of the *Ferkel* circle, now leaning toward its new and lasting name, *Vampire.* This in turn may have provided inspiration for two of the contributors to the Munch volume, Julius Meier-Graefe and Stanislaw Przybyszewski, for in their separate analyses of the paintings they stress almost exclusively their potential misogynist messages, Meier-Graefe—who was to become one of Europe's most influential critics—pressing the issue with a singular lack of vision, Przybyszewski with a creative fanaticism articulately imaginative yet rigidly confined by his own obvious bias.

Puberty and *The Hands,* in the present context viewed as expressions of Munch's compassion with the lot of woman, become in Meier-Graefe's interpretation deliberate manifestations of a special form of immorality, lewdness, which he considers an essential component of the female mystique, a character feature that fans every woman's desire to subjugate man. Thus the hovering shadows in *Puberty* and *The Day Thereafter* become the most pronounced symbol of this desire, while the paintings speak of Munch's blatant hatred for woman, an emotion Meier-Graefe calls as honest and direct as Adam's hatred for Eve.

Przybyszewski's essay is more complex. Beginning with general remarks on naturalism—"a mode of expression devoid of thought and soul"—it contrasts this with Munch's art, calling it creations of "a naked individualist... who conjures up a somnambulant, transcendental consciousness." Highly perceptive are Przybyszewski's comments on Munch's use of color as an independent symbolic feature:

> Each twinge of pain in the supreme paroxysm of exposed nerve ends has its exact counterpart in color. Pain—a red stain like blood, elongated screams of agony in strips of blue, green, and gold; unequal strips brutally splashed alongside each other.[5]

Despite this and similarly lucid flashes of insight into Munch's painterly approach and purpose, however, Przybyszewski tends to reduce the merit of his presentation by considering Munch's entire production a composite narrative on erotic issues. Viewed in this perspective *The Shriek* is seen as a final manifestation of a relentlessly downward trend in the struggle between the mind and the sex—unmistakably Strindberg's "Battle of the Brains"—the ultimate conquest of the male hero: "His sexuality has been drained from him and now he shrieks out into all nature for a new revelation."[6] This is also the stage at which Strindberg's Captain in *The Father* seizes the lighted lamp and hurls it at Laura, his wife.

In the fall of 1894 Munch was mounting his first exhibit in Stockholm. Assisting him in the venture were the art dealer, Theodor Blanch, and Helge Bäckström, Dagny's brother-in-law, who had written such a derogatory review of Strindberg's *Antibarbarus.* With seventy catalogue numbers the exhibit marked the most comprehensive Munch showing outside of Norway up to that time and aroused, at least on the opening day, a public interest approaching the sensational:

> The atmosphere among the invited artists, patrons of the arts, and gentlemen of the press was unusually exhilarated. Munch's paintings caused people to bubble over with laughter. A few took the pictures seriously, but that too was a source of amusement and only added to the general air of gaiety. The comic effect Munch's exhibit achieved with this elite public was scarcely due to malice or particular indignation. The gleeful reaction can probably partially be explained by the exceptional beauty of the autumn weather that day, and by the fact that the 1st of October was the big day for moving, so that people were happy, elated, and hectically busy. At any rate, on the occasion of its first showing Munch's art was something quite unusual and crazy compared to what had previously been shown as art in Stockholm.[7]

Critical reviews of the event were rather in keeping with the tenor and mood that had prevailed and ranged—as previously in Norway, Germany, and Denmark—from blatant ridicule to didactic admonition. Attempting to assess the paintings in terms of realism critics found them bizarre, inept, unfinished, disgusting, and downright vulgar, and many cast serious doubts on Munch's sincerity:

> We are sorry for the artist, most of all in case—which judging from previous events would not be impossible—he should succeed in gaining recognition from those who, in ignorance of the great task of art, consider it necessary to admire everything new and utter proud words about that which deserves the very opposite of praise.[8]

In the course of the next few days, however, matters calmed down considerably, and within a week a literary publication, *Figaro,* carried a detailed article discussing Munch's works not only with sympathy but a measure of controlled enthusiasm:

> In heedless contempt for form, clarity, elegance, unity, and realism he paints with the intuitive strength of talent the most subtle momentary and fleeting visions of the soul through light and darkness. The bizarre music of color is enough for him. The fantastic linear play of mood and dream satisfies him. He paints what he deeply felt, not saw with the outward eye... He paints the strongest moments of his life; whether beautiful or ugly, healthy or sick... What matters is the intensity of the soul's experience...[9]

The exhibit, though open for a full month, closed without any sales. Yet in other respects it brought the artists some highly positive results. For one thing, attendance was so good that he netted 400 Swedish crowns from his share of the entrance fees. More important, however, was that Munch during his brief stay in Stockholm had been introduced to quite a few individuals of consequence. "The Swedes are very pleasant," he notes in a letter home, "as long as I don't touch on politics"—an observation reflecting the rapidly deteriorating relationship between Sweden and Norway at that time. He goes on to report that he has met the poet, Carl Snoilsky—"model for Rosmer in Ibsen's *Rosmersholm*"—and Gustaf af Geijerstam; and at a gathering of the exclusive Edda Society had an opportunity to see "all of Stockholm's famous people."[10] Of more direct value was his meeting with two Frenchmen who happened to be in the Swedish capital that month, the Ibsen translator, Count Moritz Prozor, and the theatre authority, Lugnë-Poé, who would later commission him to make lithographs for the programs issued in connection with the French premieres of *Peer Gynt* and *Rosmersholm.*

Yet there was nothing in Stockholm to make Munch linger beyond the early days of the exhibit, and he was soon back in Berlin, intending to plunge into his new activity, graphics, but feeling he was merely wasting time visiting within his growing circle of friends. Therefore, impatient with himself and the setting he wrote home saying he would soon be going either to Paris or back to Norway, adding, "It'll be a while yet before Berlin becomes an art city."[11] Even so he remained until the beginning of June 1895, working on a series of graphics. Thereafter, during a month in Paris, he completed his *Self-Portrait with a Cigarette* (Plate 46). Later that year the painting was purchased by the National Gallery in Kristiania as a first sign of official recognition at home.

In a creative career extending over six decades Munch would at regular intervals produce pictures focusing on his own likeness. In this respect he was as determined as in his persistent pursuit of the *Sick Girl* theme, a parallel preoccupation so pronounced as to suggest the possibility he may have considered his changing attitude toward each of these subjects equally important reflections of stages in his own creative, emotional, and physical evolvement.

Of all his self-portraits none is quite as ambitious, meticulously executed, or deliberately formal, even traditional, as the one with the cigarette. Its nearest antecedent, *Self-Portrait under a Female Mask* (Plate 49), completed nearly two years earlier, is totally different, departing radically from the norm of formal portraiture by its prominent placing of the hovering, rigidly stylized representation of the likeness of Dagny Juell—as she was also featured that same year in *The Hands, Madonna,* and *The Voice*—thereby drawing the viewer's attention to matters other than the artist's portrayal of himself. Not so in the 1895 portrait in which every brush stroke and color gradation, every contrast between light and shadow serves exclusively to focus attention on and heighten the intensity of his own facial features, and where no visible symbols, no extraneous clues, provide a key to the depth of his psyche. As in his earlier portraits of others—Jensen-Hjell, Hans Jaeger, August Strindberg—it is the eyes that make the greatest impact on the viewer, their piercing, trancelike quality suggesting a wide range of subjective emotional interpretations. In terms of painterly technique, however, the portrait readily lends itself to straightforward, objective analysis. The structure, rigidly symmetric yet far less specifically defined than in earlier works, rests on a central perpendicular axis extending from the brightly lit face down along the coat to the lower edge of the canvas. The formally placed hand—Napoleonic except for its visible fingers—while belonging to the central axis, is also the terminal point of a diagonal thrust marked by the lower arm. Leitmotif for the curved texture of the brushwork is the gently spiraling smoke rising from the cigarette, whose glow must account, at least in part, for the color intensity of the face which, juxtaposed with the smoke, tends to emerge like a genie from a bottle. The color scheme—dark shadings of blue and red in dramatic contrast to the wan flesh tones of face and hands—appears deceptively simple but involves in reality a considerable diversity of values through which the entire background takes on a throbbing, restless quality.

Among other paintings completed during this concluding period of Munch's first stay in Berlin were two of his now best-known works, *Woman in Three Stages*—at first entitled simply *Woman*—and the definitive version of *Death in the Sickroom,* based on a pastel drawing already shown in the controversial Berlin exhibit of 1892. His most concerted effort at this time, however, was devoted to the field in which he was destined to make his most profound contribution, the graphic arts. He may have been led in that direction by the extreme difficulty he experienced in trying to sell his paintings, but also by the activities he had occasion to observe in the graphic studios of Ludwig Knaus and Karl Köpping, both meticulous copiers of great art works of the past. More directly inspiring just then, however, were the works of Max Klinger and Hans Thoma, whose series of etchings from the 1880s, including cycles under such titles as *Suffering, Death,* and *Love,* were widely circulated in Germany.

No one familiar with Munch's graphic works could fail to notice in them the extreme logic between the chosen medium—the copper plate, the stone, the wood block—and the expressive intent of the subject portrayed. On this basis, his careful attention to structural detail and deliberate use of linear interplays so characteristic of his paintings seem quite naturally to point toward the various graphic media in which these specific features are so essential. Consequently, he succeeds in effecting the transition from painting to graphics with the greatest of ease. Yet the presence of such natural talent and aptitude does not justify the claim made by Thiis, Gauguin, and Langaard that Munch as a graphic artist was virtually independent of outside influence. In addition to the works by Klinger and Thoma in Berlin, he certainly must have become familiar with representative works in the steadily growing body of graphics produced by French artists. Shortly after his arrival in Paris in 1889 he would have seen the show of the Society of Painter-Engravers at Durand-Ruel, with works by Redon and Moreau, and in subsequent years, when nearly all the major shows in the city contained sections devoted to the graphic arts, he must have seen etchings and lithographs by nearly all artists active in the field. Among them were three whose influence is most readily detected in his early graphic efforts. Eugène Carrière, Felix Valloton, and Toulouse-Lautrec. A unique event in this context was the 1890 showing of a carefully selected group of Japanese art works in various media at Ecole des Beaux Arts—surely as stunning a revelation to Munch as it was to the entire Parisian art community. Considering all this it was not at all remarkable that Munch should move into the graphic field at that time. The striking aspect of it was the way his own peculiar predilection for these media so quickly and apparently effortlessly enabled him to master the technique and develop an expressive range that clearly set him apart from predecessors and contemporaries alike and opened up for him new approaches to old subjects.

Gustav Schiefler, who meticulously probed the chronological sequence of Munch's graphic works and carefully catalogued those completed between 1894 and 1926[12] lists as the artist's first venture in the new field two portraits not previously attempted in any other medium. From the third entry in the Schiefler catalogue, however, and for listings representing the subsequent two years, nearly all graphics reiterate earlier paintings. Yet it would be a serious error to assume that Munch proceeded in this manner for lack of creative originality. Rather, he did so in a deliberate attempt at probing by means of such well tested subjects the particular expressive potential of this new medium with its starkly contrasting black-and-white features and uncompromising demand for direction and simplicity. On these premises he extracted from his paintings only their most essential structure and contents, hoping through such concentration to intensify the emotional-dramatic tension that is so much a part of his total compositional intent. A comparison between the painted version of *The Kiss* (Plate 28) and one of its graphic counterparts clearly testifies to the validity and purpose of this creative procedure. The painting, though by no means an extravagantly composed canvas, is still the product of a fairly elaborate scheme combining a carefully devised structure, subtle color juxtapositions, and a directly visual representation of the neutral outside world versus the inner, all-consuming existential moment implied in the title. The print, on the other hand, makes its artistic and emotional impact entirely without extraneous supportive means, relying solely on a highly imaginative exploitation of the medium through which the central figures seem to emerge organically from the grain of the wood.

The artist who produced this particular woodcut version of *The Kiss*—there was another as well as an etching—had concentrated on graphics for nearly ten years. Yet there are much earlier works that speak as convincingly of his consummate skill and artistry, among them several from 1894, his first year in this field, based on subjects previously committed to the canvas, such as a drypoint etching of *Sick Girl,* furnished with a totally separate springtime landscape as a supportive base or pedestal. There is *Puberty,* in its lithographed rendition compressed into a picture of the frightened girl and her shadow only, with no space allowed for other matters, and there is a similar rendition of *The Day Thereafter.*

In one way certain of the early graphics did not reflect a simplification of his canvas approach to the same subjects. Keenly aware of the power of color he may, at least initially, have had his doubts that forms, lines, and a rigid concentration on the essential subject matter would adequately compensate for its absence and for the peculiar surface texture resulting from its impasto. This may explain his tendency to provide his graphics with rather specific symbolic commentaries in the form of arabesques or other peripheral matters which in their subject versions, such as in the lithographs, *Self-Portrait with a Skeletal*

Arm (Plate 2) from 1895—perhaps influenced by Böcklin's superb *Self-Portrait with Death* (Plate 45)—and the *Portrait of August Strindberg* (Plate 1) from the following year, reveal a deep awareness of the psychological nature of the subject portrayed. On the other hand, there are works in which such elaborations appear both needlessly blunt and obviously redundant and hence severely threaten the quality of the finished product. His dual treatment of the subject *Death and the Maiden* (Plate 50) is a case in point. In the painting a color pattern of broken vertical streaks woven into the fabric of the background suggests a flow of sperm, while a recapitulation of the two human forms portrayed, altered to the fetal state, has been sketched into the right edge of the canvas. Such symbolic features, already superflous in the painting yet rescued by their integration into the totality of the composition, become directly obnoxious in the etching where, contained within a rigid frame and a base, the sperm and fetuses—separate and therefore too distinctly visible—result in an overstatement seriously detracting from the impact of the principal subject rendition that could well have stood in its own merit.

At the end of June, 1895, Munch came back to Norway, celebrating his return by an unusual feat of physical prowess: his first and last mountain climbing venture! Then, settling for the remainder of the summer in Åsgårdstrand, he completed several graphics, most of them based on paintings developed earlier in the same inspiring surroundings. *Lovers on the Shore*—also entitled *Attraction* (Plate 20)—is an etching showing a couple facing each other in profile against a background of the familiar chestnut trees and the phallic symbol of a full moon, its light shimmering on the surface of the fjord. *Two People* forms a simultaneous echo of the paintings *Inger on the Beach* (Plate 19) and *Melancholy;* and derived from *The Voice* is the lithograph *Summer Night* which takes its place among the most sensitively beautiful of all Munch's graphics. In the foreground is a young woman separated from the shore and those in the boat by a screen of trees, her vague longing for sexual fulfillment suggested by the erotic metaphor of the shimmering moonlight.

In September, following another trip to Paris where he was hoping to be able to exhibit, he installed himself in a studio in Kristiania, now with the prospect of a more immediate exposure to the public through a local art dealer's offer to sponsor his third hometown retrospective. With a catalogue listing of only forty numbers it was a more modest show than earlier ones, but its inclusion of the principal works in *The Frieze of Life* series made it bolder than anything the Norwegians had ever seen in an art exhibit.

The fame—or notoriety—Munch had attained in Germany, and to a lesser degree in Copenhagen and Stockholm, had by no means improved his standing at home. With *Aftenposten*'s critic leading the offensive other conservatives were quick to fall in step with the agitated beat of this chief drummer. Yet the grudging admission of talent which had been part of earlier reviews shone through this time as well, as though critics, now aware of the artist's prominence, no longer dared profess their ignorance of his position and the trends he represented. After all, Edvard Munch had received greater attention abroad than any other Norwegian painter before him.

By coincidence, the seventieth birthday of Hans Gude, celebrated National Romantic, was observed that fall—half a year late—by a retrospective sponsored by the Artists Association and running concurrently with Munch's. To proceed from Gude to Munch, a critic observed, is like going "from the ballroom to the morgue." Then followed a paragraph of that familiar, half-hearted recognition:

> But the morgue too is part of this life, and by "the morgue" we imply all that is agonizing, bitter, without harmony in our earthly existence. We have never spoken to Mr. Munch, nor have we ever seen him. But through his paintings he stands before us as one whose soul is deeply troubled, who lives with and is involved in this life's struggle and is intimately familiar with its darkest side. And as destiny seems to toss men and human conditions helter-skelter on the vast playground of existence, so the artist may have wanted to express this in his own haphazardly tossed colors.[13]

A more personal assessment of the exhibit came in the form of a private letter from someone whose specific concern must have taken Munch by surprise:

> It was with great interest and, I must confess, mixed feelings that I recently viewed your exhibit at Blomquist's. The room was full of people, but what an ignorant public they were! Although I am really not certain you might not in fact be best served by having this public remain ignorant of some of the exhibit's pictures, for if I have properly interpreted the cycle, *Woman Who Loves,* then I cannot comprehend how you could have chosen to exhibit this publically in Kristiania. Many of the pictures belong only in an environment totally different from Kristiania, where there will be a cry for the police, closing, confiscation, etc. Or is there perhaps another meaning behind these pictures of women surrounded by fetuses?
>
> Forgive me . . . for expressing my opinion of your work . . . and . . . forgive me when I ask you in the name of the friendship I know exists between you and two of my daughters and their husbands, forgive me for asking you to do me the great favor of removing our daughter Ragnhild's picture from your exhibit.

And profoundly apologetic for his interference—for he really does not want to be identified with that ignorant public—the writer, pleading for an understanding of his position as a father, signs himself, "Yours respectfully, H. Juell."[14]

Since the portrait of Ragnhild Juell Bäckström is a straightforward, totally inoffensive representation, the doctor must have wanted it removed because its presence among all the "women surrounded by fetuses" so obviously placed its named model within Munch's controversial artistic circle. It is rather puzzling that in an exhibit which also included *Madonna*—both the painting and a lithograph—*The Voice,* and other works so definitely inspired by Dagny, the doctor should have focused attention only on the portrait of Ragnhild. The reason must be that in the other paintings Munch had idealized Dagny's features to suit his symbolic intent and thereby made direct identification difficult.

As the presence of Adelsteen Normann at the 1892 retrospective had led to Munch's Berlin exhibit later that year, the convenient appearance in Kristiania of a French art authority in the fall of 1895 was to have a similar effect on Munch's forthcoming stay in Paris. The distinguished foreign visitor was the publisher of *La Revue Blanche,* Thadée Natanson, whose early enthusiasm for the Nabis and Toulouse-Lautrec made his initial reaction to Munch's painterly and graphic approach predictably favorable. Following his visit to the exhibit—where he not only carefully and with deep insight examined the works but with a mixture of amusement and consternation noted the adverse reaction of the public—he wrote a detailed account of it for his own publication, offering both critical observations and generous praise.[15] He rounded out his article with a cautionary comment of Munch's prolonged exposure to the Berlin art climate: "One would urge him after such an adequate, perhaps even too extensive, stay in Germany to proceed promptly to Paris to look at paintings, but not look for a teacher there."[16]

This was of course exactly what Munch had intended to do, for already before the exhibit he had decided that he needed a change of surroundings and would head for Paris at the first opportunity. Even so, such unqualified encouragement from the eminent Parisian must have bolstered his determination; and with his own name featured in the column of *La Revue Blanche,* not only in Natanson's article but in conjunction with a reproduction of *The Shriek* appearing in that year's December issue, he must have looked forward to this new phase of his life with much greater anticipation and confidence than would otherwise have been the case. Indeed, he must have felt a surge of that exhilarating *Machtgefühl* Strindberg had described a year earlier when an article of his had appeared in the pages of prestigious *Le Figaro*—"80,000 subscribers!"[17]—and the Parisian press seemed suddenly eager to open its columns to him. Munch would no doubt have rushed to Paris the moment his Kristiania exhibit closed had he not been detained in Norway by the unexpected recurrence of a tragic family circumstance.

14

Strindberg and Gauguin

Strindberg's Paris stay in the mid-1890s—documented in his own letters, in *Ockulta Dagboken* [The Occult Diary], and, perhaps not so reliably, in the retrospective novel, *Inferno,* as well as in certain observations by friends and acquaintances, including Munch—turned out to be a period more difficult than any he had previously experienced. Yet it was not without its moments of exaltation, beginning, ironically, with Frida's departure:

> It was with a sense of savage joy that I returned from Gare du Nord where I had parted from my little wife, who was going back to our child who had become ill in a far away country.[1]

Not long thereafter came the article in *Le Figaro*—actually the first of three installments—then a very favorable essay on Strindberg by Henri Albert in *La Revue Blanche,* and as his crowning glory in the year 1894 the December premiere of *The Father* at Lugnë-Poé's *Théâtre de l'Oevre,* an event he would later fondly recall in a lyric soliloquy spoken by Maurice, the playwright portrayed in *Crimes and Crimes:*

> Do you hear the rushing sound in the distance, like ocean waves against rocky shores, like the wind in the forest? Do you know what that is? It is Paris, whispering my name![2]

Yet this love affair between the Parisian public and its *Cher Maître Suedois* was destined to be no less turbulent than his involvement with others, and while his presence in the French capital continued to be a matter of considerable interest to the public the French did not always express themselves in terms of tender whispers. On the contrary, already a month after the successful performance of *The Father,* when *La Revue Blanche* carried his essay on *The Inferiority of Women,* they roared in indignation. "All of Paris ignited," Strindberg proudly reported to Frida, later adding, "The spirits are on the move, raging, mocking, scolding, but it's all wonderful!"[3]

A press polemic ensued, not unlike that following the closing of the Munch exhibit in Berlin, only more heated and with much broader participation. The question of women's rights had of course long been an active issue, the Paris press having given considerable space to misogynist viewpoints similar to Strindberg's. As a matter of fact, long before Strindberg appeared on the scene, *Revue des Revues* had carried articles against women's emancipation by such well-known socio-historical scholars as Herbert Spencer, Cesare Lombroso, and Lombroso's follower, Guglielmo Ferrero. *La Nouvelle Revue,* however, edited by a woman, had taken the opposite side in the argument. Even so, Strindberg's entry into this particular arena, perhaps because his reputation derived from the creative rather than the scientific field, caused much greater furor than had that of any of the previous combatants, with the result that some of France's most distinguished personalities now came rushing to the defense of women, among them Alexandre Dumas (fils), Alphonse Daudet, and Octave Mirbeau. One of the few favoring Strindberg in this matter was Huysmans, but even he had serious doubts about the basic premises of some of the former's arguments.[4]

In a life full of ironies, one of the bitterest for Strindberg must have been the circumstances surrounding his fleeting prominence in Paris which, the relative success of the *The Father* notwithstanding, was primarily the result of the controversy arising from his contribution to an already ongoing debate. Obviously, this was a far cry from the triumph he had envisioned in his ten-year struggle to gain recognition in that sophisticated center of Europe. Yet once it had happened he decided, as shown in his letter for Frida, to view it as a positive development: "...it's all wonderful!" As Stellan Ahlström suggests, the controversy, together with the success of *The Father,* did in reality lay a foundation substantial enough for Strindberg to build the kind of reputation he rightly deserved. It was only that an unfortunate set of circumstances—in Strindberg's subsequent terminology, The Powers—interfered in such a way that he was unable to reap the benefit of the existing situation. For that reason, his "name soon went into oblivion, and during the Inferno period he lived unnoticed in Montparnasse."[5]

Not quite so. Although temporarily removed from public consciousness he was by no means forgotten. Could anyone who had ever met Strindberg, either personally or through his writings, possibly ever forget him? As for living unnoticed, this, too, is not entirely in keeping with the facts. Many of his fellow Scandinavians, concerned with his strange activities and precarious state of health, kept a wary eye on him; and through the interests he chose to pursue, science and painting, he came into contact with a select group of individuals, many of considerable consequence in their own fields, who treated him with respect and admiration. The most remarkable of these entered the Strindberg annals at the Paris performance of *The Father*—from which the playwright himself chose to remain absent—when a reporter from *Le Figaro,* scanning the avant-garde audience, spotted a figure sufficiently conspicuous to rate special mention in next day's theatre column: "An unknown gentleman wearing an Astrakhan cap."[6]

It was Paul Gauguin—"a man haunted by incessant visions, an artist devoured by anguish, a seeker launched in pursuit of the undiscoverable"[7]—back in Paris after a disappointing stay in Brittany where he had tried in vain to recapture the unspoiled beauty of people and landscape he had once found there and subsequently experienced in full measure in Tahiti. Having spent two years in that remote part of the world, abandoning himself to "sheer living" and developing in his art an "Oceanic character," he had crated his total output and undertaken the long journey back to France to show the public what he had been able to accomplish in his exile. A brief stay in Paris—where his paintings had created a sensation without inspiring any buyers—convinced him that he could no longer exist in such surroundings; yet financially incapable of returning to the peace and solitude of Tahiti he had chosen as a temporary refuge Pont-Aven—perhaps thinking, as he would later state in his journals, that "from Oceania to Brittany is not very far." But this time it proved to be quite a distance, and in the fall of 1894, writing from Pont-Aven, he says:

> In December I will return to Paris and will exert myself to sell everything I have, either *en bloc* or piecemeal. The proceeds thereof once in my pocket, I will set out again for the South Seas... Nothing will stop me from going, and it will be for good. What a foolish existence European life is![8]

There is no reason to believe that Strindberg and Gauguin had met prior to that fall. They were, however, no doubt familiar with each other's activities through mutual friends, first and foremost Gauguin's one-time brother-in-law, Frits Thaulow. Then there were the Brandes brothers through whom, while in Copenhagen in the late 1880s, he may well have seen some of Gauguin's early works. At that time he was also introduced to Gauguin's wife, Mette, then already estranged from her husband.

In Paris Strindberg and Gauguin were brought together by their mutual friends, William Molard and his wife, Ida Ericson, he an amateur composer and art enthusiast of Franco-Norwegian parentage, she a Swedish sculptor. During Gauguin's absence they had served as caretakers of his studio and helped him in various other ways—as they would also be helping Strindberg. Unfortunately, no record exists of the first meeting between Strindberg and Gauguin, but it must have been a momentous occasion for both, not only because of their individual statures and long-time awareness of each other, but because of the many characteristics they had in common. Doggedly determined to pursue their creative course without regard for antecedents or consequences, they were both highly controversial figures. Too, they were total failures at providing either for their dependents or themselves and were often deprived of even the most basic physical needs; most importantly, each suffered the pangs of a self-imposed but no less agonizing separation from home and family. Yet despite all of this it is a question whether Strindberg and Gauguin felt, as Göran

Söderström claims, an instant liking for each other.[9] On the contrary, their writings, though indisputably confirming the existence of a high degree of mutual admiration, make it equally clear that while Strindberg found it difficult to appreciate Gauguin's art, Gauguin found it impossible to share Strindberg's misogynist point of view. "There are misogynists who are misogynists because they love women too well and tremble before them," Gauguin says. "I, too, love women... when they are fat and vicious, but I am no misogynist and do not tremble before them."[10]

The most tangible evidence of their exchange of ideas is found in two letters, one from Gauguin in which he asks Strindberg to write a preface to the catalogue in which he plans to list everything he wants to sell to finance his return to Tahiti, the other Strindberg's response to this request. "The idea of asking you to write this preface occurred to me," says Gauguin in his letter, "when I saw you the other day in my studio playing the guitar and singing, your Northern blue eyes studying the pictures hung on my wall." That it was not the flattering appraisal so common on such occasions Gauguin was hoping for but rather something out of the ordinary is quite apparent from his thoughts of what might have gone through Strindberg's mind at the time. "I felt your revulsion," he goes on to say—"a clash between your civilization and my barbarism... A civilization from which you are suffering, a barbarism which spells rejuvenation for me."[11]

This statement reveals Gauguin's keen perception of Strindberg's peculiar dilemma. Always eager to be considered a member of the avant-garde he still felt deeply rooted in and drawn toward a more traditional mode of life, as had been shown not so long before in his orthodox courtship of Frida during his most active participation in the activities of the *Ferkel* circle. His presence in Gauguin's radical coterie—his own guitar playing and singing notwithstanding—must, on the background of his otherwise sober pursuit of lofty scientific principles, have been an experience evoking the most ambivalent emotions. As for his view on Gauguin's art, he spelled it out in considerable detail in the long letter he wrote to explain the reason for his unwillingness to compose the requested preface, at the very outset stating that he could neither understand nor appreciate such efforts. Then follows a summary of his own attitude toward the visual arts, beginning with his first visit to Paris in 1876, when the impressionists were in the vanguard and he had looked at their new approach with calm indifference:

> But the next day I returned, I did not know just why, and discovered that there was something in these bizarre manifestations. I saw the swarming of a crowd over a pier, but I did not see the crowd itself. I saw the rapid passage of a train across a Normandy landscape, the movement of wheels in the street, frightful portraits of ugly people who had not known how to pose calmly...

The result of this, he claims, is chaos: "... utter anarchy—all styles, all colors, all subjects, historical, mythological, naturalisitic. People no longer wished to hear of schools or tendencies. Liberty was not the rallying cry." But in the midst of this turmoil he had discovered Puvis de Chavannes' *The Poor Fisherman,* a monument to order and formalism, against which Gauguin's creations appeared bewilderingly unfamiliar:

> It is too sundrenched for me who enjoy the play of light and shadow. And in your Paradise dwells an Eve who is not my ideal—for I myself have an ideal of a woman or two![12]

To this Gauguin responds that the Eve of his choice—"whom I have painted in forms and harmonies of a different world"—may one day smile on Strindberg less bitterly:

> This world I am discovering... is a Paradise the outlines of which I shall merely have sketched out. And between the sketch and the realization of the vision there is a long way to go. What does it matter! If we have a glimpse of happiness, what is it but a foretaste of Nirvana?[13]

Strindberg's mental probing of Gauguin's art does indeed lead to a deeper understanding of it, a melancholy recognition of the validity of this restless artist's search for his Nirvana. "For I too," says Strindberg in closing, "am beginning to feel an immense need to become a savage and create a new world."[14]

Not only did Gauguin decide to use this letter as his catalogue preface, but he had it printed with his own response in the daily, *L'Eclair,* where it caught the eyes of many, among them Camille Pissarro, who bemoaned Strindberg's view of the impressionists; "This author has a poor opinion of the impressionists; he understands no one but Puvis de Chavannes."[15]

While Strindberg did indeed admire Puvis de Chavannes and never seemed to come to terms with the impressionists, Pissarro drew the wrong conclusion when claiming that such preference was rooted in a lack of understanding. As he approaches the end of his Gauguin essay—for it is of course an essay rather than a letter—Strindberg makes it eminently clear that, far from lacking in understanding, he is in fact one of the very first of that singular artist's contemporaries to present a meaningful, relatively unbiased appraisal of his inspirational source and creative power:

> He is Gauguin, the savage, who hates a whimpering civilization, a sort of Titan who, jealous of the Creator, makes in his leisure hours his own little creation, the child who takes his toys to pieces so as to make others of them, who abjures and defies, preferring to see the heavens red rather than blue with the crowd."[16]

Yet between this understanding of Gauguin's drive and purpose and his own appreciation for what he saw with his "Northern blue eyes" there seemed to loom an insuperable barrier erected and maintained by the striking dualism in his soul: on the one side his strong leaning toward a traditional approach in art and on the other his unquestioned desire to support contemporary trends. In the final analysis tradition would prevail, for when asked some years later about his art preferences,[17] he placed Theodore Rousseau of the rather passé Barbizon School at the top of the list. More reflective of his own tempestuous approach to painting was his selection of Turner among British painters, while his choice of Böcklin's *The Isle of the Dead* as his single most favorite canvas may in part be explained by the happy circumstances surrounding his first exposure to that painting during the exhilarating days of his courtship of Frida. It is rather interesting that in this higher order of priorities there was room neither for Gauguin nor Munch, nor for any of the many other outstanding artists who at one time or another had belonged to Strindberg's own intimate circle of friends.

As for his personal contact with Gauguin it extended over a period of half a year but never became as close—or in times of trial as antagonistic—as his recent association with Munch in Berlin, or in a more remote past with his fellow Scandinavians in Grez, although, with experiences and attitudes of such great similarity they must at times have found each other highly compatible. "I should like to write as I paint my pictures," Gauguin says—"following my fancy, following the mood, and finding the title long afterward"[8]—a creative procedure nearly identical to Strindberg's "art by chance or accident." In December and early January they must have met quite often and under circumstances favorable enough to encourage Gauguin to solicit the catalogue preface "in memory of the winter 1894-95 when we lived behind the Institute," a wording suggesting that by then the frequency of their meetings was already on the decline. Quite naturally so, for that particular period in Strindberg's life happened to be made up of a series of days filled with physical and emotional illness. Therefore, despite his occasional presence in Gauguin's studio "playing the guitar and singing" he is not likely to have spent a great deal of time in the company of the artist once his own emotional problems began to surface.

In reality, Gauguin's life was not much better than Strindberg's, and how low each was in spirit is quite evident from some of their letters to others. It is particularly in those to their estranged wives—Frida in Dornach and Gauguin's Mette in Copenhagen—that they pour out their agony, perhaps thereby attempting to offset some of their guilt feeling about having abandoned their families. On January 7, 1895, Strindberg writes in great detail about his many problems—his shattered nerves and bleeding hands, his physical deprivation and utter loneliness, his profound regrets:

Perhaps it would have been better never to have enjoyed life, for the memory of beautiful moments is such a cruelty. And I do remember our last Christmas at Dornach with the mistletoe that killed Balder. And you gave me everything and I gave you nothing in return.[19]

In the very same month, Gauguin, equally melancholy, writes to Mette: "I am beginning to wonder whether my family knows of my existence, as my birthday, Christmas and New Year's Day all go by without a word from them."[20]

Strindberg, no longer capable of caring for himself, entered St. Louis Hospital January 11 for complete rest and for treatment of a chronic skin disorder of his hands brought about by their prolonged exposure to chemicals. Remaining until the end of the month, he would later refer to this period as his purgatory, although in reality his stay seemed to allow him to lead a life of relative normalcy. On the hospital compound he was given access to a laboratory to continue his research; he was free to take leisurely strolls to nearby places of interest, and most importantly, he had ample time to pursue his correspondence.

While there is little reason to doubt the *Inferno* implications that his St. Louis interlude in many ways was an agonizing experience, his letters—and in the course of nineteen days, part of the time with both hands bandaged, he produced thirty!—contain little of the tragic pathos of his carefully structured, imaginative observations in *Inferno.* Instead they are filled with scientific jargon, astute business considerations, and to Frida a substantial measure of bitter irony. In *Inferno* are these lyric passages:

It was my birthday. Upon my return to the hospital a letter from my wife is waiting for me. She bemoans my misfortune, she again wants to come to me to protect me and love me.

The happiness of being loved evokes, in spite of all, a need to direct my gratitude to someone . . . whom? To the unknown who for so many years has remained hidden?

My heart melts, I confess the despicable lie about my unfaithfulness, beg her forgiveness . . .[21]

But a search of his letters from that day, January 22—there are five, two of these to Frida though one is actually addressed to his infant daughter—fails to disclose anything even faintly resembling the mellow mood of reconciliation permeating the *Inferno* passages. On the contrary, the letter to Frida on his forty-sixth birthday marks one of the bitterest communications:

Do you realize one must no longer bring up children to become honorable people, for then they are lost. I also intend to write a catechism for coming generations:

First commandment: Lie! Otherwise someone will exploit your good faith.

Second commandment: Betray: otherwise you will be betrayed.

Third commandment: Steal: or you will be stolen from.

Fourth commandment: Kill: otherwise you will be killed.[22]

Yet by the time his hospital stay had come to an end much of the bitterness had vanished for, although not physically healed he had—so he says in *Inferno*—been "cured of the temptations of this world," a state of mind attained through the self-effacing example of the nuns in the hospital, one of whom, with the reverence of an obedient child, he had named mother:

> At my leave-taking I had wanted to kiss the hand of our kind mother, who without preaching had taught me the way of the cross. But a feeling of respect, as for something that must not be profaned, held me back.[23]

In that spirit he found it difficult to feel comfortable in his former circle of friends and acquaintances—that group of "anarchist artists" with their "uninhibited customs, loose morals, godlessness"—but he returned all the same, considering his own presence in the midst of all that iniquity a step on his thorny path of penitence. Besides, he could not help being fascinated with the group which, he says, represented a great deal of talent. There was one among them "with the natural gift of genius who had made an honored name for himself."[24] Gauguin, of course.

On February 15 the artist's long awaited sale had taken place, but despite his own honored name and Strindberg's evocative catalogue preface the result was most disheartening. To be sure, he must have taken some comfort in the presence of Degas and Durand-Ruel among the actual buyers, and in an encouraging letter from the poet laureate of the avant-garde, to which Gauguin responded in the most gracious terms: "In my moment of disappointment, the royal hand of Stéphane Mallarmé cordially extended gives delight and strength."[25]

Although Strindberg in the early part of *Inferno* does refer to "the honored artist who is the doyen of our dinner circle," there is little evidence to suggest that such contacts resulted in a deeper friendship between the two. In Gauguin's correspondence from that period, aside from the one letter concerning the preface, there is no reference to Strindberg at all, even though the recipient of the majority of those letters, Gauguin's Danish wife, would have read of her husband's association with her famed fellow Scandinavian with considerable interest. As for Strindberg, he brings up Gauguin in a letter of May 26 that year, to Hermann Schlittgen, the German painter, asking for his assistance in mounting a Gauguin exhibit in Munich. This may well mark the high point in the relationship between the two, for Strindberg says in the same letter: "If there is any possibility for a Gauguin exhibit this spring, Gauguin will come [with me to Munich] to arrange the matter."[26] Otherwise, it is rather clear from *Inferno* that Strindberg's social needs and commitments at that time were very limited:

> Since I have penetrated this new world into which no one can follow, I have developed a dislike for the company of people and feel an irresistable urge to divorce myself from my surroundings. Consequently, I have let my friends understand that I intend to settle for some time in Meudon to write a book, which requires solitude and silence. At the same time, trivial disagreements led to a break with my coterie at the eating place, so that one day I found myself totally isolated.[27]

In June Strindberg left Paris to spend the summer in Ystad in southern Sweden, while Gauguin, after a brief visit to Copenhagen, set out on his last voyage to Tahiti. Strindberg, back in Paris in September, received a letter from Richard Bergh requesting permission to print the Gauguin preface in conjunction with a projected article on the extraordinary French artist. While Strindberg readily gave his permission he noted in his response that he now felt "far removed from Gauguin and the fine arts," that he was totally absorbed in his scientific studies, at that time particularly busy with his *Introduction a une Chimie Unitaire,* slated for publication later that month in *Mercure de France.*

Strindberg's name did occur once more in Gauguin's correspondence, but that was two and a half years later. Dated March 1898, the letter contained reference to a strange rumor having circulated in the European press a year earlier and initially believed by a great many, including Frida and Strindberg's children in Sweden. Caused by the confusion of Nils Strindberg with his much more famous second cousin, it made it appear that the dramatist was one of three participants in the ill-fated Andree polar expedition. When the rumor at long last reached Tahiti it was accepted without the slightest doubt or suggestion of surprise by Gauguin. "I heard that Strindberg had left in a balloon for the North Pole," he writes matter-of-factly to Molard, "and that no news had been received from the three explorers for three months. I hope at any event that he will return without any broken bones."[28]

15

A Falling-Out

When Munch arrived in Paris at the end of February, 1896, and took a studio in Rue de Santé, Strindberg had only a few days earlier moved into the hotel which would figure so prominently in his *Inferno* experiences, the rather dismal Orfila in the Montparnasse section of the city. Munch makes no mention of the first meeting between them, but Strindberg refers to it in his *Inferno,* and someone else on the scene, the British composer, Frederick Delius, mentions it in his recollections, written twenty years later:

> The Norwegian painter, Edvard Munch, had just arrived in Paris and came to see me in my flat in Ruc Ducouedic. I asked him to join me for a visit to Strindberg.
>
> We found him poring over his retorts, stirring strange evil-smelling liquids, and after chattering for five or ten minutes we left in a most friendly manner.[1]

Considering that Munch's friendship with Strindberg was well established and that there is no evidence whatsoever to suggest that Munch at that time felt antagonistic toward his distinguished friend, it seems somewhat unreasonable that an outsider would be needed to bring the two together again. Therefore, Strindberg's version in *Inferno,* though affected by his particular mood and no doubt manipulated according to his creative purpose, appears more authentic. Munch, identified as the Danish Painter, makes his entry in the spring, when Strindberg, as the result of a series of strange visions and mysterious sounds, was beginning to experience the world as "a vale of tears," in which Munch's presence—they had met again a few weeks earlier—was viewed as part of a sinister plot intended to punish Strindberg for an iniquity of the past: his affair with Dagny Juell.

As in Munch's painting of death, *Springtime,* the regenerative season causing "this Gehenna to be transformed into a Sharon's Valley where not only the lilies are blooming but lilacs, robinias, paulownias," had no effect on Strindberg's own spiritual depression. "I am sorrowful unto death . . . Autumn within, spring without."[2]

While Munch must have been in Paris for quite a while before calling on Strindberg it would be erroneous to consider this an intentional slight or a lack of interest in re-establishing a fascinating friendship. A more reasonable explanation is that Munch, in the immediate aftermath of another death in the family—that of his only brother, Andreas, who had succumbed to pneumonia a few days before Christmas—preferred to keep to himself to collect his thoughts. Had Strindberg known this he might not have drawn such negative conclusions from their first accidental meeting:

> This man, who before was on friendly terms with me, had arrived in Paris six weeks ago, and when I had met him in the street he had greeted me in a strange, nearly unfriendly manner. Perhaps to compensate for this he visited me the day thereafter and invited me to his studio, while saying niceties too shallow not to leave the impression of false friendship.[3]

Munch, by nature shy, may, aside from his own reluctance to see anyone at that time, have known of Strindberg's current dislike "for the company of people" and decided not to impose on his privacy. That he had second thoughts about the matter, however, and called on him "the day thereafter"—was Strindberg's choice of words in this particular context deliberate?—suggests that he was most anxious to correct any misunderstanding that may have arisen from his reaction to the unexpected encounter the day before.

"I am with Delius and Vilhelm Krag these days," Munch writes home at the end of March. Then, in a letter dated July 1—"This I've kept in my pocket for quite a while"—he reports that he has finished a lithograph of Strindberg, implying that the two must have seen each other with some regularity and apparently on the best of terms. As Strindberg approached his mental crisis, however, his association with Munch, a constant reminder of Berlin and Dagny and Przybyszewski, became in his mind—or at least as applied creatively in *Inferno*—an ever-present threat, while to Munch, though still consciously or subconsciously influenced by Strindberg, a contact of great frequency seemed no longer as inspiring as it had once been. This comes across in an undated letter written sometime in mid-July, telling those at home that he was still with Obstfelder, "and off and on with Strindberg, who is now rather old."[4]

The lithograph referred to earlier is of course the now famous arabesqued portrait (Plate 1) with the subject's name curiously misspelled "Stindberg." In its total composition widely acknowledged to be the most meaningful visual interpretation of the controversial genius, it is certainly a far more memorable *diktarporträtt* than the Goethe-like representation Strindberg had his heart set on when first posing for Munch in Berlin two years ealier.

As Munch the preceding year had portrayed himself in a lithograph featuring a skeletal arm extending across the lower edge of the print, thereby stressing his own peculiar preoccupation with death, he had also portrayed Przybyszewski with a similar skeletal addendum, inspired, it would seem, by Przybyszewski's principal literary work, *Totenmesse* [Death Mass]. It is this portrait of Popoffsky—Przybyszewski's name in *Inferno*—that is of such pivotal importance in Strindberg's approaching *Inferno* crisis:

> It is only the head with a cloud below, and under that a pair of crossed bones as on gravestones. The decapitated head makes us shudder, and the dream I had on May 14 comes back to haunt me like a ghost.

Munch, as in his self-portrait and in this particular portrait of Przybyszewski, may in the Strindberg picture have wanted to convey his own interpretation of the Strindbergian mystique; and with the unforgettable Pole in his own as well as his sitter's mind he may well have recalled the Przybyszewski notion that in every human being there is a balance factor between the male and the female characteristics, furthermore, that in the case of Strindberg the female had taken the upper hand so that "he was incapable of judging a woman by male standards."[6] Whatever motivated Munch, in terms of technique he must have conceived of the portrait and its serpentine frame as a single composition, for the principal subject, posed slightly to the left of center, is drawn toward the elongated nude of the frame in such a way that the two provide complete pictorial balance. The manner in which the woman's hair rises as through the effect of magnetic currents is not a new feature in Munch's iconography and is therefore not, as suggested in an otherwise excellent analysis of the subject,[7] the apparent result of Munch's possible interest in the works of William Blake at that particular time. This feature is present already in paintings from 1893, among them *Vampire, Jealousy,* and *Separation,* and in several graphics preceding the Strindberg lithograph. Rather than a Blake influence, it may have been derived from Munch's awareness of Strindberg's preoccupation with pseudo-scientific investigations into the phenomenon of energy, physical and psychic. Strindberg, writing of this in *Inferno,* tells of walking between two people when he experiences a feeling of "discomfort as of a thread . . . between them." In Munch's visual application of this phenomenon, however, it is no longer a question of a thread between the two subjects but of one, the Woman, winding her irresistible power around the Man.

While this juxtaposition of the male and the female in the Strindberg portrait no doubt constitutes a deeply sincere attempt at expressive artistry, the conspicuous misspelling of the subject's name may be an example of Munch's not infrequent use of a dry form of humor and may even be a reflection of the spirit that had prompted the remark, ". . . Strindberg, who is now rather old." It is of course possible that this little detail came about quite accidentally, but if so, why was not the spelling corrected as soon as the first proof had appeared? This suggests another explanation for the slight alteration of the name into "Stindberg." While working on the portrait Munch was also in the process of producing a lithograph for the forthcoming Parisian premiere of *Peer Gynt;*

and deeply engrossed in Ibsen's strident dramatic poem he could easily have detected something vaguely familiar in Peer's retrospective musing on the appearance of the Memnon statue:

> *Han, Memnon, faldt det mig bagefter ind,*
> *lignet de såkaldte Dovregubber,*
> *slig som han sad der stiv og stind,*
> *med enden plantet på søjlestubber.*[8]

In that staid, self-centered, fat—*stind*—Egyptian colossus that sings only when caressed in a certain way by the rays of the sun Munch may have seen features of the temporarily silent northern poet posing before him in the studio that spring.

This misspelling with its possible implication, if intentional, is a harmless, rather clever jest. Not so with another lithograph from the same period, however. Entitled *In the Clinic* it shows, unmistakably, Strindberg in the foreground of an assemblage of characters suffering from various venereal diseases. Such a crude commentary on the part of Munch must be ascribed to the final falling-out between the two, an occurrence clearly referred to in *Inferno,* where the relationship between the narrator and the Danish Painter—Popoffsky's friend—runs a rocky course, its nature signified by the presence or absence of a hostile Great Dane in front of the painter's studio entrance. Toward the end of June, as verified in letters as well as observations in *Inferno,* Strindberg's guilt feelings had developed into a raging persecution complex—a condition he vehemently denied in a letter to a Swedish friend, claiming that he would soon have proof that, far from suffering from such an ailment, he was indeed being persecuted.[9]

Much of his suspicion must have been directed at Munch who, at least in *Inferno,* is viewed as an advance agent for Przybyszewski. The narrator notes that his relationship with the Danish Painter is deteriorating, while "at the same time that beast of a dog reappeared, reminding me that I must be on my guard."[10] *Ockulta Dagboken* [Diary of the Occult] contains several references to a sequence of events which in *Inferno* attain a mystic significance merely hinted at in the diary notes. "Munet [*sic*] became nervous," it says in the diary, "reacted hysterically when he covered himself with my coat; he got up and went home to go to bed."[11] On Munch's part this may of course have been motivated by nothing more profound than sheer exasperation or the onset of a chill. When placed into the *Inferno* context, however, it becomes a most astounding psychic experience:

> I am visiting with the Danish Painter in Rue de la Santé. The big dog is gone, the entrance is free. We go out to have dinner at a sidewalk cafe in Boulevard Port-Royal. My friend is cold, doesn't feel good. Since he had forgotten to bring his coat I place mine over his shoulders.

> This calms him down, he submits to me and I tame him. He no longer dares rebel against me... He confesses that Popoffsky is an evildoer and that I have him to thank for all my adversities. Suddenly he is seized by nervousness, he trembles like a medium under the influence of a hypnotist, moves about restlessly, shakes off the coat. He no longer eats, drops his fork, gets up and says good-bye after first having left me my coat.[12]

A diary note dated June 27 says simply, "... the episode with Munch," and in *Inferno* under the date July 1, having apprehensively referred to a current rumor that Popoffsky has been released from prison, the narrator tersely adds, "His friend the Dane had become my enemy."[13] With that the Danish Painter actually exits from the *Inferno* account, while the narrator himself, ravaged by physical and mental anguish, abruptly abandons his known headquarters at the Orfila, the place to which an invisible hand had once led him to have him "punished, taught, and—why not—illuminated by an inner light."[14] While his stay had certainly more than fulfilled the first of these expectations, and perhaps in part the second as well, the inner light was still missing:

> Had he lost his way in the dark woods? No, the bringer of light has led me onto the right path toward the isle of the blessed, and it is the demon that tempts me! It is a punishment placed on me.[15]

Between the *Inferno* account and Strindberg's actual escape from the Orfila, as shown in his correspondence, there are no significant discrepancies. On leaving he had let it be known that he would be visiting with the Thaulows in Dieppe, while in reality he moved only a few blocks away to the edge of *Jardin des Plantes.* Sharing this secret with Thaulow he told him that he needed to stay out of reach of certain people, Frida, for one, and "... Edvard Munch, and everything related to Juell-Przybyszewski."[16]

In the month of July Strindberg had sent some rather curious postcards to Munch, the final one, dated July 19, the day he left the Orfila, contained this sober note: "The last time I saw you I thought you looked like a murderer—or at least a murderer's handyman."[17] It was Munch's failure to break with the Przybyszewskis that brought down on him this devastating indictment, which also marked the concluding communication between the two in this trying period of their lives.

At long last it became apparent, even to Strindberg himself, that he was in need of proper rest and care, and a letter of appeal to a physician in Sweden brought the response he had been hoping for: travel money to enable him to go home. And yet, it was with disturbingly ambivalent feelings he set out on his journey: "I have the right to be afraid of Sweden, for there's raging an absolute persecution mania to have me put into a madhouse."[18] Ailing, homeless, and totally uncertain of his future he left Paris, on the eve of his departure calling out his anguish in the words of Jeremiah: "Oh, I have nearly forgotten what happiness is!"[19]

It was in 1894-95 that Munch, in a retrospective mood, had pictured himself "in hell"—much later the portrait was entitled *Inferno*—attempting, it seems, to sum up his feelings about his turbulent Berlin experiences. These had already been given memorable expression in canvases such as *Madonna, Ashes, The Shriek,* and several other works, all forming a veritable line-up of witnesses testifying to the emotional battles he had fought during that period of his life. By the time he arrived in Paris in February of 1896, however, though deeply saddened by the death of his brother, he had in reality weathered a crisis having extended over several years and come out of it strengthened, if not entirely unscathed, with a vigorous attitude toward his art and an optimistic view of the future. "I'm pretty tired of the restless life I've been leading lately," he writes home the day he has been able to arrange for a studio; and a few days thereafter, responding to a letter from his aunt, he states positively, "I'm completely organized and busy with my work."[20]

Under such circumstances it is not strange that he would postpone seeking out Strindberg, whose state of mind must have been well known to him through other Scandinavians he associated with in the Latin Quarter. This would also explain why he seemed to react with a guilty conscience when he happened to meet Strindberg in the street. Following his courtesy call the next day, however, he must have continued to see him, and the result of this restored contact, so one-sidedly negative when judged on the basis of the *Inferno* account, certainly had its positive results. On the one hand it inspired a principal work by Munch, the Strindberg portrait, and on the other an imaginative, highly poetic account of key works in Munch's *Frieze of Life* series by Strindberg in *La Revue Blanche* June 1, 1896, shortly before the opening of Munch's first one-man show in Bing's *L'Art Nouveau* gallery.

His official Paris debut had actually taken place earlier that spring when ten of his paintings were included in the *Salon des Indépendants.* From more than a thousand works on view his were among the few singled out for special mention in a new publication, *L'Aube* [The Dawn], which in its May issue carried a full-page reproduction of *Madonna* together with an article on "one of the most peculiar temperaments in the Norwegian school."[21] Yet it was Strindberg's unique appraisal in *La Revue Blanche* that caught the attention of the Parisian avant-garde, perhaps not first and foremost as a Munch review or an essay in art but an art-oriented literary miniature in pure symbolist language. Using a quotation from Balzac's Seraphita as his motto: "However incomprehensible your words are, they have charm," he begins by describing Munch as a painter of esoteric love, jealousy, death, and sadness, victim of deliberate misunderstanding by critics acting as executioners—a stab at

Strindberg's own adversaries no less than at Munch's—then goes on to discuss eight separate paintings. In Munch's words Strindberg's analyses are poems in prose, reminiscent of Przybyszewski's essay in *Das Werk des Edvard Munch*—certainly as personal in their interpretations—only much less verbose and metaphorically more creative than Przybyszewski's attempt, which Strindberg had claimed to be little more than a paraphrazing of *his* words as picked up by Przybyszewski in their daily associations back in 1893.

Those recalling Strindberg's misogynist broadside in *La Revue Blanche* half a year earlier would have little difficulty recognizing him in the Munch essay. *The Kiss* is seen as the merging of two individuals of which the smaller, in the form of a carp(!), is about to be consumed by the greater in the manner of vermin, microbes, vampires, and women. The painting *Vampire*—exhibited as *Red Hair*—represents man prostrate before woman, pleading for the privilege of being annihilated: "Rain of blood pours down over the crazed one who craves unhappiness, the divine unhappiness of being loved, which is to say, loving."

On the background of Strindberg's current pathological fear of Przybyszewski and even more of Dagny, his thoughts on *Jealousy* (Plates 47 and 48) are of special interest, for they issue forth in righteous wrath as a curse at his pursuer:

> The jealous one says to his rival: "Begone you despicable one. You are warming yourself by the fire I have lit. You will be inhaling my spirit from her mouth. You will be drinking my blood and remain my slave, for it is my spirit that rules you through the woman who has become your master."

It is highly doubtful that Munch at this juncture felt such interpretations to be in keeping with his original intent. On the other hand, never expecting his works to be seen by anyone else precisely as he himself had conceived of them but at best viewed with a measure of sincerity with which they had been painted, he could have found nothing wanting in Strindberg's imaginative visions and poetic manner of interpretation. In two paintings, *Twilight* and *Mystic Shore,* intensely emotional landscape renditions not unlike the much earlier *Inger on the Beach* and *Melancholy,* Strindberg's verbal reproductions come as close to the actual images as a rendition in a totally different medium could possibly allow. In *Twilight* the descending darkness transforms the humans into "ghosts and cadavers the moment they are ready to go home to wrap themselves in the shrouds of their beds and submit to sleep," while *Mystic Shore* shows tree trunks mauled by the surging sea. Yet their roots, still alive, crawl through the arid sand to quench their thirst at the same eternal source, the mother sea, from which Venus has risen, while Adonis has descended from mountains and villages: "They pretend to be viewing the sea lest they drown in a glance that will shake their balance and confuse them into an embrace, so that Venus will become part Adonis and

Adonis part Venus." Had it not been for Strindberg's distinguished, though highly controversial, position in intellectual-creative circles and his intriguing analysis of Munch's works, it is conceivable that the exhibit would have been all but ignored by the press, for critics who set the tone in this art capital of Europe were basically conservative. So also the art dealers. Always busy selling the preceding generations, bemoans Pola Gauguin, they had no time for the artists of the present. "They had not yet had their eyes opened to such artists as Gauguin, Van Gogh, and Seurat, the circle to which Munch seemed most closely akin."[22] Thus Munch experienced no breakthrough in Paris that spring—nor the next when as an invited artist he had his works hung in a place of honor at the *Salon des Indépendants*—and in the sea of Parisian art activities his exhibit at Bing's was a barely detectable ripple to which the press devoted only the most minimal space.

Of the critics who did take time to look in on it some came away with mixed feelings, writing of genius and exaggeration, naivité and profound thought, others with clear convictions, positive or negative. In *Mercure de France* where the untimely death in 1892 of G. Albert Aurier, principal spokesman for the symbolists, had brought about an unfortunate shift in tone, Camille Mauclair, disciple of Mallarmé and the impressionists but a thorn in the side of such artists as Toulouse-Lautrec and Gauguin, flaunted his conservatism by calling Munch's paintings brutal, messy, infantile, and of poor draftsmanship—"as is always the case with artists of this type."

The diametrically opposite point of view was expressed by Ivan Aguëli, a Swedish painter writing for *L'Encyclopedie Contemporaine,* who saw *Sick Girl* as a synthesized drama from everyday life, emotionally so strong that one instinctively senses the presence of a third actor, death. He goes on to describe Munch's dramatic use of color:

> Her reddish hair shines as in a vision, while farthest down to the right a red liquid in a glass reflects a beam of the purest scarlet. Grief, expressed in silent prayers, bends the woman's head. And over the mossy green color tones hover a cloud, pearly gray, simultaneously weighty and light, as the unknown itself. To analyze the artist's technical approach would be a sacrilege.[23]

Again, as in Strindberg's evaluation, it was the emotional quality of his paintings that made the greatest impact, and to the sensitive, unbiased viewer this experience was decidedly deepened by the artist's deliberate elimination of extraneous matter. On the other hand, someone placing primary importance on an orderly, academic approach would find such technical radicalism bewildering and come away from a Munch exhibit with a view as truncated and distorted as that of Mauclair. While Munch no doubt appreciated Strindberg's and Aguëli's imaginative visions of his works, he had little trouble with the pedestrian scorn of Mauclair, for what Zola had once said to Manet's critics applies equally well to Munch's: "Your grimaces and giggles bother him little."

16

The Last Collaboration

After Strindberg's departure from Paris late in the summer of 1896, he and Munch never again met face to face. A combination of circumstances contributed to the permanency of their separation. The geographic distance was certainly not conducive to close contact. Moreover, Strindberg must have nursed a lingering resentment toward Munch rooted in his suspicion of that conspiracy against him on the part of Munch and the Przybyszewskis, and perhaps also in his displeasure with the lithographed portrait with its unmistakable symbolism and flagrantly misspelled name. His final communication with Munch that summer—the postcard accusing him of "looking like a murderer or at least a murderer's handyman"—certainly proves that Munch had become—as stated in *Inferno*—his enemy, and an entire year would elapse before a note in Strindberg's correspondence suggests a possible thaw in his frigid attitude toward his former friend.

Munch, meanwhile, had remained in Paris until the spring of 1897 and, again participating in the Indépendants, finally received some favorable notices. On this basis he was able to sell a little and could afford to buy the small house he had been renting in Åsgårdstrand, the Oslofjord village whose gentle contours had already given so many of his paintings their lyric quality.

In Lund, where Strindberg had settled after an initial stay in Ystad and an unexpected and extended visit with little Kerstin and his in-laws in Austria—an experience of joy and agony, and of spiritual growth[1]—the final copy of *Inferno* was prepared, in May and June of 1897. In this period a mellowing seemed to have taken place in his attitude toward former friends. Thus, after a long silence he resumed his correspondence with Gustaf af Geijerstam, who proved of great help in negotiations with publishers. More surprising was his restored contact with Bengt Lidforss whose suspected treachery in the *Antibarbarus* affair and persistently friendly relations with the Przybyszewskis had at one time appeared unforgivable. Now, presumably encouraged by Lidforss, he also happened to contact Munch again. On July 20 this postcard was written:

> Dear Munch.
>
> Bengt Lidforss reported on his return here that you intended to pass through Lund on your outbound journey to Berlin. As I am living in Lund and intend to go to Berlin I would be pleased to have company on the journey, and you are cordially welcome.
>
> If you would send me a postcard informing me of your arrival I would be grateful.[2]

Nothing came of this travel plan, for Munch, at long last able to relish the simple comfort of staying in his own house, decided to remain in Norway that summer and fall to prepare for the most representative exhibit of his lifetime, scheduled for a period of three weeks in September and October. As for Strindberg, he postponed his departure until late in August, then set out for Paris alone, once more taking up residence on the Left Bank, initially buoyed by the change of scene and feeling more at home than during any previous stay. Yet gradually, inevitably, depression set in, caused in no small measure by what he considered a lack of interest in his presence on the part of earlier acquaintances, a circumstance more reasonably accounted for by the absence of those most intimate with him during his preceding stay. In that state of mind he completed the sequence to *Inferno—Legends* and *Jacob Wrestles*—and shortly thereafter began working on his most creative interpretation of the anguished years 1893 to 1897, the carefully structured yet singularly ambiguous drama, *To Damascus,* part I, his own private *Everyman.* In one of the opening speeches his prevailing mood is poignantly expressed: "I am in a strange city, have not a single friend, and the few acquaintances I do have are worse than strangers to me—I would even say enemies."[3]

With the completion of this first play in more than five years he again felt the need for a change and decided to return to Lund; but he would be a person quite different from the one he had been in his earlier stay, he warned in a letter. "I who am under the continuous scrutiny of invisible powers believe," he solemnly declares, "that I must deny myself some of those small pleasures of life that have been my downfall, most of all—the wine! When I turn homeward it is likely that I will become an ascetic in that respect . . . "[4]

Perhaps an ascetic when it came to wine, in other ways he had changed very little. Toward friends, present and past, he was as unpredictable as ever, and when someone happened to suggest the possibility of another contact with Munch—it would turn out to be the last—he reacted as though his cordial postcard had never been written.

Instrumental in this attempt at bringing the two together again—if only within the covers of a publication—was Emil Schering, then on the threshold of becoming a German translator of Strindberg's most recent works and already the editor of a new avant-garde publication, *Quickborn,* launched for the purpose of presenting a broad international spectrum of modern creative trends. Well in advance of Strindberg's fiftieth birthday, which would occur January 22, 1899, Schering was planning a special edition of his periodical devoted to samples of Strindberg's writings, and, as a particularly bright inspiration—or so Schering himself thought—he had decided to ask Munch to provide illustrations. It would appear, however, that in his initial contact with Strindberg regarding the matter no mention was made of Munch's part, for Strindberg's response—rather lukewarm at the best—concerns literary matters only. "Is it really an advantage to be read in such a fragmentary manner?" he appropriately asks. "I for one think not." But after additional pleas he agrees to let the project proceed, although he feels unable to promise an original manuscript for the occasion. Then follows his reaction to Munch's possible participation:

> As regards Munch, who is my enemy, I sense an unwillingness to cooperate with him, in particular since I am certain he will not miss the opportunity to stab me with a poisoned knife, especially if it is intended that he is to illustrate my pieces. In any event, if we are to be placed together I must ask to see his drawings so that I may exclude whatever is scandalous. These are not idle suspicions but reasonings well rooted in experience.[5]

Assuming that such feelings would be mutual, he adds that it would be best if Schering did not mention to Munch that he, Strindberg, would be contributing to an issue in which *his* drawings would appear.

Why this renewed bitterness? A possible explanation is that Munch, a notoriously poor letter writer, had failed to respond to Strindberg's postcard, on Munch's part no more than a simple oversight but in Strindberg's eyes a deliberate rejection of the extended hand. It could also be that the "new" Strindberg, writer of *Inferno* and *To Damascus,* felt that Munch's particular approach to human emotions was ill suited to the contemporary self-image Strindberg wanted to convey, hence his fear of something "scandalous" in Munch's visual interpretations. Yet deeply obligated to Schering, in particular for his translation of *To Damscus,* he finally relents, though he does not cease grumbling: "I'd be happy if Munch didn't come with his outdated phallic motifs but instead chose his motifs from purely aesthetic considerations, which do not necessarily exclude psychological insight."[6]

The Strindberg-Munch issue of *Quickborn* appeared in October, 1898, and Strindberg, deliberately ignoring Munch's contribution, reacts sullenly to the product: "Many thanks for the copies of *Quickborn.* The name was not a happy choice, the color on the cover is unsympathetic and the reproductions are not first class."[7]

Munch's response to Schering's proposal must from the very outset have been as favorable as Strindberg's was negative, and since he happened to be in Berlin at the time and was in regular contact with Schering he may well have been involved in the plan from its inception, seeing in it a unique opportunity to reciprocate for the article in *La Revue Blanche.* Quietly accepting Strindberg's terms, which must have been relayed to him by Schering, he contributed a series of illustrations—some already familiar to the initiated, others produced for the occasion—which together may be viewed as a brief retrospective of his own career, a testimony to his indebtedness to Strindberg, and a sincere gesture toward reconciliation.

To four contributions by Strindberg—two prose pieces, one of which, despite his original reluctance to promise anything new, was written expressly for that issue of *Quickborn,* a selection of poetry, and a one-act play—Munch provided a dozen illustrations, only a few of these actually inspired by the accompanying text material, but all in one way or another relating to their common source of creative energy and the spirit in which they had associated in Berlin and Paris.

Readers were furnished with visual images of the artists through Munch's *Self-Portrait with a Skeletal Arm* (Plate 2) and his very sensitive lithographed Strindberg portrait. In his prevailing spirit of reconciliation, however, Munch had eliminated the arabesque in the Strindberg portrait, thereby not only reducing its artistic merit but taking away the deeper meaning of the juxtaposition of these particular pictures: Munch with Death and Strindberg with Woman. The cover illustration, however (Plate 51) gives poignant expression to one of the principal wellsprings of each artist: the anguish of the human condition. "One should paint one's inner emotions," Strindberg had said, a statement equally applicable to his writing, and what Munch was attempting to portray "... human beings who breathe and feel and suffer and love." The picture with its stylized decorative features and highly romantic overtones unquestionably indebted to current art nouveau trends, represents a man in deep agony pressing a hand to his heart from where a stream of blood gushes forth to nourish the roots of a stately flower rising to full picture height, the agony and the glory symbolizing the artist's sacrificial devotion to the creative process.

The inclusion of black-and-white reproductions of *Sick Girl* and *Puberty* appears to have retrospective significance to Munch only, but with *Madonna* the reminiscences go back to his early Berlin days with Strindberg, and its inclusion may therefore signify the beginning of their joint presence there, an event of particularly crucial consequence in the development of German creativity.

New and closely related to the text material are two drawings for a prose piece entitled *Toward the Sun,* describing an Alpine ascent Strindberg had once undertaken to break through to the source of light which had remained hidden behind the clouds for three oppressive weeks. Again, in his illustration of the rising sun—a subject Munch would be using again, and monumentally, in his murals in the Aula of Oslo University—his approach is characterized by elegantly flowing, decorative lines in art nouveau manner. The second picture, however, providing a stark contrast to the exuberance of the first and inspired by the text's reference to the people still moving about, trembling, in the dismal grayness below, shows a funeral procession in the pouring rain, drawn with a simplicity and a directness reminiscent of Daumier.

For Strindberg's new piece, a short story entitled *The Silver Moor,* Munch drew a coastal landscape not particularly faithful to the literary description, incorporating instead his own Åsgårdstrand shoreline featuring a tree trunk with demonstratively tentacled roots, as in the painting *Mystic Shore* described by Strindberg in the article in *La Revue Blanche.*

The poetry section of the issue—excerpts from Strindberg's *Sömngångarnätter* [Sleepwalker Nights]—provided the inspiration for Munch's rather grotesque picture, *The Girl and the Heart.* Strindberg, having seen a dripping heart displayed in a butcher shop window, recalled that experience in a poem, comparing it to the melancholy sight of a frugal volume put on view by a book dealer:

> There hangs in the book shop window
> A thinly clad little book.
> It is a heart carved out,
> Suspended there on its hook.[8]

In an article dealing with this special edition of *Quickborn,*[9] Torsten Svedfelt, while stating that Munch's etching cannot have been placed into that particular context entirely without forethought, still claims that it is highly doubtful there is a deeper relationship between poem and picture—a rather surprising and debatable conclusion. That Strindberg intends to parallel the still trembling heart of the slaughtered animal with the creative inspiration and the emotional sacrifice inherent in its ultimate delivery seems self-evident. Munch, picturing a young woman holding in her ritually extended hands a bleeding heart, that of the poet or painter, does of course make use of the very same parallel, except that by placing Woman unmistakably in the pose of a sacrificing priestess he elevates the simile to a universal symbol, showing Woman as the central source of the artistic inspiration, simultaneously creative and destructive. This visual interpretation, though certainly speaking directly to the contents of the poem, is also rooted in Munch's familiarity with a Strindberg far more complex than the one who had written this poem more than ten years earlier. Therefore the picture symbolizes Strindberg in a much broader context, providing, in fact, a more than adequate compensation for Munch's conciliatory elimination of the crucial arabesque in the portrait.

Of a similar ritual quality are Munch's lithographs, *The Kiss of Death* and *Harpy,* free fantasies on the one-act play, *Simoom,* written in 1889 in the acknowledged spirit of Edgar Allan Poe, Strindberg's "literary soul mate,"[10] whose writings became known to him through Ola Hansson back in the days of the Scandinavian Experimental Theatre in Copenhagen. Munch's Poe enthusiasm, no less ardent, was most likely generated by Przybyszewski—though possibly by Strindberg, too—in their early Berlin days, as evidenced in certain paintings from that period, *Death and the Maiden,* for one, possibly *Vampire* and *Ashes,* and quite definitely in many of his subsequent graphic works. It is that shared admiration for Poe that is brought out in Munch's interpretation of *Simoom,* a play by Strindberg himself described as "a brilliant Edgar Poe piece,"[11] but actually departing from its paragon in many essentials:

> The terror of the victim of irrational forces is not its substance... Even less Poesque is the management of the motif of fear-by-suggestion that results in death, a phenomenon that had been reported in current psychiatric literature.[12]

Taking place in a burial chamber in the desert region of Algeria the play deals with the Bedouin craving for revenge against the French usurpers on their land and takes its name from the relentlessly hot, arid desert wind that drives the outsider to madness or death. A Frenchman finds himself at the mercy of a Bedouin girl, Biskra, whose psychic powers are even more destructive than the dreaded desert wind. While Strindberg's interest in the subject extended beyond the Poe motifs into "the battle of the brains... the stronger's conquest of the weaker,"[13] Munch's emphasis is on the macabre, the terrorizing, which of course lends itself far better to the momentary and single image than does the fear-by-suggestion motif which for its effect depends on an extended narrative rendition.

In *The Kiss of Death* Munch takes as his point of departure a scene where the female character, the Bedouin girl Biskra, shows the French officer a skull, making him believe he is seeing his own reflection and thereby, at the zenith of her suggestive power, bringing about his actual death. Munch's lithograph, while unquestionably illustrative of this *Simoom* scene, may also be viewed as a sequel to an earlier graphic work, *Lovers,* representing man and woman, their separate features nearly indistinguishable, as in *The Kiss,* rocking in passionate ecstacy on a sea of desire, only in the *Simoom* version one of the two has been transformed into a skull. The Munchian leitmotif of undulant lines, equally prominent in both, forms a line between this moribund vision of love and desire and such earlier, more elaborate renditions as *Madonna* and, most relevant in the present context, the arabesque in the Strindberg portrait.

Harpy, the second illustration to the Strindberg play, shows the mythological bird-woman monster possessively hovering over a decomposing, nearly skeletal figure on the verge of being buried in the desert sand. Retaining through its arid landscape a point of reference to *Simoom* it presents in reality a profoundly pessimistic image of the inevitably destructive consequence of the relationship between man and woman, and is therefore a commentary on Strindberg's persistent misogynist view.

Ingrid Langaard and Torsten Svedfelt both stress that in the Strindberg-Munch edition of *Quickborn* it is not a question of a collaboration between two artists but rather an attempt on Munch's part to provide the Strindberg texts with picture material that at least in its broadest context would appear relevant. Yet a careful analysis of text and pictures clearly shows that Munch, whether using old or new material, approached his task with total sincerity and entirely without the satire or bias Strindberg had feared. Accepting his own role as subservient to Strindberg's he succeeded not only in providing meaningful illustrative material to the available texts but through his own instinctive and intimate knowledge of the Strindbergian mystique gave the entire presentation a cohesive quality that would otherwise have been missing.

Strindberg must have failed to detect any such merit in the finished product, for in a letter to Richard Bergh, written shortly after the publication of the *Quickborn* edition, he acidly observes:

> Tomorrow I'll be sending you Munch's latest masterpieces in the grotesque, which I abhor. In seven years he has found no new purpose, has not even discovered a new cause he may caricature.[14]

Thus, instead of effecting the reconciliation Munch may have been hoping for, this last direct manifestation of their relationship appears rather to have intensified Strindberg's hostility toward the artist he had once closely and proudly associated with and acclaimed as a key figure in "the Scandinavian Renaissance."

As for Munch, although he left no special record of his disappointment in this adverse reaction on the part of Strindberg, he must have felt deeply disheartened at the outcome of the project and more specifically the finality of the break. That the bitterness was not mutual is shown in Munch's continued feeling of admiration for Strindberg as verified in statements to friends, such as those recalled by Inger Alver Gløersen, who in her reminiscences of Munch notes that whenever their conversation turned to Strindberg—"and that was not infrequently"—his facial expression invariably became troubled, so much so that it was easy to understand that the loss of Strindberg's friendship was one of the great sorrows life had bestowed on him. "Spiritually giving, that's what we must be," she remembers Munch saying—"especially in the arts. And Strindberg kept giving."[15]

Although this unique friendship between two of the most extraordinary members of the Scandinavian creative community in the 1890s extended over a mere four years, during which the direct contact between them was actually limited to periods of a few troubled months in Berlin and Paris, it is clearly reflected in the works of each artist, first and foremost those produced during or immediately following the actual days they were together but also in many of their subsequent efforts. Strindberg's autobiographical writings from the 1890s, in which their relationship was a feature of some importance, led to dramas that would revitalize that entire medium of expression: *To Damascus, A Dream Play,* and ultimately his highly concentrated, visually simplified and synthesized chamber plays. One of these, *The Ghost Sonata,* despite its final coda of a tremulously ethereal sound of the harp and a vision of Böcklin's otherworldly serene *Isle of the Dead,* comes across as a haunting, dissonant echo of the decadence, sickness, and death so characteristic of Munch's early paintings. The awesome display of the devastating relationship between man and woman in *The Dance of Death* certainly had its close parallels in Munch's paintings and graphics from the 1890s, most of which evolved from experiences and associations with Strindberg and his gradually diminishing entourage.

When discussed in the broader context of modern art history Munch's contribution is more often than not limited to his works from the late 1880s and throughout the 1890s, those in the latter group, as these pages have attempted to show, to a great extent influenced or inspired by Strindberg. However, in Munch's life "Strindberg kept giving." This is shown not only in Munch's continued preoccupation with earlier themes—*Jealousy, Woman in Three Stages, Vampire* and their starkly synthesized graphic versions, his equivalent of Strindberg's chamber plays—but in many later works as well, such as his planting sequences with Adam and Eve and the implicit temptation, the pronounced misogynist canvases variously entitled *The Murderess* and *The Death of Marat,* and certainly *The Dance of Life* with its pessimistic view of the power of Eros. On the opposite side of the coin is the possibility, already suggested, that Munch's monumental manifestation of his slowly, painfully gained belief in a positive force behind all human striving, his mural *The Rising Sun,* may also have been inspired by Strindberg.

Many years after their friendship had been dissolved a token of Munch's continued admiration must have reached Strindberg, most likely on the occasion of his sixtieth birthday, for in the archives of the Munch Museum in Oslo there is an acknowledgement of this in a postcard from Strindberg, containing one single word which in its sincere simplicity may speak equally for both artists: *"Tack."*

Appendix

Notes on Personalities Mentioned in the Book

[Individuals of broad international fame, e.g., Ibsen, Grieg, Gauguin, Sibelius, etc., have not been included.]

Ancher, Anna, (1859-1935) and Michael (1849-1927), wife and husband. Danish painters who belong to the so-called Skagen group, Realists gathering in the summer months at the northernmost point of the Jutland peninsula and depicting life among the fisherfolk there. Anna concentrated on the women and interior views; Michael dealt with the out-of-doors; both with an increasingly bright palette as they approached the change of the century.

Backer, Harriet (1845-1932), Norwegian impressionist painter whose sunny interiors blended a quality of preciseness learned in Munich and an intriguing interplay of light and shadow acquired in Paris, where she studied with Leon Bonnat, who later became Munch's teacher. She herself established a private art academy in Norway and was of great influence in the development of Norwegian art.

Ballin, Mogens (1871-1914), Danish painter and craftsman who in 1889-1892, while in France, belonged to Gauguin's inner circle of friends. In Denmark he became a principal spokesman for Symbolism. His production as a painter was limited, but in the growing creative crafts movement he was a pioneer.

Bang, Herman (1857-1912), Danish prose writer whose 1890 novel *Generations without Hope* was symptomatic of early *fin de siècle* decadence in Scandinavia. From such rather fashionable emphasis on the pessimistic in society he developed into an exceptionally sensitive short-story writer compassionately siding with the poor, the neglected, and the downtrodden.

Bergh, Richard (1858-1919), Swedish painter known for his realistic genre pictures, among which is *An Hypnotic Seance* (1887), now in Stockholm's National Museum. A lifelong friend of Strindberg, Richard Bergh produced one of the most sensitive of the many portraits painted of the dramatist in the 1890s.

Bjørnson, Bjørnstjerne (1832-1910), Norwegian poet, novelist, and dramatist whose popularity and influence in Norway clearly surpassed that of his far more internationally famous contemporary, Henrik Ibsen. Bjørnson's robustly extrovert attitude, his often parochial patriotism and, not the least, his traditional view of the visual arts, made him a thorn in Munch's side.

Böcklin, Arnold (1827-1901), Swiss painter. Because much of his early creative life was spent in Düsseldorf, Weimar, and Munich, Böcklin is often haphazardly included in discussions of nineteenth century German art. However, he maintained his allegiance to his Swiss homeland and tradition. To Strindberg and Munch he was a source of inspiration, but in reality only through his serenely moody *Isle of the Dead* (1881). Versions in Dresden, Basel, and New York.

Brandes, Edvard (1847-1931), Danish writer and politician, with his brother Georg one of the most influential of Scandinavian literary critics. He was instrumental in bringing Strindberg to Copenhagen in 1888.

Brandes, Georg (1842-1927), Danish critic whose lecture series *Main Currents in 19th Century European Literature* ushered in Scandinavian realism. No Scandinavian writer of any consequence remained unaffected by Brandes's demand for a new, contemporary approach to the art of writing. His voluminous biographical studies of such personalities as Michelangelo, Shakespeare, and Goethe have become classics in the field.

Bull, Ole (1810-1880), Norwegian violinist and cultural leader. The first nineteenth century Norwegian to gain Europe-wide fame, Ole Bull served his nation as a cultural ambassador and at home inspired the development of national literature and drama.

Cappelen, August (1827-1852), Norwegian painter, educated in Düsseldorf under his countryman Hans Gude. His moody representations of forests and rivers are a foreshadowing of expressionistic landscape art.

Cederström, Gustaf (1845-1933), Swedish history painter, famed in particular for his *Funeral of Charles XII* exhibited at the Paris World's Fair in 1878. Subjects of more contemporary orientation show Cederström's indebtedness to Courbet.

Dahl, Johan Christian (1788-1857), Norway's foremost landscape artist, educated in Copenhagen and Dresden where he became a professor at the Academy and a close friend of Caspar David Friedrich. Dahl's monumental landscapes of Norwegian fjords and mountains, his intimately poetic renditions of crofts and farms, made him the principal exponent of National Romanticism in the arts.

Dauthendey, Max (1867-1918), German poet drawn to the instantenous inspiration of Impressionism and the psychologically oriented subject matter of Expressionism. In the early 1890s he appeared in Berlin and was deeply influenced by Munch's emotional approach to the visual arts.

Dehmel, Richard (1863-1920), German lyric poet, member of Strindberg's Berlin group and one of the founders of the periodical *Pan.* His poetry, initially inspired by Impressionist tendencies, later became pondrously introvert and erotic, no doubt a result of the company he kept.

Delius, Frederick (1863-1934), British Neo-Romantic composer deeply indebted to Scandinavian creativity, the music of Sibelius and especially Grieg, whose spirit re-echoes in a tone poem such as *On Hearing the First Cuckoo in the Spring;* also to the Danish novelist Jens Peter Jacobsen, whose Naturalistic work *Niels Lyhne* provided the libretto for his opera *Fennimore and Gerda,* and to Munch, who portrayed him in a sensitive lithograph.

Drachmann, Holger (1846-1908), Danish painter and poet, a Neo-Romantic influenced by the life and work of Lord Byron. An extended stay in London in the early 1870s put him in contact with

British and French revolutionaries and brought an end to his Romantic view, although a certain extravagant flair stayed with him throughout his creative life. His poetry, among the finest in Danish literature, is strongly marked by a keen sense of the visual clearly attributable to his training as a painter.

Ekström, Per (1844-1935), Swedish landscape artist inspired by Corot and the Barbizonians. Spent fifteen years in Paris (1876-1901) but remained dedicated to the Swedish landscape which he reproduced in pictures characterized by a moody, mystic twilight. The character, Sellén, in *The Red Room* is modeled on Ekström.

Eugen, Prince of the House of Bernadotte (1865-1947), Swedish painter deeply inspired by Romantic landscape art, not the least that of the Norwegians Dahl and Gude. His stay in Paris in the late 1880s deepened his poetic sensitivity and subsequent landscapes such as *The Old Castle* (1893), Valdemarsudde Collection, Stockholm), and *The Cloud* (1895, Gothenburg Art Museum) are mood paintings inspired by sources as diverse as French Symbolism and Swedish Neo-Romantic literature.

Gallén-Kallela, Axel (1865-1931), one of Finland's leading painters. Initially a Naturalist and open-air artist he later submerged himself in the Finnish national idiom and, no doubt inspired by Sibelius, produced a series of stylized, expressive images rooted in the Kalevala epic. In Berlin in the 1890s he painted an exceptionally sensitive portrait of Munch.

Garborg, Arne (1851-1924), Norwegian poet and novelist, a central figure in late nineteenth and early twentieth century Scandinavian culture; principal exponent of the Norwegian vernacular language movement. While his novels from the 1880s bear the imprint of Naturalism and the Bohème attitude of Hans Jaeger and his coterie, later works in prose and poetry, such as the novels *Peace* (1892), *The Lost Father* (1892), and in particular the collection of poetry *The Hill Maiden* (1895), reflect the tendencies of Symbolism and Neo-Romanticism.

Gauguin, Pola (1883-1961), the son of Paul Gauguin, born in Paris but grew up in Denmark when his mother and father separated prior to the father's departure for Oceania. Pola Gauguin settled in Norway, initially as a painter and teacher but later as a journalist and art critic. He wrote very subjective but highly readable biographies of Munch, Christian Krohg, and his own father.

Geijerstam, Gustaf af (1858-1909), Swedish novelist and critic, a leader of the so-called "Young Sweden" group dedicated to the creation of a modern Swedish literature in keeping with the issues put forward by Georg Brandes in 1871. While important in his own days and successful with two particular novels, *Erik Grane* (1885) and *Pastor Hallin* (1887), Geijerstam's significance waned quickly.

Goldstein, Emanuel (1862-1921), Danish poet. His 1886 collection entitled *Vekselspill* (Exchanges) was reissued in 1892 with a new title *Alruner* (Mandrakes) and a frontispiece by Munch derived from the subject *Melancholy*. He also translated French *fin de siècle* literature into Danish.

Gude, Hans (1825-1903), leading Norwegian landscape artist and distinguished teacher, first in Duesseldorf then in Karlsruhe and Berlin. His influence on the subsequent generation of painters in Norway and also Sweden was considerable. His own landscapes bear the indelible imprint of Romanticism as practiced in Dusseldorf, although his journeys in the British Isles in the 1860s freed his approach to the out-of-doors.

Hansson, Ola (1860-1925), Swedish author and journalist whose sexually oriented *Sensitiva Amorosa* (1887) marked a new attitude in Swedish prose. It was that work that brought his name to the attention of Strindberg, with the result that Hansson, who from 1889 resided in Berlin, invited Strindberg to join him there and be part of the new and exciting creative life that was brewing in the Prussion capital. Hansson produced novels, poems, and essays in Swedish as well as in German but in his later years never attained the lyric tone, the sensitive perception, or intriguing mysticism that made him triumph in his youth.

Hartleben, Otto Erich (1864-1905), German writer; naturalist and social critic in his early works. A free attitude toward eroticism is perhaps influenced by his presence in the *Ferkel* group in the early 1890s. His tragedy, *Rosenmontag* [Monday of Roses], first performed in 1900, remained his greatest success.

Heiberg, Gunnar (1857-1929), next to Ibsen Norway's leading dramatist. Rooted in the spirit of the 1880s with its Bohème movement and Ibsen's pioneering plays on contemporary issues, Heiberg became an active spokesman for a new generation of writers and artist, including Munch, although the friendship between them, dating from *The Black Pig* group in Berlin, did not last.

Heidenstam, Verner von (1859-1940), Swedish novelist and Nobel laureate. Early friend and supporter of Strindberg in whose company he visited Italy in 1885. Heidenstam's essay collection *Renaissance* (1889) contributed to a renewed interest in aesthetic ideals and imagination and the ushering in of the Neo-Romantic movement.

Hill, Carl Fredrik (1849-1911), Swedish Impressionist painter. By the age of thirty he was beginning to suffer from emotional disturbances which would ultimately keep him in confinement until his death. Prior to that, however, he had produced some magnificently sensitive representations of the French countryside in a manner inspired by Corot and the Barbizonians, but with colors and brushwork closely related to that of the Impressionists. Most of his works are in Stockholm's National Museum.

Jaeger, Hans (1854-1910), Norwegian writer and social rebel, leader of the movement he described in his novel *From the Life of the Kristiania Bohème* (1885). An attack on the establishment in the Norwegian capital—government bureacracy, church, the judicial system—it caused his indictment for public indecency and his imprisonment. Munch, who remained an admirer of Jaeger, painted his portrait in 1889.

Jensen-Hjell, Karl (1861-1888), Norwegian painter, student of Frits Thaulow, and close friend of Munch who portrayed him in 1885.

Josephson, Ernst (1851-1906), Swedish painter, inspired by Courbet and Manet but with a tendency toward Romanticism and symbolic imagery. *The Water Sprite* (1882) in Stockholm's National Museum combines traditional Romanticism with a strong emotional element pointing toward Expressionism. *Spanish Blacksmiths* (1882) in the National Gallery in Oslo shows his admiration for the Venetians, Velazquez, and Rembrandt. Josephson was instrumental in the opposition to Swedish academic art in the 1880s and thereby contributed immeasurably to the progressive spirit characteristic of Swedish visual creativity in the latter part of the century.

Kielland, Valentin (1866-1944), Norwegian sculptor, friend of Munch, who shared living quarters with him in Paris in 1889. His works are marked by a strong social awareness rooted in French Naturalism.

Krag, Vilhelm (1871-1933), Norwegian poet whose early efforts echoed much of Munch's creative concern. Such psychological probings, however, soon yielded to his overwhelming love for his home territory on the rocky south coast of Norway, a landscape Munch would later depict in his murals in the Festival Hall of Oslo University.

Krohg, Christian (1852-1925), Norwegian Realist-Impressionist painter, adviser to Munch and other young Norwegians in the 1880s. Born into a distinguished and conservative family, not unlike that of Munch, Krohg broke with his past and became in words and pictures a spokesman for the most progressive tendencies of the day. His *Albertine* or *In the Waiting Room of the Police Physician* (1886-1888) is generally considered to be the prototype of Naturalism in Norwegian art. Later works have a color exuberance and a brush technique decidedly acquired through his prolonged stays in Paris.

Kronberg, Julius (1850-1921), Swedish painter trained in Munich, where his continued exposure to works of the Baroque period determined his own mastery of color and composition. While he carried out the monumental decorations of the ceiling in the entry hall of Stockholm's Royal Palace—completed with a Tiepolo-like bravura—his most popular work remains The *Hunter's Nymph* (1875) in the National Museum, a painting much admired by Strindberg.

Krøyer, Peter (1851-1909), Denmark's most popular painter in the last decades of the nineteenth century, adept at interior genre paintings but a virtuoso with his treatment of the interplay of light and shadow in open-air canvases depicting people and landscape at the northernmost point of the Jutland penisula, where he painted with the Anchers and Christian Krohg.

Larsson, Carl (1853-1919), one of Sweden's most beloved painters and illustrators, and long-time friend of Strindberg. In 1883 Strindberg left Sweden to join Larsson and his family at Grez-sur-Loing on the edge of the Fontainebleau Forest in France. The National Museum in Stockholm shows a major oil painting of Larsson's brilliantly depicting a Swedish winter landscape, and the entry hall of the museum contains his monumental ceiling paintings. However, his principal strength as an artist is found in his intimate watercolors from his rustic home in Dalecarlia where the activities of his wife and children, indoor and out and in the shifting seasons, continually inspired his creativity.

Leistikow, Walter (1865-1908), German painter. Active participant on the side of the visiting artist in the turmoil following the closing of the Munch exhibit in Berlin in 1892 and later a prime mover in the Berlin Secession. His moody landscapes in impressionist style favor the spacious heaths and moors of North Germany.

Munch, Andreas (1811-1884), Norwegian poet and dramatist, relative of Edvard Munch. He was the first recipient of the Norwegian government's artist's annuity and was given the honorary title 'professor' for his contribution to national literature.

Munch, Peter Andreas (1810-1863), Norway's foremost historian in the nineteenth century; Edvard Munch's uncle. His history books were read aloud in the home of his brother Christian, the physician who was Edvard's father. P.A. Munch's enormous contribution to Norwegian historical scholarship—his *History of Norway,* brought to the year 1397, numbered 8 volumes—constitutes a key element in the nations' drive for cultural independence.

Nilssen, Jappe (1870-1931), Norwegian writer and art critic, was a friend of Edvard Munch who posed him on the boulders on the shore of the Oslofjord in the series of paintings and graphics entitled *Melancholy*. His progressive reviews of contemporary art in *Dagbladet* paved the way for a broad acceptance of newer trends among art patrons and the public. Nilssen understood and appreciated Munch's particular approach long before the artist gained general acceptance.

Nordström, Karl (1855-1923), Swedish landscape artist, member of the group residing in Grez-sur-Loing in the 1880s. At that time his paintings moved ever closer to French Impressionism with airy skyscapes and sunbaked fields. Back in Sweden he gradually developed a new and independent approach in which form and color contributed to a particularly dramatic representation of his subjects.

Normann, Adelsteen (1848-1918), Norwegian painter trained in Duesseldorf whose glossy West Norwegian landscapes became very popular in Prussia in the 1880s. He took the initiative for Munch's first exhibition in Berlin in 1892.

Obstfelder, Sigbjørn (1866-1900), Norwegian poet, perhaps the single most admired lyricist in the generation following Ibsen and Bjørnson. His free-flowing style, his veiled but highly imaginative metaphors, and his pessimistic bent are by many considered the literary parallels to Munch's visual expressions. Munch's lithograph of Obstfelder (1897) is one of his finest achievements in portraiture.

Paul, Adolf (1863-1943), Swedo-Finnish author, a radical Naturalist who in the 1890s wrote some works dealing so openly with erotic subject matter that one of them, *The Ripper* (1891) was confiscated by the authorities. During Strindberg's early days in Berlin Paul served as his principal mentor and protecter, not always to Strindberg's satisfaction. Paul's *My Strindberg Book,* memoirs of their mutual stay in Berlin, is considered rather biased.

Schlittgen, Hermann (1859-1930), German painter, illustrator, and printmaker. As a portrait artist he is represented in museums throughout Germany, and as an illustrator in the publication *Fliegende Blätter* he established himself as a leading caricaturist in the manner of Daumier.

Segelcke, Severin (1867-1940), Norwegian portrait artist and lithographer who produced a number of successful pictures of Norwegian cultural personalities but whose single most successful work is his portrait of Strindberg painted in Berlin in 1893.

Snoilsky, Carl (1841-1903), Swedish poet and cultural leader, a pioneer in the new literary trends of the 1880s and 1890s. His three collections published in 1883, 1887, and 1897 are among the finest achievements in Swedish poetry. Snoilsky is generally assumed to have been Ibsen's model for Johannes Rosmer in *Rosmersholm,* which in part accounts for Munch's excitement at having met him in Stockholm in 1894.

Stuck, Franz von (1863-1928), German artist, leading spirit in the Munich Secession. His painting *The Sin,* a sensual portrait of a woman, seems inspired by Munch's *Madonna,* while Munch's later lithograph, also entitled *The Sin,* may in turn have been influenced by Stuck.

Sudermann, Hermann (1857-1928), German writer, naturalist. When meeting Strindberg in Berlin in 1893 he had already made a name for himself with the novel *Frau Sorge* (1887) and two very successful plays, *Honor* (1889) and *Homeland* (1891).

Tavaststjerna, Karl August (1860-1898), Swedo-Finnish writer. In 1886 the publication of his *Barndomsvänner* [Childhood Friends] marks the beginning of realism in the Swedo-Finnish novel. In his brief career Tavaststjerna wrote a play, short stories, and several collections of poetry, much of this considered essential in the development of modern Finnish literature.

Thaulow, Frits (1847-1906), Norwegian painter and spokesman for modern trends in the visual arts. Trained by Gude in Karlsruhe, 1873-1875, he soon settled in Paris where he gained much from his exposure to and friendship with Impressionists and Post-Impressionists. From the early 1880s until his death he exhibited regularly at the Paris Salon and received widespread recognition as a fine colorist. His early discovery of Munch's exceptional talent is much to his credit.

Thegerström, Robert (1857-1919), Swedish portrait artist who belonged to the Grez-sur-Loing group and also painted with Strindberg in the Stockholm archipelago.

Thiis, Jens (1870-1942), Norwegian art historian and museologist. As director of Norway's National Gallery and lecturer in art history at Oslo University, Thiis exerted greater influence on Norwegian art than any other theoretician. He was instrumental in the acquisition of Munch's principal works for the National Gallery. In 1933 his *Edvard Munch og hans samtid* (Edvard Munch and His Time) was published simultaneously with Pola Gauguin's volume on the same subject. Ragna Stang (1909-1978), whose *Edvard Munch: the Man and His Art,* was published in 1977, was Jens Thiis's daughter.

Tidemand, Adolf (1814-1876), Norwegian painter, portrayer of folk life and tradition. As a teacher at the Duesseldorf Academy he exerted great influence on Norwegian and Swedish students, and his formal canvases incorporating multicolored national costumes and silvery ornaments elevated him into a position of prominence not only in Norway but throughout the Germanic world. Late in his career he felt drawn toward naturalistic subjects, and his painting *Starvation* (1874) in the Kristiansand Permanent Gallery brings the social-realist element into Norwegian art.

Vigeland, Gustav (1869-1943), Norway's leading sculptor, creator of the vast layout of Oslo's Frogner Park. Although influenced by Rodin and Maillol, Vigeland demonstrates in most of his works a rich and original imagination funneled into a deep admiration for the creative spirit itself—shown in his monuments to such individuals as the mathematician Abel, the composer Nordraak, and the poet Wergeland. Initially part of the group gathering at *The Black Pig* in Berlin, he soon had a falling-out with Munch and the two, although spending most of their mature years within easy reach of each other in Oslo, remained estranged for the remainder of their lives.

Wahlberg, Alfred (1834-1906), Swedish artist known for his moody landscapes in the manner of Daubigny of the Barbizon School. Strindberg, especially, was impressed with this sort of intimate portrayal of nature and remained a faithful admirer of his compatriot's paintings, which also gained the approval of the Paris Salon and the French public in general.

Welhaven, Johan Sebastian (1807-1873), Norwegian poet, essayist, and arbiter of taste. Favoring a continuation of the nation's cultural relationship with Denmark he became the spokesman for a conservative group of writers and intellectuals in opposition to the radical, patriotic element gathering around Henrik Wergeland, whose writings and viewpoint Welhaven considered primitive and narrow. His poetry, particularly balladry rooted in Norwegian legend and folklore, reveals a fine sensitivity toward his medium and a deep love for tradition and landscape.

Wentzel, Gustav (1859-1927), Norwegian realist painter, student of Christian Krohg but without his teacher's broad outlook and flexible attitude toward the creative act. His two canvases entitled *Breakfast* (1882 and 1885) in the National Gallery in Oslo remain the prototypes of detached realism in Norwegian art.

Werenskjold, Erik (1855-1938), distinguished Norwegian painter and illustrater who in his art combined a healthy naturalistic attitude with a deep sensitivity toward Norwegian landscape and folklore. Educated in Munich and Paris, where he learned to appreciate the French for their treatment of color, form, and their attitude toward nature. Werenskjold was an early and consistent admirer of Munch.

Wergeland, Henrik (1808-1845), Norwegian poet and national leader, the nation's "uncrowned king" in the first half of the nineteenth century. Many consider Wergeland to be the greatest literary genius Norway has fostered, and his principal competitors for the distinction, Ibsen and Bjørnson, would no doubt have concurred. His immense popularity, which made him a legend in his own time, derived not only from his profuse literary activities but also his ceaseless strivings for the betterment of the masses. He was without doubt the single most important socio-cultural figure in nienteenth century Norway.

Werner, Anton von (1843-1915), German painter. Early in his career Werner became a professor of the Berlin Academy, later its director. His monumental paintings depicting historical battle scenes and imperial public events were highly favored by the kaiser and established the artist as a principal spokesman for a traditional approach to the arts. In the turmoil following the closing of the Munch exhibit in 1892 he represented the conservative element.

Weyr, Rudolf (1847-1914), Austrian sculptor, married to Marie Uhl, Frida's sister. He gained prominence with his successful entry in a competition for a medal design for the Vienna World's Fair in 1873. His best known major work is the complex monument to the dramatist Grillparzer, designed in 1878 and completed several years later in cooperation with Carl Kundmann. Throughout Austria there are monuments by Weyr, among them that to Johannes Brahms in Vienna. His works, decorative, skilled, imaginative, are rooted in naturalist tendencies but with strong leanings toward the Baroque.

Willumsen, Ferdinand (1863-1958), Danish painter, graphic artist, sculptor, and architect. In France in the 1880s he became a member of Gauguin's group in Brittany, and his inclination toward bright, broad color surfaces remained a permanent feature in his paintings. Next to Munch, Willumsen was probably the most widely acknowledged Scandinavian painter of that generation. His works are found in museums throughout Europe, but his principal collection is housed in his home at Frederikssund, not far from Copenhagen.

3. J.C. Dahl: *Stugunøset Mountain.* 1851.

4. J.C. Dahl: *Fjord Landscape in Sogn.* 1827.

5. Chr. Krohg: *In the Waiting Room of the Police Physician.* 1886-87.

6. Chr. Krohg: *Sleeping Mother and Child.* 1883.

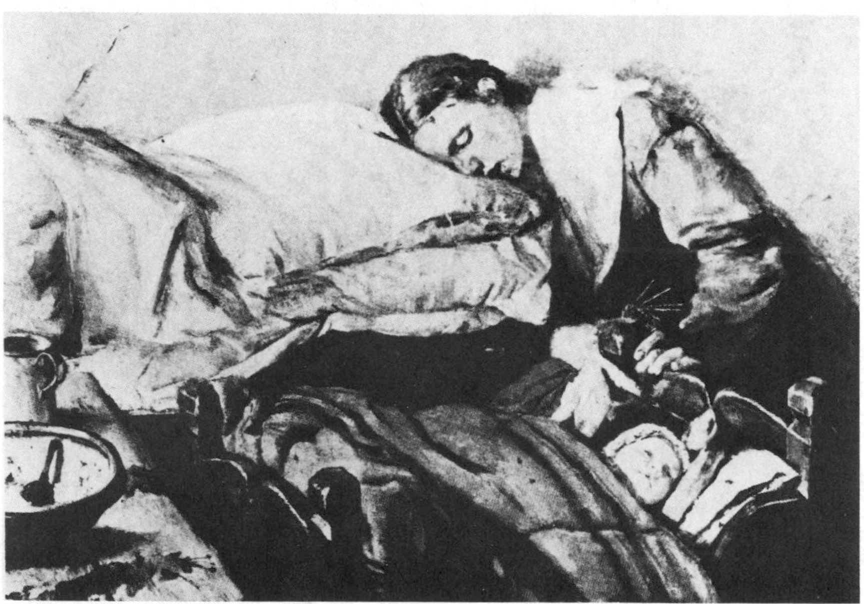

7. Edv. Munch: *Early Morning.* 1883.

8. Edv. Munch: *Portrait of Jensen-Hjell.* 1885.

9. Edouard Manet: *The Absinth Drinker.* 1859-60.

10. Edv. Munch: *Morning*. 1884.

11. Edv. Munch: *Tête-à-tête*. 1884.

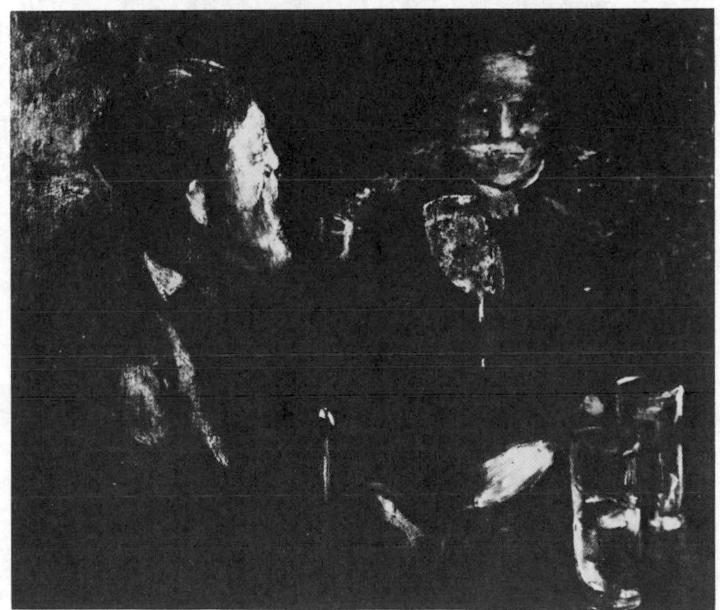

12. Edv. Munch: *Sick Girl.* 1885-86.

13. Chr. Krohg: *Sick Child.* 1880.

14. Edv. Munch: *Sick Girl.* 1885-86. Detail.

15. Edv. Munch: *Sick Girl.* 1896. Lithograph.

16. Edv. Munch: *Springtime.* 1889.

17. Edv. Munch: *Portrait of Hans Jaeger*. 1889.

18. Edouard Manet: *Portrait of Stéphane Mallarmé*. 1876.

19. Edv. Munch: *Evening (Inger on the Beach)*. 1889.

20. Edv. Munch: *Attraction.* 1896. Lithograph.

21. Edv. Munch: *Separation.* 1896. Lithograph.

22. Aug. Strindberg: *White Sailing Mark*. 1892.

23. Aug. Strindberg: *Sailing Mark*. 1892.

24. Edv. Munch: *Music at Karl Johan Street.* 1889.

25. Edv. Munch: *Rue Lafayette.* 1891.

26. Edv. Munch: *Summer Day at Karl Johan Street.* 1891.

27. Edv. Munch: *Evening at Karl Johan Street.* 1892.

28. Edv. Munch: *The Kiss*. 1892. Drypoint and aquatint.

29. Pierre Puvis de Chavannes: *The Poor Fisherman.* 1881.

30. Arnold Böcklin: *The Isle of the Dead.* 1880.

31. Edv. Munch: *A Swan (Vision).* 1892.

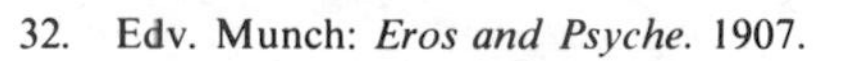

32. Edv. Munch: *Eros and Psyche.* 1907.

33. Edv. Munch: *Puberty*. 1893-94.

34. Edv. Munch: *The Day Thereafter*. 1893-94.

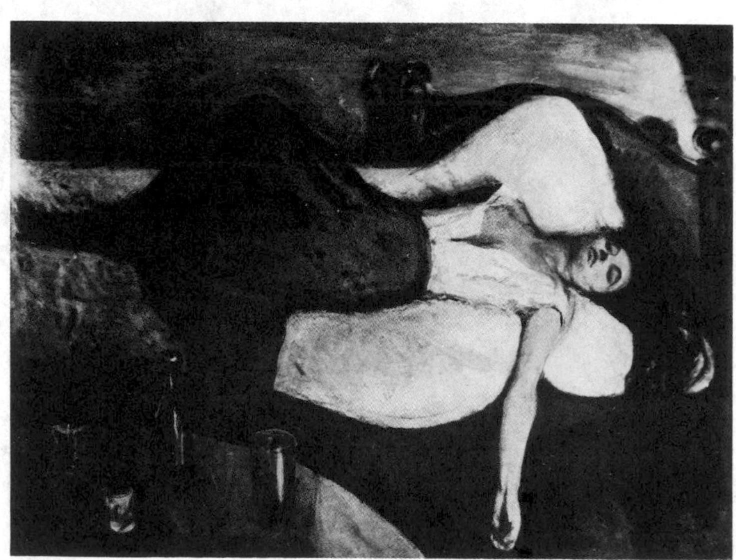

35. Edv. Munch: *Portrait of Strindberg.* 1892.

36. Chr. Krohg: *Portrait of Strindberg.* 1893.

37. Edv. Munch: *Portrait of Dagny Juell Przybyszewska.* 1893.

38. Edv. Munch: *Portrait of Stanislaw Przybyszewski.* 1893.

39. Edv. Munch: *The Hands.* 1893.

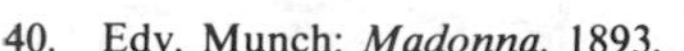

40. Edv. Munch: *Madonna.* 1893.

41. Edv. Munch: *Vampire*. 1893.

42. Edv. Munch: *The Shriek*. 1893.

43. Aug. Strindberg: *Night of Jealousy*. 1893.

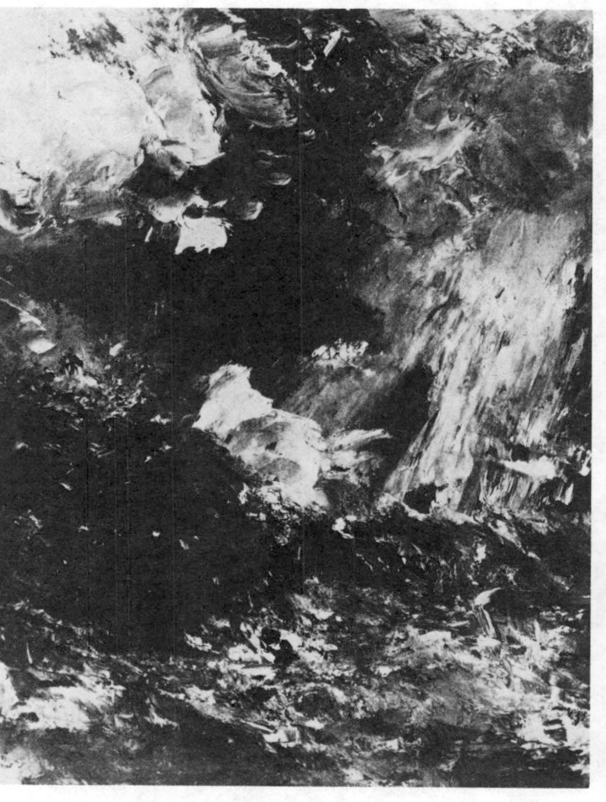

44. Aug. Strindberg: *The Wave*. 1892.

45. Arnold Böcklin: *Self-Portrait with Death Playing the Fiddle.* 1872.

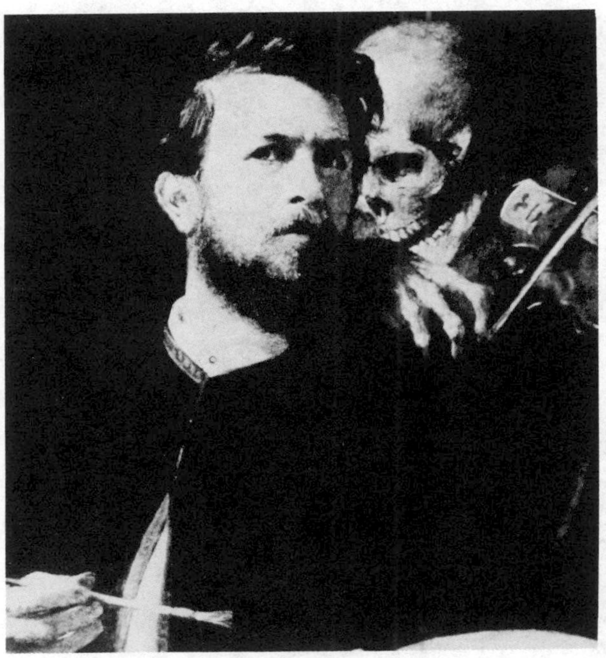

46. Edvard Munch: *Self-Portrait with Cigarette.* 1895

47. Edv. Munch: *Jealousy.* 1895.

48. Edv. Munch: *Jealousy.* 1901.

49. Edv. Munch: *Self-Portrait under a Female Mask.* 1892-93.

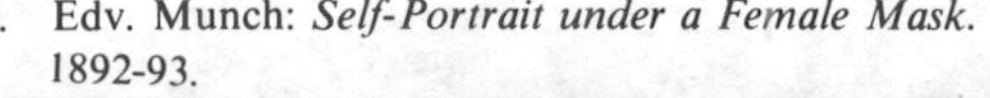

50. Edv. Munch: *Death and the Maiden.* 1893-94.

51. Edv. Munch: *The Blossom of Pain.* 1897. (Cover for *Quickborn* publication).

Notes

Chapter 1

1. The Norwegian capital, in the Middle Ages called Oslo, was renamed Christiania when the Dano-Norwegian king, Christian IV, rebuilt the city in the seventeenth century. In 1880 the spelling was changed to Kristiania, and the name was retained until the medieval name was restored in 1924.

2. August Strindberg, *August Strindbergs Brev*. Utgivna av Torsten Eklund. Stockholm: Albert Bonniers Förlag, 1948 to 1974. Vol III, pp. 296, 300. (Strindberg's letters as quoted have been translated by the author.)

3. Ibid., pp. 307-8.

4. August Strindberg, *Dikter på vers och prosa*. Stockholm: Albert Bonniers Förlag, 1883. p. 216 (trans.).

5. *Strindbergs Brev*, vol. III, pp. 325, 365-66. (The article and the poem, with the three-column photo of Strindberg, appeared in January 1884.)

6. Curiously, a then virtually unknown Frenchman, Paul Gauguin, happened to be represented at the same exhibit with three canvases.

7. Ingrid Langaard, *Edvard Munch: Modningsår*. Oslo: Gyldendal Norsk Forlag, 1960. p. 12 (trans.).

8. Ibid.

Chapter 2

1. *Stockholm och dets omgifningar*. 7th edition. Stockholm: Albert Bonniers Förlag, 1897. p. 8 (trans.).

2. August Strindberg, *Samlade Skrifter*. Utgivna av John Landquist. Stockholm: Albert Bonniers Förlag, 1911-1922. Vol. V, p. 351. (All quotes from *Samlade Skrifter* have, unless otherwise indicated, been translated by the author.)

3. *Perspektiv på Röda rummet*. Erend och Ulla-Britta Lagerroth, editors. Stockholm: Rabén & Sjögren, 1971. P. 82 (trans.).

4. *Samlade Skrifter*, vol. V, p. 374.

5. Birgitta Steene, *The Greatest Fire: A Study of August Strindberg*. Carbondale, Illinois: Southern Illinois University Press, 1973. P. 21.

6. A few days after her marriage to Strindberg, Siri von Essen gave birth to a child that died within a week. While no source of contention in the first years of their marriage this evoked much ill feeling and suspicion on the part of Strindberg as the marriage entered its most turbulent state in the 1880s.
7. *Samlade Skrifter,* vol. IX, pp. 179, 263.
8. Ibid., vol. X, pp. 69-71 and 87-99.
9. August Strindberg, *August Strindbergs Brev.* Utgivna av Torsten Eklund. Stockholm: Albert Bonniers Förlag, 1948 to 1973. Vol. III, p. 5.
10. *Strindbergs Brev,* vol. III, pp. 6-7 and 10-11. (Carl Larsson was being threatened with a paternity suit.)
11. Ibid., pp. 47-48 and 52.
12. Ibid., vol. III, pp. 188, 199.
13. Ibid., vol. III, p. 242.
14. Ibid., p. 267.
15. Carl Larsson, *Jag.* Stockholm: Albert Bonniers Förlag, 2nd ed., 1961. pp. 159-160 (trans.).
16. *Samlade Skrifter,* vol. IV, pp. 149-50, and vol. XIX, p. 196.

Chapter 3

1. August Strindberg, *Samlade Skrifter.* Utgivna av John Landquist. Stockholm: Albert Bonniers Förlag, 1911-1922, vol. V, p. 351.
2. Ibid., p. 34.
3. Rolf Stenersen, *Edvard Munch, Close-Up of A Genius.* Translated and edited by Reidar Dittmann. Oslo: Gyldendal Norsk Forlag, 1961. P. 56.
4. *Samlade Skrifter,* vol. XVIII, p. 92.
5. Ibid., pp. 12-13.
6. Stenersen, *Edvard Munch,* p. 67.

Chapter 4

1. August Strindberg, *Strindbergs Brev.* Utgivna av Torsten Eklund. Stockholm: Albert Bonniers Förlag, 1948 to 1974. Vol. III, p. 308.
2. August Strindberg, *Samlade Skrifter.* Utgivna av John Lundquist. Stockholm: Albert Bonniers Förlag, 1911 to 1922. Vol. XVII, p. 33.
3. Ibid., vol. XIX, p. 227.
4. Ibid., vol. XVII, p. 34.
5. *Strindbergs Brev,* vol. IV, p. 359.
6. Erik Hedén, *Strindberg: En ledtråd ved studiet av hans verk.* Stockholm: Tidens Förlag, 1926. p. 157 (translated).
7. *Strindbergs Brev,* vol. IV, p. 361.

8. Ibid., vol. V, p. 41.
9. Ibid., pp. 68-69.
10. Ibid., vol. V, p. 129.
11. Ibid., pp. 97, 110.
12. Ibid., p. 158.

Chapter 5

1. Jens Thiis, *Edvard Munch og hans samtid.* Oslo: Gyldendal Norsk Forlag, 1933. pp. 164, 170 (trans.).
2. To be discussed in a different context. Other works reflecting the Bohème influence are *Morning, Tête-à-Tête, Dance, Studio Brawl,* and the portraits of Jensen-Hjell and Hans Jaeger.
3. August Strindberg, *Strindbergs Brev.* Utgivna av Torsten Eklund. Stockholm: Albert Bonniers Förlag, 1948 to 1974. Vol. V, p. 81. (The Brasserie was Café de la Régence.)
4. Recorded in a letter to Paul Gauguin written in 1895 and included in *Samlade Skrifter,* vol. LIV, p. 327.
5. Theodore Duret, *Manet and the French Impressionists.* Translated by J.E. Crawford Flitch. Philadelphia: Lippincott Company, 2nd edition, 1912. p. 6.
6. Lawrence and Elisabeth Hanson, *Impressionism, Golden Decade.* New York: Holt, Rinehart & Winston, 1961. pp. 182-83.
7. Raymond Cogniat, *The Century of the Impressionists.* New York: Crown Publishers, Inc., n.d. p. 76.
8. Pola Gauguin, *Edvard Munch.* Oslo: Aschehoug & Co., 1933. p. 50 (trans.).
9. *Aftenposten,* November 18, 1885 (trans.).
10. Ingrid Langaard, *Edvard Munch: Modningsår.* Oslo: Gyldendal Norsk Forlag, 1960. p. 20.
11. Johan Rewald, *The History of Impressionism.* New York: Simon and Schuster, 1946. p. 44.
12. Letter to Harald Nørregård. Munch Museum Archives, Oslo. Undated.
13. Jens Thiis, *Edvard Munch,* pp. 135-36.
14. Oskar Kokoschka, "Edvard Munch's Expressionism." *College Art Journal,* vol. XII, no. 4. New York, 1953.
15. Langaard, *Edvard Munch,* p. 30.

Chapter 6

1. August Strindberg, *Strindbergs Brev.* Utgivna av Torsten Eklund. Stockholm: Albert Bonniers Förlag, 1948 to 1974. Vol. III, p. 301.
2. Martin Lamm, *August Strindberg.* Translated and edited by Harry G. Carlson. New York: Benjamin Blom, Inc., 197. p. 199.
3. *Strindbergs Brev,* vol. V, p. 306.

4. Ibid., p. 467.

5. August Strindberg, *Samlade Skrifter.* Utgivna av John Landquist. Stockholm: Albert Bonniers Förlag, 1911-1927. Vol. LIV, p. 178.

6. *Strindbergs Brev,* vol. V, p. 178.

7. Ibid., vol. VI, p. 148.

8. Gunnar Ollén, *Strindbergs dramatik.* Stockholm: Prisma, 1961. p. 49 (trans.).

9. Strindberg's letters, his *Confessions of A Fool,* and an account by the couple's oldest daughter, Karin Smirnoff, *Strindbergs første hustru.* Copenhagen: Branner, 1948, contain frequent references to the mounting tension in the household at this particular time.

10. Birgitta Steene, *The Greatest Fire: A Study of August Strindberg.* Carbondale, Ill.: Southern Illinois University Press, 1973. p. 41.

11. *Strindbergs Brev,* vol. VI, p. 137.

12. *Strindbergs Brev,* vol. VI, p. 262.

13. August Strindberg, *Pre-Inferno Plays.* Translations and Introductions by Walter Johnson. Seattle: University of Washington Press, 1970. P. 11.

14. *Samlade Skrifter,* vol. XVII, p. 287.

15. Smirnoff, *Strindbergs forste hustru,* p. 122.

16. Aage Welblund, *Omkring den literaere Café.* Copenhagen: Branner, 1951. p. 33 (trans.).

17. *Strindbergs Brev,* vol. VII, p. 203.

18. *Pre-Inferno Plays,* p. 81.

19. Ibid., p. 77.

20. *Strindbergs Brev,* vol. VII, p. 161.

21. Ollén, *Strindbergs dramatik,* p. 69.

22. *Strindbergs Brev,* vol. VII, p. 276.

23. Ollén, *Strindbergs dramatik,* p. 86.

24. Stellan Ahlström, *Strindbergs erövring av Paris. Strindberg och Frankrike 1884-1895.* Uppsala: Almquist & Wiksell, 1956. pp. 121-23 (trans.).

25. *Strindbergs Brev,* vol. VII, p. 310.

26. Ibid., p. 313.

27. Ibid., p. 321.

Chapter 7

1. Munch willed his entire property "and everything therein" to the city of Oslo. Upon his death in 1944 it was discovered that he had retained the vast majority of his paintings since 1909, more than 1,500, and several copies of each of his more than 700 graphic works.

2. *Dagbladet,* May 3, 1889. (trans.).

3. Pola Gauguin, *Edvard Munch.* Oslo: Aschehoug & Co., 1933. p. 70.

4. Ingrid Langaard, *Evard Munch: Modengsår.* Oslo: Gyldendal Norsk Forlag, 1960. p. 38.

5. *Dagbladet,* April 27, 1889.

6. For example, *Puberty* and *The Day Thereafter,* several interiors from his home, and a few landscapes.

7. Rolf Stenersen, *Edvard Munch: Close-Up of a Genius.* Translated and edited by Reidar Dittmann. Oslo: Gyldendal Norsk Forlag, 1969. p. 53.

8. Besides Dr. Munch, who could not take time away from his practice, there were Andreas, a medical student, Laura and Inger, and the aunt, Karen Bjølstad, who kept house.

9. His house, occupied by the Germans, had been severely damaged together with a great many paintings stored there.

10. Langaard, *Edvard Munch,* p. 50.

11. John Rewald, *Post-Impressionism from Van Gogh to Gauguin.* New York: The Museum of Modern Art, n.d. pp. 194-95. (The definition in Rewald's volume is quoted from an article in an 1889 isssue of *Revue Indépendant* by Eduard Dujardin.)

12. *Aftenposten,* October 5, 1889.

13. Inger Munch, ed., *Evard Munch Brev.* Oslo: John Grundt Tanums Forlag, 1949. p. 67.

Chapter 8

1. Richard Bergh's enthusiasm for this particular work did not extend to its flagrant expression of the author's current antidemocratic tendencies. Karl Nordström, on the other hand, chose to ignore them.

2. August Strindberg, *Samlade Skrifter.* Utgivna av John Landquist. Stockholm: Albert Bonniers Förlag, 1911-1927. Vol. XXIV, p. 10.

3. Ibid., p. 224.

4. A Danish acquaintance from their Grez period, Marie David, whom Strindberg had accused of lesbianism. The court, deciding in her favor, imposed a fine on Strindberg.

5. Per Ekström (1844-1935), portrayed as Pelle in *The Son of A Servant* and Sellén in *The Red Room,* an open-air painter, admirer of the Barbizon School, who no doubt influenced Strindberg with his views and painterly approach.

6. *Samlade Skrifter,* op. cit., vol. XIX, p. 9.

7. Ibid.

8. Josephson (1851-1906), painter and poet, acclaimed in the Paris *Salon* of 1881, remained a controversial figure in Sweden. During a visit to Norway in 1872 he was inspired by the folk tradition of the water spirit and in 1882 completed a canvas with that title and by many considered Scandinavia's first expressionist painting.

9. Thegerström (1857-1919), member of the Grez circle, favored the archipelago but made his principal contribution as a portrait artist. His large canvas representing girls dancing in a meadow decorates the grand staircase of Stockholm's *Dramatiska Teatern.*

10. August Strindberg, *August Strindbergs Brev.* Utgivna av Torsten Eklund. Stockholm: Albert Bonniers Förlag, 1948 to 1974. Vol. VIII, p. 300.

11. Göran Söderström, *Strindberg och bildkonsten.* Stockholm: Forum, 1972. p. 168 (trans.). (Quote from Strindberg's *Vivisektioner.*)

12. From responses to questions submitted to him on the occasion of his sixtieth birthday in 1909. Questions and answers published in *Bonniers Magazine* that year and included in *Samlade Skrifter,* vol. LIV, p. 472.

13. *Himmelrikets nycklar* [The Keys to the Kingdom], 1892.

14. Söderström, *Strindberg och bildkousten,* p. 175. (This, too, is a quote from Strindberg's *Vivisektioner.*)

15. Ibid., p. 412, and elsewhere throughout the volume.

16. Torsten Måtte Schmidt, ed., *Strindbergs måleri.* Malmö: Allhems Förlag, 1972. p. 14.

17. His observations on botany, chemistry, and on color photography have been judged to have considerable merit. All in all, however, his scientific objectivity, particularly in his Inferno period, was severely threatened by his leanings toward the occult.

18. Söderström, *Strindberg och bildkousten,* p. 181.

19. This difficult play, in some ways foreshadowing *To Damascus,* was premiered in the Swedish Radio Theatre. (Gunnar Ollén, *Strindbergs dramatik.* Stockholm: Prisma, 1961. p. 94.)

20. *Strindbergs Brev,* vol. IX, p. 65.

21. Ibid., p. 69.

22. Ibid., pp. 70-71. (Müggelschloss is a lakeside restaurant, Priapus a Polish lawyer who liked to dance to a Russian funeral march. Oscar Blumenthal, director of the Lessing Theatre, had promised to perform Strindberg's plays and had written about him in the *Börsen-Kurier.*)

Chapter 9

1. From the nineteenth century there were representative works by Ingres, Gericault, Delacroix, Cabanel, Couture, and Puvis de Chavannes. Bonnat willed his collection to his hometown, Bayonne, giving the city one of the finest art galleries of France.

2. John Rewald, *Post-Impressionism from Van Gogh to Gauguin.* New York: The Museum of Modern Art, n.d. p. 150.

3. Philippe Jullian, *The Symbolists.* London and New York: Phaidon, 1973. p. 225 (The statement is a quote from Paul Verlaine.)

4. Des Esseintes is said to be modeled on Count Robert of Montesquiou-Fezensac, writer and man-about-town in Paris and London.

5. U-K Huysmans, *Against the Grain.* Introduction by Havlock Ellis. New York: Illustrated Editions, 1931.

6. Born in 1786, Chevreul was still living when the neoimpressionists made their entry. He died in 1889.

7. Munch Museum Archive.

8. Inger Munch, ed., *Edvard Munchs Brev.* Oslo: Johan Grundt Tanums Forlag, 1949. p. 71.

9. Ibid., p. 74.

10. Ingrid Langaard, *Evard Munch: Modningsår*. Oslo: Gyldendol Norsk Forlag, 1960. p. 116.

11. *Munchs Brev*, p. 99.

12. Rewald, *Post-Impressionism*, pp. 415-16.

13. Langaard, *Edvard Munch*, pp. 130-31.

14. Rewald, *Post-Impressionism*, p. 302.

15. Langaard, *Edvard Munch*, pp. 126-27, 440.

16. Rewald, *Post-Impressionism*, p. 55.

17. *Dagbladet*, December 16, 1891.

18. Rolf Stenersen, *Evard Munch: Close-Up of a Genius*. Translated and edited by Reidar Dittmann. Oslo: Gyldendal Norsk Forlag, 1969. p. 101.

19. Munch Museum Archive.

20. Later bound by Munch and inscribed with the title *The Tree of Knowledge*.

21. The poetic prose of Sigbjφrn Obstfelder and the strange orthography of Hans Jaeger. This is an example of Munch's Norwegian and its lack of punctuation: "Gå in i en billiardsal—Når du har seet en stun på dette intense grφnne betraek se da op—Hvor forunderli alt er rφdli omkring—de herrerne som der ved var sortklaedt de har fået karmosinrφde dragter—og salen et rφdli vaeg og tag." Munch Museum Archive.

22. Roy McCullen, *Victorian Outsider. A Biography of J.A.M. Whistler*. New York: E.P. Dutton & Co., 1973. pp. 244-45.

23. Munch Museum Archive.

24. Munch Museum Archive: "Hva der φdelaegger den moderne kunst—det er de store udstillinger—kunstens store bon marcheer."

25. Munch Museum Archive.

26. Originally shown with the title *Jealousy*, this painting was later renamed *Melancholy* to avoid confusing it with subsequent works dealing more specifically with the subject of jealousy.

27. Munch Museum Archive.

28. Munch Museum Archive.

29. One of the few early Munch paintings not in Norway, *Despair* is in Stockholm's Thiel Gallery, which has the largest Munch collection outside of Norway.

30. There is disagreement about the exact time when the versions now in the National Gallery in Oslo may have been repainted. It is likely, however, that those in the 1892 retrospective were different canvases.

31. *Aftenposten*, October 9, 1892.

32. Ibid.

33. Charles Chassé, *The Nabis and Their Period*. Translated by Michael Bullock. New York: Frederick A. Praeger, 1969. p. 13.

34. Munch Museum Archive.

Chapter 10

1. Henrik Cornell, *Den svenska konstens historia:* Andra delen. *Från nyantiken til Konstnärsförbundet.* Stockholm: Aldus/Bonniers, 1959. p. 109 (trans.).
2. Ola Hansson, *August Strindberg och Ola Hanssons brevväxling.* Stockholm: Albert Bonniers Förlag, 1933. p. 142 (trans.).
3. Ibid., p. 147.
4. August Strindberg, *August Strindbergs Brev.* Utgivna av Torsten Eklund. Stockholm: Albert Bonniers Förlag, 1948 to 1974. Vol. IX, p. 76.
5. Ingrid Langaard, *Evard Munch: Madningsår.* Oslo: Glydendal Norsk Forlag, 1960. p. 177.
6. *Strindbergs Brev,* vol. IX, p. 95.
7. Ibid., p. 93.
8. Inger Munch, ed., *Edvard Munchs Brev.* Oslo: Johan Grundt Tanums Forlag, 1949. p. 137.
9. *Aftenposten,* November 11, 1892.
10. *Munchs Brev,* p. 121.
11. Ibid., p. 120.
12. Gerhard Mazur, *Imperial Berlin.* New York and London: Basic Books, Inc., 1970. pp. 225-26.
13. *Munchs Brev,* pp. 122-23.
14. Stanislaw Przybyszewski, *Erinnerungen an das literarische Berlin.* Munich: Winkler Verlag, 2nd edition, 1965. pp. 190-91 (trans.).
15. *Strindbergs Brev,* vol. IX, p. 104.
16. *Strindbergs Brev,* vol. IX, p. 124.
17. Stellan Ahlström, *Strindbergs erövring av Paris. Strindberg och Frankrike 1884-1885.* Uppsala: Almquist & Wiksell, 1956. pp. 169-70.
18. *Strindbergs Brev,* vol. IX, p. 121.
19. During the Swedish-Norwegian union the Norwegian flag, a white and blue cross on a red field, contained a miniature Swedish flag in the upper section closest to the mast. Flying the "pure" flag implied an overt demonstration against the union.
20. Jens Thiis, *Edvard Munch og hans samtid.* Oslo: Gyldendal Norsk Forlag, 1933. p. 205.
21. Ibid.
22. Langaard, *Edvard Munch,* p. 234.
23. Adolf Paul, *Min Strindbergsbok.* Stockholm: Nordstedt, 1930. p. 52 (trans.).
24. *Munchs Brev,* p. 124.
25. This accounts for Munch's frequent copying of his own pictures. If a sale involved a key work he would immediately begin working on a copy so that his own collection would remain intact. To Rolf Stenersen he confided that he could hardly sleep when his works were on exhibit outside of Norway.

Chapter 11

1. Frida Strindberg, *Strindberg och hans andra hustru.* Stockholm: Albert Bonniers Förlag, 1933. Vol. I, pp. 19-21 (trans.). The second quote is a strikingly close description of Strindberg as he appears in the portrait painted by Christian Krohg at that exact time.
2. August Strindberg, *August Strindbergs Brev.* Utgivna av Torsten Eklund. Stockholm: Albert Bonniers Förlag, 1948 to 1974. Vol. IX, p. 123.
3. Ibid., p. 128.
4. August Strindberg, *The Cloister.* C.G. Bjurström, ed. Translated and with commentary and notes by Mary Sandbach. New York: Hill & Wang, 1961. p. 33.
5. Gunnar Brandell, *Strindberg in Inferno.* Translated by B. Jacobs. Cambridge, Mass.: Harvard University Press, 1974. p. 30.
6. By referring to Munch as the *Danish* painter he may of course have wanted to conceal the identity of the character but may also have wanted to get back at those who had ignorantly called *him* a *Norwegian* poet.
7. *The Cloister,* p. 47.
8. *Strindbergs Brev,* vol. IX, pp. 153, 155.
9. *The Cloister,* p. 47.
10. Jens Thiis, *Edvard Munch og hans samtid.* Oslo: Gyldendal Norsk Forlag, 1933. p. 211.
11. Frida Strindberg, *Strindberg,* p. 316.
12. Stanislaw Przybyszewski, *Erinnerungen an das literarische Berlin.* Munich: Winkler Verlag, 1965. p. 225.
13. Ibid., p. 196.
14. *Strindbergs Brev,* vol. X, pp. 107-8. A similar view on Dagny Juell, entirely without further supporting evidence, is presented by Evert Sprinchorn in his introduction to *Inferno, Alone, and Other Writings* by Strindberg. New York: Anchor Books, 1968.
15. Ibid., p. 54, n. 1.
16. Frida Strindberg, *Strindberg och hans andra hustru,* p. 318.
17. Pola Gauguin, *Edvard Munch.* Oslo: Aschehoug & Co. (W. Nygaard), 1933. p. 106.
18. Portrayed on the canvas *Melancholy.*
19. Mentz Schulerud, *Norsk Kuntnerliv.* Oslo: J.W. Cappelens Forlag, 1960. p. 346 (trans.).
20. Frida Strindberg, *Strindberg och hans andra hustru,* p. 181.
21. August Strindberg, "Kvinnohat och kvinnodyrkan," *Samlade Skrifter.* Utgivna av John Landquist. Stockholm: Albert Bonniers Förlag, 1911-1927. Vol. XXVII, p. 576.
22. *The Cloister,* p. 52.
23. Ibid., pp. 37-38.
24. Later Irma Mudocci would play a similar though less decisive role.
25. Munch Museum Archive.

26. Frida Strindberg, *Strindberg och hans andra hustru,* p. 181.

27. A later version, identical in size and compositional approach but different in color scheme and devoid of the transfigured expression too pronounced in the first version, can be seen in the Hamburg Kunsthalle.

28. Stanislaw Przybyszewski, ed., *Das Werk des Edvard Munch.* Berlin: S. Fischer Verlag, 1894. pp. 47, 19.

29. Munch Museum Archives.

30. Another early Munch painting presently in Stockholm's Thiel Gallery.

31. Göran Lindström, "Edvard Munch i Strindbergs *Inferno.*" *Ord och Bild,* no. 3, 1955. p. 138.

32. *Das Werk des Edvard Munch,* p. 20.

33. Munch Museum Archive.

34. Munch Museum Archive.

Chapter 12

1. Gunnar Brandell, *Strindberg in Inferno.* Translated by Barry Jacobs. Cambridge, Mass: Harvard University Press, 1974. p. 1.

2. Stanislaw Przybyszewski, *Erinnerungen an das literarische Berlin.* Munich: Winkler Verlag, 1965, p. 189.

3. August Strindberg, *August Strindbergs Brev.* Utgivna av Torsten Eklund. Stockholm: Albert Bonniers Förlag, 1948 to 1974. Vol. IX, p. 111.

4. Frida Strindberg, *Strindberg ach hans andra hustru.* Stockholm: Albert Bonnier Förlag, 1933. pp. 45-46.

5. Carl Ludwig Schleich, *Hågkomster om Strindberg.* Translated by G. Lindelöf. Stockholm: Björck & Börnesson, 1917. pp. 8, 7 (trans.).

6. *Strindbergs Brev,* vol. X, p. 51.

7. Jens Thiis, *Edvard Munch og hans samtid.* Oslo: Gyldendal Norsk Forlag, 1933. p. 205.

8. Rolf Stenersen, *Edvard Munch: Close-Up of a Genius.* Oslo: Gyldendal Norsk Forlag, 1969. p. 25.

9. Przybyszewski, *Erinnerungen an das literarische Berlin,* p. 190.

10. Göran Lindström, "Edvard Munch i Strindbergs *Inferno,*" *Ord och Bild,* no. 3, 1955. p. 129.

11. H. Schlittgen, *Erinnerungen.* Munich: A. Langen Verlag, 1926. p. 239 (trans.).

12. Ingrid Langaard, *Edvard Munch: Madningsår.* Oslo: Gyldendal Norsk Forlag, 1960. p. 234.

13. Frida Strindberg, *Strindberg,* p. 216.

14. In a letter to Paul, dated May 9, 1893, Strindberg asks, "Can't you calm down Mr. Türke with a little gift...?"

15. Torsten Måtte Schmidt, ed., *Strindbergs måleri.* Malmö: Allhems Förlag, 1972. pp. 341-42.

16. Frida Strindberg, *Strindberg,* p. 100.

17. Böcklin (1827-1901), though born in Switzerland, is considered a key figure in German art. Following a roving existence in his homeland and Germany he ultimately settled in Florence, where some of his finest works were created, among them *The Isle of the Dead,* existing in at least three versions.

18. Elizabeth G. Holt, ed., *From the Classics to the Impressionists: Art and Architecture of the Nineteenth Century.* New York: Anchor Books, 1966. p. 94.

19. Konstantin Bazarov, "Arnold Böcklin." *Art and Artists,* June 1971. pp. 24-25.

20. Letter to Johan Rohde, Munch Museum Archive.

21. Frida Strindberg, *Strindberg,* pp. 101, 103.

22. Göran Söderström, *Strindberg och bildkonsten.* Stockholm: Forum, 1972. p. 209. These artists, she says, have banned nature and art from their creations and left colors only. On that basis her professed admiration for Munch in her memoirs seems rather unbelievable and may be an adjustment after the fact.

23. Frida Strindberg, *Strindberg,* p. 100.

24. August Strindberg, *The Chamber Plays.* Translated by Evert Sprinchorn, Seaburn Quinn, Jr., and Kenneth Petersen. New York: E.P. Dutton & Co., Inc., 1962. p. 152.

25. Frida Strindberg, *Strindberg,* pp. 350-52.

26. In her farsical account of the two before the officiating German clergyman Strindberg, suddenly forgetting his German, responds to the vows in an incomprehensible linguistic melange, while Frida herself unsuccessfully fought an attack of the giggles: "I laughed loudly, wildly, despite the traditional requirement that brides weep..."

27. *Strindbergs Brev,* vol. IX, pp. 184-85.

28. August Strindberg, *The Cloister,* C.G. Bjurstrom, ed., translated and with commentary and notes by Mary Sandbach. New York: Hill & Wang, 1961. pp. 62-63.

29. *The Cloister,* p. 69.

30. *Strindbergs Brev,* vol. IX, p. 249.

31. Frida Strindberg, *Strindberg,* vol. II, p. 111.

32. *The Cloister,* p. 104.

33. Frida Strindberg, *Strindberg,* vol. II, p. 121.

34. *The Cloister,* p. 104.

35. *The Cloister,* p. 111.

36. *Strindbergs Brev,* vol. IX, pp. 306, 312-13.

37. Frida Strindberg, *Strindberg,* p. 188.

38. *Strindbergs Brev,* vol. X, p. 15.

39. Frida Strindberg, *Strindberg,* vol. II, p. 206.

40. Frida Strindberg, *Strindberg,* vol. II, pp. 202-3.

41. Söderström, *Strindberg och bildkousten,* p. 398. The quote is from an article in a Kristiania newspaper, written by Munch as an obituary when he had learned of Dagny's murder by a

jealous lover in June of 1901. The article emphasizes Dagny's organizational talent, her contribution through the introducing of Norwegian art in Germany, her musical talent, her ability as a translator—aspects of her life, the writer claims, totally ignored by the press.

42. *Strindbergs Brev,* vol. X, p. 40.

43. August Strindberg, *Samlade Skrifter.* Utgivna av John Landquist. Stockholm: Albert Bonniers Förlag, 1911-1927. Vol. IV, p. 149.

44. *Strindbergs Brev,* vol. X, pp. 178-79.

45. *The Cloister,* p. 125.

46. *Strindbergs Brev,* vol. X, p. 94.

47. Ibid., p. 267.

48. Ibid., p. 314.

Chapter 13

1. Ingrid Langaard, *Edvard Munch: Modningår.* Oslo: Gyldendal Norsk Forlag, 1960. p. 189.

2. Inger Munch, ed. *Edvard Munchs Brev.* Oslo: Johan Grundt Tanums Forlag, 1949. p. 129.

3. Stanislaw Przybyszewski, *Das Werk des Edvard Munch.* Berlin: S. Fischer, 1894. pp. 36-37.

4. *Das Werk des Edvard Munch,* p. 41.

5. Ibid., pp. 24, 18-22.

6. Ibid.

7. *Edvard Munch.* Catalogue issued for the exhibit in Malmö Konsthall, Malmö, Sweden, March 22-Mary 25, 1975. p. 25.

8. Ibid., p. 27.

9. Malmö Exhibit Catalogue, p. 29.

10. *Munchs Brev,* p. 145.

11. *Munchs Brev,* p. 146.

12. Gustav Schiefler, *Verzeichniss des graphischen Werks Edvard Munchs.* Vol. I: 1894-1906; vol. II: 1906-1926. Photostatic reprint of the original edition. Oslo: J.W. Cappelens Forlag, 1974.

13. Henning Gran, "Edvard Munchs møte med norsk kritikk 1895." *Kunst og Kultur,* vol. XLVI. p. 206 (trans.).

14. *Munchs Brev,* p. 154. Munch graciously acceded to the request.

15. In the future Natanson would be more reserved in his attitude toward Munch's art, but this first time he found much to admire, and his review, knowledgable and unbiased, provided a refreshing contrast to the tone prevailing in the local press.

16. Langaard, *Edvard Munch,* pp. 357-58.

17. August Strindberg, *August Strindbergs Brev.* Utgivna av Torsten Eklund. Stockholm: Albert Bonniers Förlag, 1948-1974. Vol. X, p. 310.

Chapter 14

1. August Strindberg, *Samlade Skrifter.* Utgivna av John Landquist. Stockholm: Albert Bonniers Förlag, 1911-1927. Vol. XXVIII, p. 7.

2. Ibid., vol. XXX, p. 152.

3. August Strindberg, *August Strindbergs Brev.* Utgivna av Torsten Eklund. Stockholm: Albert Bonniers Förlag, 1948-1974. Vol. X, pp. 361-366.

4. Stellan Ahlström, *Strindbergs erövring av Paris. Strindberg och Frankrike 1884-1895.* Uppsala: Almquist & Wiksell, 1956. pp. 256-61.

5. Ibid., p. 7.

6. Ibid., p. 252.

7. Wladislawa Jaworska, *Gauguin and the Pont-Aven School.* New York: New York Graphic Society, 1972. p. 12.

8. Paul Gauguin, *Letters to His Wife and Friends.* Edited by Maurice Malingue and translated by Henry J. Stenning. New York: World Publishing Company, 1941. p. 195.

9. Göran Söderström, *Strindberg och bildkonsten.* Stockholm: Forum, 1972. p. 274.

10. Paul Gauguin, *The Intimate Journals.* Translated by Van Wyck Brooks, prefaced by Emile Gauguin. London: William Heinemann, Ltd., 1923. p. 58.

11. Gauguin, *Letters,* p. 197.

12. Gauguin, *The Intimate Journals,* p. 18.

13. Gauguin, *Letters,* pp. 197-98.

14. Gauguin, *Journals,* p. 19.

15. Söderström, *Strindberg och bildkonsten,* p. 280.

16. Gauguin, *Journals,* p. 19.

17. In a questionnaire sent to him by Georg Bröchner, Danish freelance writer, who planned to publish the results in a British periodical.

18. Gauguin, *Journals,* p. 1.

19. *Strindbergs Brev,* vol. X, p. 343.

20. Gauguin, *Letters,* p. 196.

21. *Samlade Skrifter,* vol. XXVIII, p. 15.

22. *Strindbergs Brev,* vol. X, pp. 372-73.

23. *Samlade Skrifter,* vol. XXVIII, p. 20.

24. Ibid., p. 21.

25. Gauguin, *Letters,* p. 200.

26. *Strindbergs Brev,* vol. XI, p. 19.

27. *Samlade Skrifter,* vol. XXVIII, p. 36.

28. Gauguin, *Letters,* p. 212.

Chapter 15

1. From Delius' letters and memoirs, here quoted from John Boulton Smith: "Edvard Munch og Frederick Delius," in *Kunst og Kultur,* vol. 48, no. 3, p. 140.

2. August Strindberg, *Samlade Skrifter.* Utgivna av John Landquist. Stockholm: Albert Bonniers Förlag, 1911-1927. Vol. XXVIII, p. 63.

3. Ibid., p. 65.

4. Inger Munch, ed., *Edvard Munchs Brev.* Oslo: Johan Grundt Tanums Torlag, 1949. pp. 156, 158.

5. *Samlade Skrifter,* vol. XXVIII, p. 76.

6. Stanislaw Przybyszewski, *Das Werk des Edvard Munch.* Berlin: S. Fischer, 1894, p. 182.

7. Gösta Svenaeus, "Strindberg och Munch i Inferno." *Kunst og Kultur,* vol. 50, p. 18.

8. Henrik Ibsen, *Samlede Vaerker.* Kristiania og København: Gyldendalske Boghandel, 1914. Vol. III, p. 265. Verbatim translation:

   He, Memnon, it occurred to me later,
   looked like the so-called Dovre Kings,
   as he sat there, self-centered and fat,
   with his tail planted on broken columns.

9. August Strindberg, *August Strindbergs Brev.* Utgivna av Torsten Eklund. Stockholm: Albert Bonniers Förlag, 1948 to 1974. Vol. XI, p. 224.

10. *Samlade Skrifter,* vol. XXVIII, pp. 78-79.

11. *Ockulta Dagboken.* Manuscript, Strindbergs Collection, Royal Library, Stockholm. Carton 72, p. 4.

12. *Samlade Skrifter,* vol. XXVIII, pp. 72-73.

13. Ibid., p. 79.

14. Ibid., p. 26.

15. Ibid., p. 89.

16. *Strindbergs Brev,* vol. XI, p. 278.

17. Ibid., p. 277.

18. Ibid., p. 245.

19. Ibid., p. 289.

20. *Munchs Brev,* p. 155.

21. Ingrid Langaard, *Edvard Munch: Modningsår.* Oslo: Glydundal Norsk Forlag, 1960. p. 363. (The present discussion on Strindberg's Munch essay is based on Ingrid Langaard's and on the essay itself as reproduced in full in Göran Söderström, *Strindberg ach bildkousten.* Stockholm: Forum, 1972. pp. 304-5.

22. Pola Gauguin, *Edvard Munch.* Oslo: Aschehoug & Co., 1933. p. 150.

23. Langaard, *Edvard Munch,* pp. 368-69.

Chapter 16

1. The *Inferno* account stresses this ambivalence: "It was a baby of six weeks I had left behind, and I returned to find a little girl two and a half years old. At our first meeting she gazes into the depth of my soul, her manner not severe but very serious, apparently looking to see whether I had come for her or her mother. Reassured, she allows herself to be kissed, and puts her arms around my neck." Further on, having been told of a person possessed by the devil, and of his exorcism, he says, "Stories such as these and others strengthened my conviction that this particular district had been predestined as a place of penance, and that there was a mysterious correspondence between this country and the places depicted in Swedenborg's Hell." August Strindberg, *Samlade Skrifter.* Utgivna av John Landquist. Stockholm: Albert Bonniers Förlag, 1911-1927. Vol. XXVIII, pp. 124-25, 144.

2. August Strindberg, *August Strindbergs Brev.* Utgivna av Torsten Eklund. Stockholm: Albert Bonniers Förlag, 1948 to 1974. Vol. XII, p. 129 (Bengt Lidforss, having visited Kristiania, had met Munch under rather peculiar circumstances at the Grand Cafe, an episode referred to in a letter to Geijerstam in August 1897, then included in *Legender, Skrifter,* vol. XXVIII, p. 287.

3. *Samlade Skrifter,* vol. XXIX, p. 8.

4. *Strindbergs Brev,* vol. XII, p. 286.

5. Ibid., vol. XII, p. 319.

6. Ibid., p. 338.

7. Ibid., vol. XIII, p. 32.

8. *Samlade Skrifter,* vol. XIII, p. 210:

   Där hänger på boklådfönstret
   en tunnklädd liten bok.
   Det är ett urtaget hjärta
   som dinglar där på sin krok.

9. Torsten Svedfelt, "Strindberg, Munch och *Quickborn.*" *Bokvännen,* vol. 24, pp. 51-56.

10. Birgitta Steene, *The Greatest Fire: A Study of August Strindberg.* Carbondale, Ill.: Southern Illinois University Press, 1973. p. 70.

11. *Strindbergs Brev,* vol. VII, p. 272.

12. Carl L. Anderson, *Poe in Northlight. The Scandinavian Response to His Life and Work.* Durham, N.C.: Duke University Press, 1973. p. 134.

13. Gunnar Ollén, *Strindbergs dramatik.* Stockholm: Prisma, 1961. p. 89.

14. *Strindbergs Brev,* vol. XIII, p. 86.

15. Inger Alver Gløersen, *Den Munch jeg møtte.* Oslo: Gyldendal Norsk Forlag, 1962. p. 91.

Bibliography

Ahlström, Gunnar, *Det moderna genombrotet i nordens litteratur.* Stockholm: Kooperativa Förbundet, 1947.

Ahlström, Stellan, *Strindbergs erövring av Paris. Strindberg och Frankrike 1884-1895.* Uppsala: Almquist & Wiksell, 1956.

Askeland, Jan., Norsk malerkunst: hovedlinjer gjennom 200 år. Oslo: J.W. Cappelens Forlag, 1981.

Bazarow, Konstantin, "Arnold Böcklin." *Art and Artists,* June 1971.

Bjørnsen, Johan Faltin, *Sigbjørn Obstfelder: Mennesket, poeten, grubleren.* Oslo: Gyldendal Norsk Forlag, 1959.

Bouret, Jean, *The Barbizon School and 19th Century French Landscape Painting.* New York: New York Graphic Society, 1973.

Brandell, Gunnar, *Strindberg in Inferno.* Translated by Barry Jacobs. Cambridge, Mass.: Harvard University Press, 1974.

Brandell, Gunnar, ed., *Synspunkter på Strindberg.* Stockholm: Bokförlaget Aldus/Bonnirs, 1964.

Chassé, Charles, *The Nabis and Their Period.* Translated by Michael Bullock. New York: Frederick A. Praeger, 1961.

Cogniat, Raymond, *The Century of the Impressionists.* New York: Holt, Rhinehart & Winston, 1961.

Cornell, Henrik, *Den svenska konsten historia. Från nyantiken till Konstnärsförbundet.* Stockholm: Aldus/Bonniers, 1959.

Dahlström, Carl, *Strindberg's Dramatic Expressionism.* Ann Arbor, Mich.: The University of Michigan, 1930.

Durban, Arne, *Malerskikkelser fra 80-årene.* Trondheim: F. Bruns Bokhandel, 1943.

Duret, Theodore, *Manet and the French Impressionists.* Translated by J.E. Crawford Flitch. Philadelphia: Lippincott Co., 1912.

Gauguin, Paul, *The Intimate Journals. Translated by Van Wyck Brooks,* prefaced by Emile Gauguin. London: William Heinemann, Ltd., 1923.

Gauguin, Paul, *Letters to His Wife and Friends.* Edited by Maurice Malingue and translated by Henry J. Stenning. New York: World Publishing Company, 1949.

Gauguin, Pola, *Edvard Munch.* Oslo: Aschehoug & Co. (W. Nygaard), 1933.

Gilson, Etienne, *Painting and Reality.* New York: World Publishing Company, 1961.

Gløersen, Inger Alver, *Lykkehuset: Edvard Munch og Åsgårdstrand.* Oslo: Gyldendal Norsk Forlag, 1970.

______, *Den Munch jeg møtte.* Oslo: Gyldendal Norsk Forlag, 1962.

Gran, Henning, "Edvard Munchs møte med norsk kritikk 1895." *Kunst og Kultur,* vol. XLVI, 1963.

Gustafson Alrik, *A History of Swedish Literature.* Minneapolis: The University of Minnesota Press, 1961.

Hanson, Lawrence and Elisabeth, *Impressionism: Golden Decade*. New York: Holt, Rhinehard & Winston, 1961.

Hansson, Ola, *August Strindbergs och Ola Hanssons brevväxling*. Stockholm: Albert Bonniers Forlag,
1938.

———, *Sensitiva amorosa*. Hälsingborg: Hans Österling, 1887.

Hedén, Erik, *Strindberg: En ledtråd ved studiet av hans verk*. Stockholm: Tiden Förlag, 1926.

Heller, Reinhold, *The Scream*. New York: Viking Press, 1973.

Hodin, Joseph Paul, *Edvard Munch*. New York: Praeger Publishers, 1972.

Huysmans, Joris Karl, *Against the Grain*. Introduction by Havlock Ellis. New York: Illustrated Editions, 1931.

Ibsen, Henrik, *Samlede Vaerker*. Kristiania og København: Gyldendalske Boghandel, Nordisk Forlag, 1914.

Jaeger, Hans. *Fra Kristianiabohemen*. American reprint in Norwegian. Minneapolis: William Kridt, 1893.

Jaworska, Wladislawa, *Gauguin and the Pont-Aven School*. Translated by Patrick Evans. New York: New York Graphic Society, 1972.

Johannesson, Eric O., *The Novels of August Strindberg. A Study in Theme and Structure*. Berkeley and Los Angeles: University of California Press, 1968.

Kingbury, Martha, "The Femme Fatale and Her Sisters." Chapter in *Woman as a Sex Object: Studies in Erotic Art 1730-1970*. Thomas B. Hess and Linda Nochlin, eds. New York: Newsweek, Inc., 1972.

Kokoschka, Oskar, "Edvard Munch's Expressionism.' *College Art Journal*, vol. XII, no. 4, New York, 1953.

Lamm, Martin, *August Strindberg*. Translated and edited by Harry G. Carlson. New York: Benjamin Blom, Inc., 1971.

Langaard, Ingrid, *Edvard Munch: Modningsår*. Oslo: Gyldendal Norsk Forlag, 1960.

Langaard, Johan, and Revold, Reidar, *Edvard Munch, fra år til år*. En håndbok. Oslo: Aschehoug & Co. (W. Nygaard), 1961.

———, *Edvard Munch: Masterpieces from the Artist's Collection in the Munch Museum in Oslo*. New York: McGraw-Hill Book Company, 1964.

Larsson, Carl, *Jag*. Stockholm: Albert Bonniers Förlag, 1961.

Laurin, Carl, Hannover, Emil, and Thiis, Jens, *Scandinavian art*. New York: The American-Scandinavian Foundation, 1922.

Lexow, Einar, *Norges Kunst*. Oslo: Steenske Forlag, 1942.

Lindström, Göran, "Edvard Munch i Strindbergs *Inferno*." *Ord och Bild*, no. 3, 1955.

Mazur, Gerhard, *Imperial Berlin*. New York and London: Basic Books, Inc., 1970.

McCullen, Ray, *Victorian Outsider*. A biography of J.A.M. Whistler. New York: E.P. Dutton & Co., Inc., 1973.

McGill, V.J., *August Strindberg, the Bedeviled Viking*. New York: The Macmillan Company, 1930.

Messer, Thomas S., *Edvard Munch*. New York: Harry N. Abrams, Inc., 1974.

Meyer, Michael, *Ibsen, A Biography*. New York: Doubleday & Co., Inc.,1971.

Moen, Arve, *Edvard Munch: Kvinnen og Eros*. Et billedverk. Oslo: Norsk Kunstreproduksjon, 1957.

———, *Edvard Munch: Samtid og miljø*. Et billedverk. Oslo: Norsk Kunstreproduksjon, 1956.

Munch, Inger, ed., *Edvard Munchs Brev*. Oslo: Johan Grundt Tanums Forlag, 1949.

Nochlin, Linda, ed., *Impressionism and Post-Impressionism 1874-1904*. Sources and Documents. Englewood Cliffs, N.J.: Prentice-Hall, Inc., 1966.

Ollén, Gunnar, *Strindbergs dramatik*. Stockholm: Prisma, 1961.

Østby, Leif, *Norges kunsthistorie.* Oslo: Gyldendal Norsk Forlag, 1962.
Paul, Adolf, *Min Strindbergsbok.* Stockholm: Nordstedt, 1930.
Przybyszewski, Stanislaw, *Erinnerungen an das literarische Berlin.* Munich: Winkler Verlag, 1965.
______, *Totenmesse.* Berlin: S. Fischer, 1893.
______, *Das Werk des Edvard Munch.* Berlin: S. Fischer, 1894.
Reid, Louis Arnoud, *Meaning in the Arts.* New York: Humanities Press, 1969.
Rewald, John, *Camille Pissaro.* New York: Harry N. Abrams, n.d.
______, *The History of Impressionism.* New York: Simon and Shuster, 1946.
______, *Post-Impressionism from Van Gogh to Gauguin.* New York: The Museum of Modern Art, n.d.
Rosemblum, Robert, *Modern Painting and the Northern Romantic Tradition.* Friedrich to Rothko. New York: Harper & Row, 1975.
Schiefler, Gustav, *Verzeichnis des graphischen Werks Edvard Munchs.* Vol. I: 1894 to 1906; vol. II: 1906 to 1926. Photographic copies of the original German editions. Reprint preface by Pål Hougen. Oslo: J.W. Cappelens Forlag, 1974.
Schleich, Carl Ludwig, *Hågkomster om Strindberg.* Translated by G. Lindelöf. Stockholm: Björck & Börjesson, 1917.
Schlittgen, Hermann, *Erinnerungen.* Munich: A. Langen Verlag, 1926.
Schmidt, Torsten Måtte, ed., *Strindbergs måleri.* Malmö: Allhems Förlag, 1972.
Schulerud, Mentz. *Norsk Kuntnerliv.* Oslo: J.W. Cappelens Forlag, 1960.
Selz, Jean, *Edvard Munch.* Translated by Eileen Hennessy. New York: Crown Publishers, 1974.
Smirnoff, Karin, *Strindbergs første hustru.* København: Branner, 1948.
Smith, John Boulton, "Edvard Munch og Frederick Delius." *Kunst og Kultur,* vol. 48, no. 3.
Söderström, Göran, *Strindberg och bildkonsten.* Stockholm: Forum, 1972.
Sorell, Walter, *The Duality of Vision: Genius and Versatility in the Arts.* New York: The Bobbs-Merrill Co., Inc., n.d.
Sprigge, Elizabeth, *The Strange Life of August Strindberg.* New York: Macmillan Co., 1949.
Stang, Nic., *Edvard Munch.* Illustrations edited by Ragna Stang. Translated by Carol J. Knudsen. Oslo: Tanums Forlag, 1972.
Stang, Ragna, *Edvard Munch: the Man and His Art.* New York: Abbeville Press, 1979.
Steene, Birgitta, *The Greatest Fire: A Study of August Strindberg.* Carbondale Ill.: Southern Illinois University Press, 1973.
Stenersen, Rolf, *Edvard Munch: Close-Up of A Genius.* Translated and edited by Reider Dittmann. Oslo: Gyldendal Norsk Forlag, 1969.
Stenstadvold, Håkon, *Norsk malerkunst i norsk samfunn.* Oslo: Dreyers Forlag, 1960.
Stockholm och dets omgifningar. Seventh edition. Stockholm: Albert Bonniers Förlag, 1897.
Strindberg, August, *August Strindbergs Brev.* Utgivna av Torsten Eklund. Vols. I through XIII. Stockholm: Albert Bonniers Förlag, 1948-1974.
______, *Samlade Skrifter.* Utgivna av John Landquist. Stockholm: Abert Bonniers Förlag, 1911-1927.
______, *The Chamber Plays.* Translated by Evert Sprinchorn, Seaburn Quinn, Jr., and Kenneth Petersen. New York: E.P. Dutton & Co., Inc., 1962.
______, *The Cloister.* Edited by C.G. Bjurström. Translated and with a commentary and notes by Mary Sandbach. New York: Hill & Wang, 1969.
______, *Dikter på vers och prosa.* Stockholm: Albert Bonniers Förlag, 1883.
______, *Inferno, Alone,* and *Other Writings.* In new translations. Edited and introduced by Evert Sprinchorn. New York: Anchor Books, 1961.
______, *Pre-Inferno Plays.* Translations and introductions by Walter Johnson. Seattle and London: The University of Washington Press, 1970.
Strindberg, Frida, *Strindberg och hans andra hustru.* 2 vols. Stockholm: Albert Bonniers Förlag, 1933.

Svedfelt, Torsten, "Strindberg och Munch i *Inferno.*" Bokvännen, vol. 24.
Svenaeus, Gösta, *Edvard Munch: Das Universum der Melancholie.* Lund: Gleerup, 1968.
———, "Strindberg och Munch i *Inferno.*" *Kunst of Kultur,* vol. 50.
Sypher, Wylie, *Rococo to Cubism in Art and Literature.* New York: Vintage Books, 1960.
Thiis, Jens, *Edvard Munch og hans samtid.* Oslo: Gyldendal Norsk Forlag, 1933.
Welblund, Aage, *Omkring den literaere Café.* København: Branner & Koch, 1951.
Willett, John, *Expressionism.* New York: McGraw-Hill Book Company, 1970.

Selected Exhibit Catalogues

(In chronological order)

New York, Museum of Modern Art in collaboration with Institute of Contemporary Art, Boston. *Edvard Munch.* 1950. Essay by Frederick B. Deknatel, introduction by Johan Langaard, bibliography by Hannah B. Muller.
Stockholm, Moderna Museet, *August Strindberg.* 1963. Essay by Göran Söderström.
Oslo, Munch Museet. *Katalog no. 3.* 1964. Introduction by Johan Langaard.
New York, The Solomon R. Guggenheim Museum. *Edvard Munch.* October 1965-January 1966. Texts by Sigurd Willoch, Johan Langaard, Louise Averill Svendsen.
Los Angeles, Los Angeles County Museum of Art. *Edvard Munch: Lithographs, Etchings, Woodcuts.* January 28-March 9, 1969.
Washington, D.C., The Phillips Collection. *The Work of Edvard Munch.* Introduction by Alan M. Fern, catalogue notes by Jane Van Nimmen.
Oslo, Munch Museet. Katalog A-3. *Edvard Munch: Tegninger, skisser, og studier.* 1973. Introduction by Pål Hougen, notes by Bente Torjusen.
Malmö, Malmö Konsthall. Edvard Munch. March 22-May 25, 1975. Introduction by Eje Högestätt, essays by Pål Hougen, Arne Eggum, Felix Hatz, Jan Torsten Ahlstrand.
Bergen, Norway, Vestlandske Kuntindustrimuseum. *Edvard Munch og Henrik Ibsen.* May-June 1975. Essay by Pål Hougen.
Humlebaek, Denmark, Louisiana Museum. *Edvard Munch.* October 11, 1975-January 4, 1976. Introduction by Hugo Arne Buch, essays by H.E. Nørregård-Nielsen, Ole Sarvig, Henrik Nordbrandt, Trygve Nergaard, Arne Eggum, Pål Hougen, and Øystein Hjort.
Washington, D.C., The National Gallery. *Edvard Munch: Symbols and Images.* November 11, 1978-February 19, 1979. Introduction by Robert Rosenblum, essays by Arne Eggum, Reinhold Heller, Trygve Nergaard, Ranga Stang, Bente Torjusen, and Gerd Woll.

Index

This index is organized according to Library of Congress alphabetization and not that of the national languages involved. All titles of literary and art works—with a few specific exceptions—have been given in English, whether published translations are available or not. The names August Strindberg and Edvard Munch are in the index only as they relate to their works. Page numbers in italics refer to note references.